Violent Storms

Other Books in the
DISCOVERING EARTH
SCIENCE SERIES

VOLCANOES AND EARTHQUAKES (No. 2842)

The first book in the series, this volume concentrates on the geologic phenomenon of Earth, and how this phenomenon has affected life on our planet. Also included is a history of the planet's geology.

MYSTERIOUS OCEANS (No. 3042)

The third volume in the series looks at the hydrologic phenomenon of Earth—its origin, purpose, mechanisms, and effect on life. The book concentrates on oceans' role on our planet.

THE LIVING EARTH: THE COEVOLUTION OF THE PLANET AND LIFE (No. 3142)

The fourth book in the series focuses on the biological phenomenon of Earth. It looks at the origins, history and future of life, as well as the effects that the geologic, climatic, and hydrologic phenomena have on life.

EXPLORING EARTH FROM SPACE (No. 3242)

The final volume in the series deals with the technologic advances that enable us to view our planet from space. It covers the way man-made satellites can provide us with better information on the geologic, climatic, biologic, and hydrologic phenomena of our planet and enable us to better predict disasters, locate and monitor natural resources, and explore our Solar System.

Violent Storms

JON ERICKSON

TAB BOOKS Inc.
Blue Ridge Summit, PA

FIRST EDITION

SECOND PRINTING

Printed in the United States of America

Library of Congress Cataloging in Publication Data

Erickson, Jon, 1948—
   Violent storms.

   Bibliography: p.
   Includes index.
   1. Storms. 2. Severe storms. I. Title.
QC941.E75 1988   551.5′5   88-8570
ISBN 0-8306-9042-5
ISBN 0-8306-2942-4 (pbk.)

TAB BOOKS Inc. offers software for sale. For information and a catalog, please
contact TAB Software Department, Blue Ridge Summit, PA 17294-0850.

Questions regarding the content of this book
should be addressed to:

   Reader Inquiry Branch
   TAB BOOKS Inc.
   Blue Ridge Summit, PA 17294-0214

Cover photograph courtesy of Woods Hole Oceanographic Institution.

Edited by Suzanne L. Cheatle
Series design by Jaclyn Saunders

Contents

Acknowledgments

The following are recognized for their help in providing photographs and editorial assistance: the U.S. Department of Agriculture (USDA), the U.S. Geological Survey (USGS), the National Aeronautics and Space Administration (NASA), the National Oceanic and Atmospheric Administration (NOAA), the U.S. Air Force, the U.S Army Corps of Engineers, the U.S Navy, family members, and friends.

Introduction

Of all nature's forces, storms are perhaps the most destructive and take the most lives. Storms also serve a very useful purpose by distributing the Sun's energy around the world. This distribution of energy keeps the Earth from having great extremes of temperature, thereby allowing nearly every place to be inhabited by one form of life or another. Storms are also responsible for providing life-giving rain so desperately needed on a planet that is fast becoming overcrowded with human inhabitants. Excessive rain in one part of the world might be matched by dry weather somewhere else, often bringing floods in one area and droughts in another. Storms also cleanse the Earth by removing pollutants, both natural and man-made. These poisons are eventually swept into the ocean where they are further diluted. Although man would like to alter the weather to his advantage, it is not certain how this tampering with nature would affect the delicate balance of the atmosphere. It might bring on calamity.

An imaginary weather radar station standing on the very top of the world keeps an eye out for dangerous storms. This is no ordinary radar, for it can see the weather way back into the past and predict the weather far off into the future. The mighty radar beams sweep across the surface of the entire planet, searching for hurricanes, tornadoes, and other violent storms. The radar looks for such things as dramatic changes in the climate, abrupt departures in the flow of the ocean currents, rapid surges of the glaciers, and the deadly contamination of the atmosphere. Once the radar finds the problem, it gives the inhabitants of Earth fair warning of the impending danger. The radar cannot stop the peril, however—only people can do that.

The powerful radar beam can penetrate deep into the interior of the Sun. Within the Sun's core, hydrogen is fused into helium, releasing tremendous amounts of energy as light and heat, along with strong particle radiation, which is responsible for the solar wind. The energy explodes through the Sun's surface, producing fiery fountains that leap hundred of thousands of miles into space. On the surface of the Sun are violently swirling masses of hot gases.

Some areas are cooler than others and appear as huge dark patches, or *sunspots*. The Sun has an atmosphere composed of a high-temperature plasma, which glows an eerie red when seen during a total eclipse.

The Sun radiates its energy at the speed of light; it takes the energy about eight minutes to reach Earth. The Earth receives only one-billionth of the Sun's energy. Yet, the amount of solar energy striking Earth at any given moment is greater than all the fossil fuels used by man since the discovery of fire.

The radar eye can delve deeply into the past and discover the creation of the Earth. Chunks of matter, possibly leftovers from a nearby exploding supernova, were scooped up out of the solar nebula as the protoplanet swung around the Sun. As the Earth became larger, it began to melt from the inside out by the extreme heat generated by radioactive elements and by the frictional heat from the bombardment of meteors. All of a sudden, out of deep space came a wayward asteroid about the size of Mars, striking the Earth with a glancing blow. As the asteroid bounced off into space, it sucked out a streamer of molten rock, which coalesced to form the Moon. Eventually, the earth cooled and formed a crust, and deluge after deluge filled the basins with water, which overflowed and combined into a single ocean that covered the entire planet. At first, only tiny pieces of land appeared, roaming freely about on a sea of molten magma. These pieces became attached to one another and steadily grew into a single large supercontinent, called Pangaea.

The earliest storms can be detected by the radar. These storms were much more violent that they are today and were responsible for creating life. Tremendous lightning bolts provided the spark of life by combining the right chemicals in the right order. Rainwater washing off the land flowed into the ocean, bringing with it carbon chains of every description. The pull of the Moon brought tides, which flowed and ebbed over the shore. Buried in the mud flats was an unusual group of molecules, which had the ability to replicate themselves, drawing from energy stored in the mud by the successive tides. Soon the seas were teeming with single-celled organisms, which slowly evolved into more complex forms of life. Only after a tenuous layer of ozone was formed in the upper atmosphere as protection from the Sun's deadly ultraviolet radiation did life take to the land.

The radar sees the individual continents split off Pangaea and drift apart. This rearrangement of the land mass dramatically changed the climate of the world, and ice ages came and went almost on a regular basis. Just about every major ice age coincided with the extinction of large numbers of species. Perhaps the greatest ice age took place over 200 million years ago and killed 95 percent of all life on Earth. Something extremely catastrophic must have happened to the world to cause such a disaster.

One explanation for the extinction of the dinosaurs and three-fourths of other species 65 million years ago is that the Earth was bombarded by a massive meteor that blasted huge quantities of dust into the atmosphere and cooled the planet. The last major ice age began some 100,000 years ago and ended a mere 10,000 years ago. Following the retreat of the ice northward, our ancestors, the Cro-Magnon, settled into territories that were already occupied by the Neanderthal, a primitive offshoot of *Homo sapiens*. It is often suggested that Cro-Magnon was a natural-born killer and massacred his stocky cousins until they became extinct. Now humanity appears again to be on the brink of extinction, having at its disposal powerful weapons that can create a storm vastly more destructive than anything nature is capable of.

1

The Solar Connection

THE greatest storm ever imagined lasted for 100,000 years and involved nearly all the matter in the universe. From the onset, huge swirling masses of high-temperature plasma composed of elementary particles flew out into space in all directions at near the speed of light. Currents and eddies flowed violently through this primordial soup, forcing matter to clump together and thereby sowing the seeds of the galaxies. Protostars ignited, and pervaded what was once empty space with light.

By the time the universe was 1 billion years old, but still less than one-tenth its present width, most of the galaxies had formed. The galaxies combined into clusters, which gathered into superclusters and wandered around in space in seemingly haphazard motions. Also at this time, most of the massive stars collapsed into black holes or exploded into supernovas, providing raw materials for new stars.

The Milky Way Galaxy formed somewhat later than the original galaxies, which are now so far away that they are on the very fringes of the most powerful telescopes. Many of the stars of the older galaxies have already passed through their life cycles and exist as burnt-out hulks. Because of the relative youth of the Milky Way, it will take some time to go before most of its stars, including the Sun, burn themselves out. When the universe has ceased its expansion—about 40 billion years from now—gravity will take hold and pull all matter back together again into a dense cosmic soup. Then the universe will again bounce back into new life.

THE SOLAR NEBULA

Around 5 billion yeas ago, a giant star over 100 times the size of the Sun exploded in what is called a *supernova*, and debris was blown outwards in all directions (FIG. 1-1). The giant gas bubble was composed mostly of hydrogen and helium, but also contained dust particles of nearly every element found in the universe. After traveling 10,000 years in empty space, debris from the supernova collided with other galactic matter that existed in a diffused cloud of gas and dust particles called a *nebula*. This

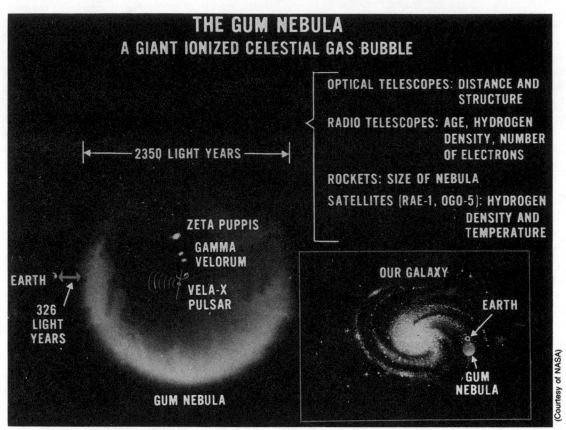

Fig. 1-1. The Gum Nebula, a giant gas bubble created by an exploding star.

galactic cloud was somewhat spherical and had a diameter some 10,000 times larger than the Sun and a density less than the thinnest atmosphere. The shock wave and intermingling of matter caused the nebula to rotate slowly in a counterclockwise direction as viewed from Polaris, the North Star. This rotation triggered a collapse of the nebula toward the axis of rotation by mutual gravitational attraction, forming a pancake-shaped disk.

The rotational force of the solar nebula is called *angular momentum*. It is that property of a spinning body which cannot be created or destroyed, but can only be transferred from one body to another. As the solar nebula condensed further, it spun faster, like an ice skater spins faster when she pulls in her outstretched arms, and its angular momentum is said to have been *conserved*. The faster spinning impeded further collapse because of centrifugal force (which

tends to fling matter outward from the center of rotation).

In order for a planetary system to form, most of the angular momentum must be transferred from the center of the disk to the outside. One way this transference could be accomplished is by gravitational torques. The outward matter spinning slower causes a tug on the center, slowing it down and forming spiral arms similar to those of a spiral galaxy. The formation of a single protostar from a slowly rotating cloud is relatively rare; therefore, single stars are a minority in our Galaxy. The vast majority of stars are created from rapidly spinning nebulae, which fragment into several protostars.

As the solar nebula continued to collapse, the center of the system became quite hot, while the outside remained relatively cold. If the solar nebula had continued its compression unabated, a lone, planetless star might have formed, spinning on its axis at great speed. However, a slowly rotating nebula has a better chance of differentiating into concentric rings of planetesimals because centrifugal forces because centrifugal forces keep the planetesimals from falling inward toward the center of the system. The planetesimals eventually coalesced into planets, lying in nearly the same plane, with most rotating in the same direction as the protostar.

Nearly all the angular momentum of the solar system resides with the planets, mostly Jupiter, which, with one-tenth the Sun's diameter, could have become a small star had it grown somewhat larger. The Sun has nearly all the mass of the solar system, yet it has hardly any of the angular momentum. This lack of angular momentum keeps the Sun from spinning off its outer layers and keeps the planets in their orbits.

At some point during the ongoing accumulation of gases and other materials, about 4.8 billion years ago, the increasing overlying weight caused the core of the protosun to heat up by compression. When the temperature of the core reached 20 million degrees Centigrade, hydrogen was fused to helium, and the Sun caught fire after only 100,000 years from the time the nebula began to collapse.

The infant Sun was only about 70 percent as bright as it is today, but was more active. Much of its energy was used for the creation of strong solar winds and powerful solar flares, which reached tens of millions of miles into space. The young Sun rotated much faster on its axes, completing a turn every few days. This rapid rotation created strong magnetic fields, which caused considerable turbulence on the Sun's surface, resulting in numerous giant sunspots. The Sun was very unstable and periodically puffed itself up, returning to its original size after the core began to cool.

THE SUN

The Sun is an ordinary star in terms of its size and brilliance, and lives among 100 billion similar stars in a Galaxy stretching 100,000 light-years across. The Sun resides in one of three principal spiral arms of the Milky Way Galaxy, 28,000 light-years from the center. It takes 200 million years to make one complete circuit around the Galaxy in a clockwise direction as viewed from Andromeda, our nearest galaxy, which is similar to the Milky Way, and some 2 million light-years away.

The Sun belongs to a minority of single stars, whereas the vast majority exist as binary star systems or clusters of multiple stars. The Sun is composed of 73 percent hydrogen and 25 percent helium, with minor amounts of other elements. The *solar disk*, the visible portion of the Sun, has a diameter of 864,000 miles, or roughly 100 times the diameter of the Earth.

The Sun is divided into three layers (FIG. 1-2). The core, about one-third the radius of the Sun, is mostly composed of helium. Above the core is a dense radiative zone of hydrogen which diffuses thermal energy outward from the surface of the core to the upper layer by atomic emission and absorption. The convection zone occupies the outer one-third of the Sun, but has only 1 percent of its mass. It is also mostly composed of hydrogen and transfers thermal energy (several million degrees Centigrade) to the surface through rising and falling eddies of gas.

The visible surface of the Sun is called the *photosphere*, and is only a few hundred miles thick with a temperature of 6000 degrees Centigrade. A granular pattern is displayed on the photosphere which changes by the minute, indicating vigorous turbulence in gases immediately below the surface.

The Sun's atmosphere is called the *chromosphere*, and is composed of reddish glowing gases thousands of miles thick. The chromosphere can be observed during the total eclipse of the Sun. During this time, giant solar flares (FIG. 1-3) can also be seen leaping as high as a million miles into space, gracefully arching over, and falling back into the Sun.

Surrounding the chromosphere is an intensely hot halo, called the *corona* (FIG. 1-4). It extends for millions of miles into space.

The solar wind is a stream of electrically charged particles that spew out from the surface along the Sun's magnetic lines of force. The solar wind in-

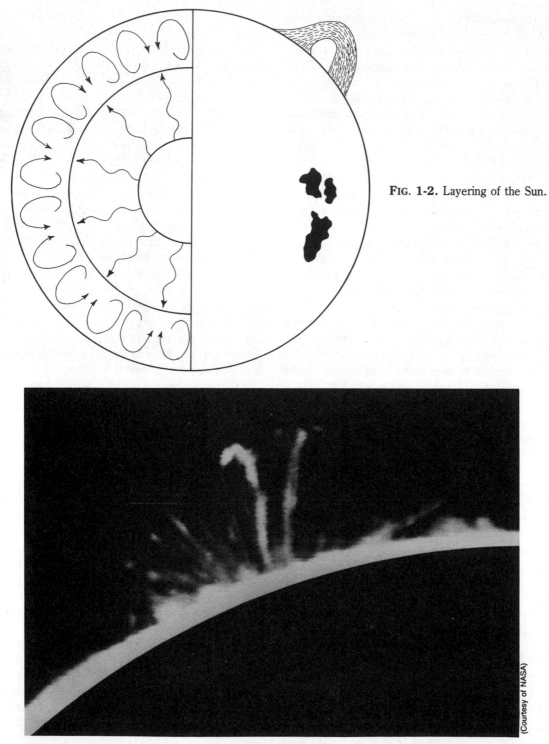

FIG. **1-2.** Layering of the Sun.

FIG. **1-3.** Solar flares.

(Courtesy of NASA)

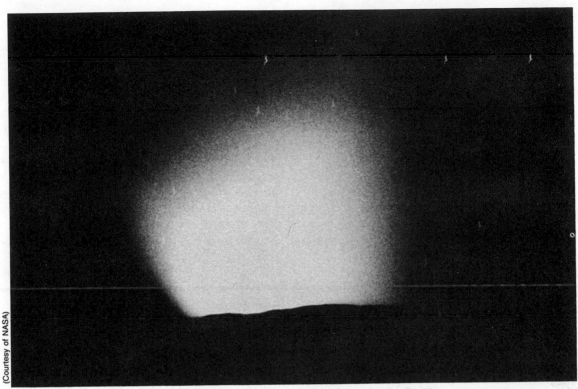

FIG. 1-4. The solar corona as photographed by Apollo 15.

creases during times of increased solar activity. The charged particles are funneled into the polar regions of the Earth's magnetic field and produce magnificently colored lights of the aurora borealis in the Northern Hemisphere and the aurora australis in the Southern Hemisphere. A strong solar wind also might be responsible for the formation of noctilucent clouds which are composed of minute ice crystals and are some 50 miles above the earth, far above normal clouds.

When the Sun was much younger, the solar wind was quite strong, enough to blow the volatile gases of the formative terrestrial planets outward toward the large gaseous planets that incorporated them into their atmospheres. The solar wind also might have aided in the transfer of the Sun's angular momentum to the planets, since now the Sun has only a meager portion of its original momentum and the solar wind is presently very feeble. It has even been suggested that the solar wind could be har-

nessed to propel spaceships around the Solar System. Giant sails could catch the charged particles, like the billowing sheets of seagoing ships catch the wind.

Solar *cosmic rays* are radioactive atomic nuclei expelled by the Sun at velocities near the speed of light. They possess extremely penetrating power, and are associated with solar flares, which are indicative of increased solar activity. When they interact with the Earth's atmosphere, solar cosmic rays produce secondary radioactive isotopes, or *radionuclides*, and radioactive particles which, along with cosmic radiation from space, are responsible for much of the background radiation on the earth's surface.

The background radiation can be measured by a *scintillometer* through the interaction of radioactive particles with a sodium-iodide crystal. This instrument gives an average background reading of about 50 counts per second (CPS). The Earth's magnetic field, or *magnetosphere*, deflects most of the cosmic radiation which could prove to be particularly harmful to life on Earth.

The Sun generates a strong magnetic field as a result of the large difference in rotation rates between the core and the surface. The core probably retained much of its original angular momentum, possibly because of low friction between it and the overlying layer, causing it to spin much faster than the surface. The Sun's present period of rotation is one rotation in about 25 days at the equator and 33 days near the poles. The interior of the Sun, however, completes one rotation in only a few days. The difference in rotation rates generates the Sun's magnetic field by what is called the *magneto effect*. (The faster a magneto turns, the larger the electrical current or magnetic field it generates.) About every 22 years, for unknown reasons, the Sun reverses its magnetic polarity, during which time the strength of the magnetic field runs through a minimum and then a maximum.

The surface of the Sun is often marred with *sunspots* (FIG. 1-5). These are large patches of relatively cool gas associated with magnetic vortices and energetic solar flares. Sunspots occur on the average in 11-year cycles, running through a maximum and minimum period in about 22 years. During a sunspot maximum, there might be as many as 100 sunspots at any one time. A sunspot maximum creates magnetic storms in the Earth's atmosphere which adversely affect the ionosphere because of the high influx of solar cosmic radiation. The disruption of a layer of ions between 50 and 200 miles above the Earth's surface causes a deterioration of radio communication, which uses the ionosphere to bounce radio waves around the world. Sunspots also can adversely affect the weather, a topic that will be discussed in further detail in Chapter 5.

(Courtesy of NASA)

FIG. 1-5. The Sun's surface, showing sunspots and a solar storm (upper right).

The Sun obtains its energy from thermonuclear reactions by the fusion of hydrogen to helium on or just below the surface of the core. There are three possible nuclear reactions that can take place in the Sun. The first is a reaction of hydrogen with deuterium, an isotope of hydrogen called *heavy hydrogen* containing one proton and one neutron. The second reaction is hydrogen with tritium, an even heavier isotope of hydrogen containing one proton and two neutrons. The third reaction is deuterium with tritium, which provides a leftover neutron for possible use in the first reaction.

The reactions produce helium, which contains two protons and two neutrons and a tremendous amount of thermal energy. Since helium is heavier than hydrogen, it falls inward toward the center of the Sun by the influence of gravity, building up a residue of helium *ash* in the core. Eventually, the buildup of helium will pollute the core, and fusion reactions will either cease altogether or take place higher, in the conductive zone.

The Sun regulates the temperature of the core by expanding when the core gets too hot from an increase of thermal pressure. This expansion provides a larger surface area in which to radiate the excess energy. If the core gets too cool, the loss of thermal pressure causes the overlying layers to compress by the force of gravity, and the heat of compression raises the temperature of the core.

The so-called *neutrino problem* raises serious questions about the thermonuclear reactions taking place in the Sun. Neutrinos are particles of near-zero mass, sometimes called *little neutrons*. They are produced by nuclear reactions, like those at nuclear-generating stations, and should be flying out from the Sun in copious amounts. Yet scientists find only about one-third of the expected number of neutrinos emanating from the Sun. One theory suggests that since neutrino production decreases substantially as the temperature falls, the core could be cooling down and could presently exist at a temperature much lower than expected. The problem is that, as the core cools, the Sun should be shrinking by detectable amounts because there is less thermal pressure pushing outward against the weight of the overlying layers. It could be that a strong magnetic field substituted magnetic pressure for the loss of thermal pressure in maintaining the Sun's observed radius. If the core is indeed cooling down, there could be dire implications for the future climate on Earth.

THE PLANETS

While the Sun was first stoking its furnace, the inner terrestrial planets—Mercury, Venus, Earth, and Mars—were completing their accumulation, layer upon layer, or *planetesimals*, which are chunks of stony material about the size of a pebble. This whole process probably took less than 100 million years, making the planets contemporary in age with the Sun. The outer Jovian, or gaseous, planets—Jupiter, Saturn, Uranus, and Neptune—probably formed in a similar manner as the Sun: by the local concentration of nebular gas and dust that collapsed into a planet by self-gravitation. Most of the volatiles of the terrestrial planets were probably blown toward the gaseous planets by the then strong solar wind.

After the terrestrial planets completed their growth, they heated up from the inside out and partially melted. This melting process divided the interior of the planets into their respective layers, with the heaviest in the center and the lightest on the outside. One effect of this meltdown was that gases and water vapor were boiled off and, caught by the solar wind, were taken out to the orbits of the larger planets and incorporated into their atmospheres. The source of heat was intense, short-lived radioactive elements, called *radionuclides*, which generated heat as they decayed into stable daughter products. After these radioactive elements decayed away, radioactive elements with longer half-lives maintained the interiors of the planets in a semimolten or plastic state.

The Solar System occupies a vast amount of space, having a radius of several billion miles. The Sun's family consists of nine known planets, an asteroid belt between Mars and Jupiter (possibly leftover planetesimals or debris from a planet that disintegrated), and the Oort Cloud out beyond the orbit of Pluto, where the comets reside.

Not all comets behave in a well-ordered manner. Some swing close by the Sun in highly elliptical orbits and shoot out into deep space again at great speeds. Not all of these comets are so lucky however; some actually plunge into the Sun with no chance of escape. Considering their relatively small size, their effect on the Sun is of no consequence except to cause a slight brightening of the corona.

Some 20 billion miles from the Sun lies a region of empty space—empty only in the sense that there are no solid bodies. It is not a perfect vacuum, but is composed of gas and dust particles, possibly remnants of the original solar nebula. From this far out in space, the Sun looks as though it were nothing more than an overly bright star, and its nearest neighbor, Alpha Centauri, is some 4.2 light-years, or 25 trillion miles (40 trillion kilometers) away.

Having planets does not make the Sun unique among stars. Although single stars are definitely in a minority, most of them can be expected to have planets, since the formation of a planetary system is the natural consequence of the formation of a single star. Planets of other stars are too dim to be studied from Earth, but they can be observed to cause a wobble in the orbit of the mother star. The orbits of the planets can be expected to be slightly elliptical to nearly circular, nearly coplanar, and spaced well apart; so, there is no close approach between two planets.

Our Solar System seems to have an exception to this rule because the orbit of Pluto swings in and out of the orbit of Neptune. Actually, there is no danger of collision because Pluto's orbit is also inclined 17 degrees to the solar plane. It is because of this unusual behavior that Pluto is thought to have once been a moon of Neptune that somehow was knocked out of orbit.

Other unusual characteristics distinguish our Solar System. Venus is the only planet whose rotation is *retrograde*, or backwards, in relation to the other planets. The axis of rotation of Uranus lies 8 degrees from the plane of its orbit, making it appear to be rolling along like a bowling ball. The Earth is unique in that the planet has an atmosphere abundant in oxygen and appears to be drowning in water. No other planet has so much water in the liquid state.

THE EARTH

The Earth completed most of its growth about 4.6 billion years ago. Repeated meteor and aster-oid impacts, along with internal radiogenic heating kept the Earth in a molten state for quite some time, allowing the interior of the Earth to differentiate into its various layers by gravitational segregation (FIG. 1-6). The heavier metals, mostly iron and nickel, settled toward the center of the Earth to make up the core.

The Earth's core is composed of an inner layer of a solid crystalline structure surrounded by a liquid outer layer. A small difference in rotation rates between the inner and outer core sets up a magnetic field similar to that of the Sun, although it reverses polarity considerably less often than the Sun's. The core is surrounded by a heavy iron-magnesium-rich rock material, which comprises the lower mantle. The lower mantle conducts heat away from the core and from its own internal radiogenic heating to the upper mantle. This heating from below produces convection cells in the lighter rocks of the upper mantle, which transports the excess heat to the crust where it is radiated into space.

The lightest rock materials floated to the surface, like slag on top of molten iron ore, and formed the early crust. The Earth was probably devoid of any atmosphere in its early life, as volatiles and gases boiled off and were blown away by the solar wind. This was a time of intense volcanic activity, and there were probably thousands of volcanoes popping off at any one time.

Volcanoes were a key factor in the formation of the original atmosphere, which was composed of nitrogen, carbon dioxide, methane, and water vapor, and enveloped the Earth in a continuous dense cloud. When the Earth cooled sufficiently, water vapor condensed into rain, which poured down on the still-hot surface and immediately evaporated. Eventually, the surface became cool enough for water to collect in small basins. (The early storms were highly energetic and released tremendous amounts of power, making the most destructive hurricanes of today puny and insignificant by comparison.) As the water became deeper, the entire surface of the planet was flooded. Finally, the only features that broke the surface of the 2-mile-deep ocean were tall volcanic peaks. Otherwise, the entire Earth was covered with water.

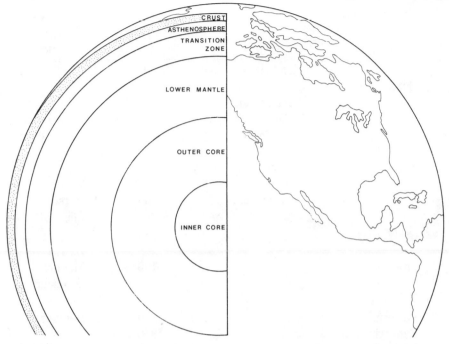

FIG. 1-6. The composition of the Earth.

CRUST
ASTHENOSPHERE
TRANSITION ZONE
LOWER MANTLE
OUTER CORE
INNER CORE

When the Earth was about 1 billion years old, massive extrusions of basalt and intrusions of granite built up layer upon layer until slivers of land, called *cratons*, were able to break the water's surface. These ancient rocks became the seeds from which the protocontinents grew. They exist today as stable regions in the interior of continents.

Because the Earth's interior was still considerably hot and viscous, the thin protocontinents roamed about freely on a sea of molten rock called the *asthenosphere*, colliding and bouncing off each other with considerable ease. Further cooling of the earth's interior caused the protocontinents to lose some of their mobility and they stuck together, forming two supercontinents. The southern continent, named *Gondwanaland*, was composed of present-day Africa, South America, Antarctica, Australia, and India. The northern continent, named *Laurasia*, was composed of the remaining continents of the Northern Hemisphere. The two supercontinents were temporarily separated by what was called the *Tethys Seaway*, which during this time was teeming with life.

Successive bumps and grinds between the continents created many of the world's major mountain ranges. Finally, according to German meteorologist Alfred Wegener, the continents joined into one large supercontinent called Pangaea, meaning *all land*, which stretched from pole to pole. Pangaea was surrounded by an ancient sea called Panthalassa, meaning *universal sea*, and by this time, plants were taking root on land.

By the time the dinosaurs roamed the land some 180 million years ago, Pangaea began to break up into our present-day continents (FIG. 1-7). Great rift systems pushed the continents apart at a rate of about 1 inch per year. The Atlantic, Arctic, and Indian oceans were created, and animals, which had freely roamed from one continent to another, were cut off from each other except by passage over a few temporary land bridges.

The Atlantic Ocean widened at the expense of the Pacific, and since the earth was not expanding, the excess ocean crust had to be disposed of. According to the plate tectonics theory (FIG. 1-8), new lithosphere is created at the midocean ridges, while

Table 1-1. Geologic Time Scale

ERA	PERIOD	EPOCH	AGE IN MILLIONS OF YEARS	FIRST LIFE FORMS
Cenozoic	Quaternary	Holocene	.01	
		Pleistocene	2	Man
		Pliocene	10	Mastodons
		Miocene	25	Saber-toothed tigers
	Tertiary	Oligocene	40	
		Eocene	60	Whales
		Paleocene	65	Horses Alligators
Mesozoic	Cretaceous		135	Birds
	Jurassic		180	Mammals
	Triassic		230	Dinosaurs
Paleozoic	Permian		280	Reptiles
	Pennsylvanian		310	Trees
	Mississippian		345	Amphibians Insects
	Devonian		405	Sharks
	Silurian		425	Land plants
	Ordovician		500	Fish
	Cambrian		570	Sea plants
Protozoic			3300	Invertebrates Oldest rocks
Archaean			4600	Meteorites

the old lithosphere is assimilated into the mantle by subduction in the deep ocean trenches. The plate boundaries are zones of intense tectonic activity that are responsible for mountain building and most of the earthquakes and volcanic eruptions.

As time goes on, the Pacific Ocean will continue to shrink; California will slice its way northward, where it will disappear down the Aleutian trench; and the isthmus connecting North and South America will sink below the ocean as the two continents go their separate ways. The Mediterranean Sea will get squeezed dry as the African and Eurasian plates continue to press against each other; a new subcontinent will tear itself free from East Africa and crash into India; and Australia will drift northward and collide with Southeast Asia. Eventually, continents will rearrange themselves into a totally new supercontinent, called *Neopangaea*, whereupon new continents will break off and drift apart, forming a strange new world with no resemblance to the Earth we know today.

As the Earth continues to age, the interior will cool to the point that lithospheric plates first become sluggish and then cease their movements altogether. When this occurs, some 2 billion years from now, the Earth will become deathly quiet, volcanoes and earthquakes will cease their activity, and the Earth will become in all respects a dead planet.

THE MOON

The origin of the Moon still remains a paradox, even though astronauts have visited it on several occasions and have brought back moonrocks for scientists to study. One theory has it that the Moon was plucked out of the Earth during the Earth's molten state by the tidal pull of the Sun and other planets. It could also have spun off by centrifugal force when the Earth was turning wildly on its axis, which would have left a large gouge in the Earth. According to one theory, this gouge became the deep Pacific basin. At that time, the day was only a few hours long and the Moon completed an orbit, much closer to the Earth, in a matter of hours. Gradually, as the Earth's rotation slowed down from tidal friction, the Moon's orbit grew outward to its present position.

The problem with the so-called fission theories is that the Moon does not orbit the Earth in the equatorial plane as it should in this case. Also, had the Moon originated in this manner, it is unlikely either the Earth or the Moon could have survived the gravitational forces involved, and both would have disintegrated.

Yet the Moon is definitely receding from the Earth at a rate of about 2 inches per year, and the Earth's rotation has decreased through time. As tidal currents drag across the bottom of shallow seas, they dissipate tidal energy, thereby lengthening the day. At the present rate the Earth is slowing down, however, the Moon and Earth would have been so close less than 2 billion years ago that the surface would have completely melted. The Earth could have captured the Moon, but in so doing, the Earth's surface would have melted because of the increased

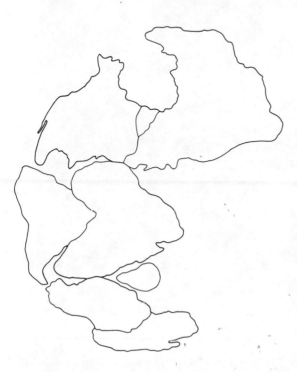

FIG. 1-7. Initial breakup of Pangaea 180 million years ago.

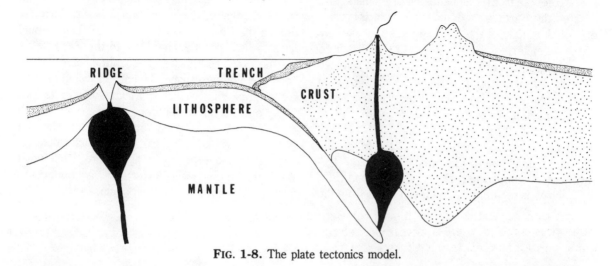

RIDGE   TRENCH   CRUST

LITHOSPHERE

MANTLE

FIG. 1-8. The plate tectonics model.

FIG. 1-9. The surface of the Moon.

(Courtesy of NASA)

angular momentum of the Earth-Moon system. In either case, no such evidence of melting is indicated anywhere in the geologic record.

Accretion from the same planetesimals that created the Earth is an equally unsatisfactory theory for the origin of the Moon because, unlike any of the other terrestrial planets, the Moon has little or no iron in its core and consists almost entirely of rock. Another theory suggests that the Moon might have been blasted out of the Earth when it was still molten as a result of a collision with a Mars-sized asteroid. If this so-called "big splash" theory is correct, then the mantle rocks of the Moon and the Earth should be of the same composition. Unfortunately, comparing rocks from the Moon (FIG. 1-9), which is tectonically dead, and rocks from the Earth, which is still tectonically active, will not give perfect matches because the Earth's mantle has changed in composition in the intervening period.

Another problem with the theory is getting these mantle rocks out into a nearly circular orbit around the Earth. A small planet sized body would have to deliver a glancing blow to the Earth; a direct hit would splash up huge quantities of rocks and send them off into space. The object would have to barely graze the Earth, vaporizing some of its own rocky outer layer in the process and mixing it with that of the Earth. All this material would then be blown into orbit in a long streamer, which would accumulate into a near spherical satellite, while what was left of the wayward asteroid would bounce off into space, never to be seen again.

2

What a Gas

THE Earth, viewed from space (FIG. 2-1), looks as though it is shrouded in an ocean of air with wisps of clouds floating lazily by. The atmosphere is a unique mixture of 77 percent nitrogen, 20 percent oxygen, 2 percent water vapor, and 1 percent other gases, the most important of which is carbon dioxide. No other planet in our Solar System has so much free oxygen or oxygen bonded to hydrogen, making water. It is for this reason that no other planet in the Solar System could possibly have life as we know it. If the level of oxygen rose just a few percent higher than it presently is, however, the entire surface of our planet could incinerate in one great conflagration.

Ninety percent of all the air in the atmosphere lies in a zone only 10 miles thick. This makes for a thin shell roughly 0.1 percent of the diameter of the earth and one-millionth of its mass. It is also the area where the weather is generated.

The atmosphere is divided into five major layers (FIG. 2-2), which extend out to the very reaches of space. The atmospheric pressure at sea level is about one ton per square foot; at Death Valley, California, which is 280 feet below sea level, the atmospheric pressure is much greater. The reason we do not feel the difference is that the air pressure is also equalized on the inside of our bodies, pressing outward with an equal amount of force.

THE DISCOVERY OF AIR

The first to speculate on the nature of air were the ancient Greek philosophers. Anaximenes (560-500 B.C.) argued that air was the chief element of nature from which all substances were made. Empedocles (490-430 B.C.) took this idea one step further and added the elements of earth, water, and fire. Various combinations of these four elements created all things, which can change and perish, but the elements remained unchangeable and indestructible.

Perhaps the most famous of the Greek philosophers, Aristotle (384-322 B.C.), refined these ideas and included the notion that one element could

FIG. 2-1. The Earth viewed from Apollo 8.

change into another, such as water to air when it boils. He also argued against the existence of a vacuum, stating that nature abhors a vacuum, and he believed outer space had to be filled with air or some other substance. Aristotle also said that air is weightless, and a 5-pound weight would fall five times faster than a 1-pound weight. Although many of them were incorrect, Aristotle's meteorological theories were held to be infallible in Western civilization for nearly twenty centuries.

It was not until the Renaissance period, around the sixteenth century, that there was a rebirth of inquisitiveness about the nature of things, and some of the dogma arising from revered Greek philosophers was questioned. Before this time, people were mystified about wind and air, and consid-

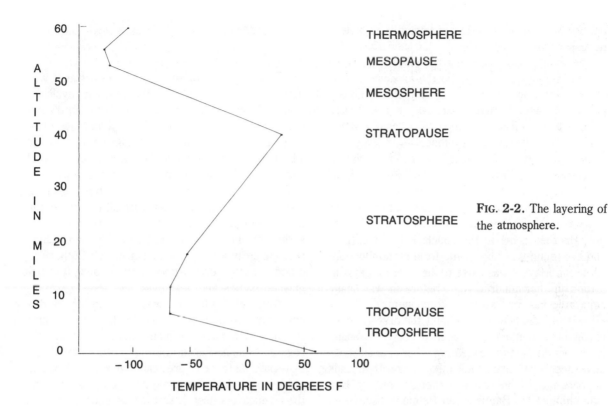

FIG. 2-2. The layering of the atmosphere.

ered them spirits and not part of this world. Perhaps, the most vigorous exponent of this new science was the Italian astronomer and physicist Galileo Galilei (1564-1642), who not only was considered to be the first modern scientist but might well be the greatest scientist of all time.

Galileo proved that air did indeed have weight because compressed air weighed more than the same volume of normal air. He made a vacuum by pulling down on a plug inserted in an inverted tube of water, producing a void space above the water at the top of the apparatus. What Galileo is most popularly known for, however, was his famous gravity experiment. On top of the Tower of Pisa, he dropped two iron balls of different sizes to prove that the acceleration of gravity and air friction would cause the balls to hit the ground at the same instant. Again, another of Aristotle's ideas went by the wayside.

Borrowing from the design of the German inventor Otto von Guericke, the English scientist Robert Boyle and his young assistant Robert Hooke built a much more superior air pump, with which they conducted a series of experiments on air and combustion in 1660. The air pump operated on the same principle that Galileo used to create a vacuum. A piston inside a cylinder was moved up and down, while valves were opened and closed to achieve a vacuum in an attached vessel. Inside this vacuum jar, Boyle dropped a weight and a feather to prove that Galileo was correct in asserting that all objects traveled at the same speed in a vacuum.

Boyle also found that sound could not travel in a vacuum, and neither could combustion take place in a vacuum. What he was most famous for however, was his discovery of what is known as *Boyle's law*, which states that the volume of a gas varies inversely with the pressure, provided the temperature remains the same. In other words, doubling the pressure on a confined gas will cause it to occupy half the space.

About the same time that Boyle and Hooke were conducting their vacuum experiments, the English scientist John Mayow was investigating combustion and respiration. It was known that air was necessary for keeping a flame or an animal alive; for neither could exist very long in a closed jar. Since not all the air was used up in the process, something else in the air was left behind. Repeated experiments with burning materials and with live animals inside a flask inverted over a basin of water led Mayow to the conclusion that air was composed of two substances. One was removed from the air by combustion, drawing water up into the flask, while what was left behind could not support burning or breathing. Therefore, some part of air supports combustion and life, while an inert part does not. He then came to the conclusion that burning and breathing were the same form of combustion. Although Mayow was close to discovering oxygen, it took another hundred years before air was finally separated into its two main components.

Carbon dioxide was probably the first gas ever recognized. It must have been observed bubbling from vats during the fermenting process of alcoholic beverages ever since their introduction thousands of years ago. In the early seventeenth century, Belgian chemist Jan Baptista van Helmont discovered that the gas given off by breweries was the same as that occurring from the reaction of acid on sea shells and from the burning of charcoal. This gas became known as *fixed* air because it was in a fixed form in certain solids and liquids. Van Helmont was the first to coin the term *gas* even though most scientists preferred using the terms *air*, or *airs*.

Over 100 years later, in 1755, Helmont's gas was rediscovered by the Scottish chemist Joseph Black. In one of Black's earlier experiments, he mixed acid with chalk in a tall glass cylinder and noticed a strong effervescence, which produced a gas that overflowed and extinguished a burning candle next to the container. Then he tried dipping a burning piece of paper into the container and observed that the flame immediately went out. He even poured the heavy gas over a burning candle, extinguishing the flame. Black also wanted to prove that the gas given off in alcoholic fermentation was the same as fixed air. He knew that blowing through a tube immersed in limewater would turn it cloudy because his breath contained fixed air. He collected a

phial of brewery gas and shook it vigorously with limewater which, to his satisfaction, also turned cloudy.

The inert part of air, or *residual air* as it was then called, was isolated by the Scottish physician-chemist Daniel Rutherford in 1772. Rutherford's experiments were similar to those of John Mayow: he burned various substances in an inverted jar set in a basin of water. He wanted to remove all the vital part of air (oxygen) so all that remained was the residual air. He hit upon the idea of burning phosphorus because it combined with all the oxygen in the air and produced fumes that were readily absorbed by the water in the basin. This left behind residual air in a fairly pure form, which Rutherford called *nephitic*, or poisonous, air because it extinguished flames and destroyed life.

Although Rutherford was credited for the discovery of nitrogen, at the time he did not recognize that he had isolated the main constituent of air. He regarded this gas as common air saturated with the material substance of fire, called *phlogiston*, which made it noxious. The name nitrogen was given by the French chemist J.A. Chaptal because it was found in saltpeter, a nitrate used in making gunpowder.

Scientific historians granted equal credit for the discovery of oxygen to the Swedish chemist Carl Scheele and the English chemist Joseph Priestley. In 1771, Scheele produced oxygen, which he called *fire air*, by heating saltpeter with sulfuric acid. He lowered a flame into a container of this gas, and it blazed brilliantly. He mixed fire air with foul air (nitrogen), creating an air whose properties tested exactly the same as common air.

Three years later, Priestley heated mercuric oxide in a tube inverted in a bowl of mercury. A gas was liberated whose pressure forced the mercury down the tube. Priestley inserted a burning candle into the tube, and the candle burned more vigorously than in ordinary air. He concluded after further tests of this "new air" that it was about five times purer than common air. Mice confined in a jar of new air would remain conscious twice as long as they would in a jar of common air.

In 1777, the French chemist Antoine Lavoisier,

called the father of modern chemistry, made the important connection that air was not a simple substance but a mixture of pure air (oxygen) and noxious air (nitrogen). Only pure air supported combustion and respiration, while the leftover noxious air, which he called *azote* (Greek, meaning no life) played no part at all.

Although Lavoisier did not discover oxygen, he was the first to grasp its vital role in combustion and oxidation. He proved that pure air was different from common air and was consumed in the process of combustion. He gave this air the name *oxygene*, meaning acid producer, because of the mistaken belief that oxygen was a constituent of all acids. Lavoisier also proved that fixed air was composed of carbon and oxygen and gave it the name *carbon dioxide*.

In 1784, the English scientist Henry Cavendish was the first to determine accurately the composition of dry air which, according to his calculations, consisted of 79.16 percent nitrogen and 20.84 percent oxygen. Although he did not know at the time that argon constitutes nearly 1 percent of the air, his values were remarkably close to the currently accepted dry air values of 78.084 and 20.948.

ORIGIN OF THE ATMOSPHERE

The first atmosphere was composed of the original hydrogen and helium left over from the solar nebula. During the Earth's first billion years, the light from the Sun was as feeble as it now is on Mars. The Sun was much more active then, however, with giant solar flares reaching millions of miles into space. A strong solar wind swept the light gases of the early atmosphere out into space, leaving the Earth in a near vacuum, much like the Moon is now. Without an atmosphere and oceans to distribute the Sun's energy, the surface of the Earth baked at the temperature of molten iron during the day and froze to lower than −100 degrees Fahrenheit at night.

The vacuum allowed meteors to speed their way to the surface, unmolested by air friction, which would otherwise burn them up. Some meteorites were stony, composed of rock and metals; some were icy, composed of frozen water, dry ice (carbon dioxide), and other frozen gases; and some contained carbon, like coal raining down from the heavens.

Comets (FIG. 2-3) also plunged into the Earth, bringing huge quantities of water. These cosmic visitors made quite a splash in the thin crust that was forming at the time, and great craters were excavated out of the young rocks. The shocks from the impacts split open the crust, forming large fissures. From these bled molten rock which paved over the surface. Eventually, the Earth became as pockmarked as the moon, with thousands of giant craters and flat basaltic plains.

One of the significant results from this battering of space junk was that a second atmosphere was formed when the Earth was about 0.5 billion years old. Trapped volcanic gases and lava exploded through the surface during the bombardment. These gases, combined with gases from the impact of comets and meteorites, created an atmosphere of nitrogen, carbon dioxide, water vapor, ammonia, and methane. Any free oxygen formed by the disassociation of water and carbon dioxide was permanently tied up in chemical reactions. The atmospheric pressure rose slowly until it was equal to or greater than that of today.

Even though the Sun was dimmer than it is now, the early climate on Earth was very hot because the early atmosphere acted like a greenhouse, allowing sunlight in but little of the Earth's radiant heat out. Between the water vapor that rose through volcanic pores and cracks in the Earth and the ice that fell out of the sky, the Earth acquired a vast supply of water. Because of the intense heat, however, all water evaporated, and any raindrops that did manage to fall evaporated before hitting the ground, leaving the entire surface hot and dry.

When the Earth cooled and the rains finally came, they came in torrents. Raging floodwaters cascaded down the slopes, gouging out deep gullies and canyons, and any high ground was soon carved down to the level of the plain. Water collected in craters and basins, which overflowed and combined to form shallow seas. The seas started out fresh, but gradually obtained salts and nutrients as streams washed over the land.

Storms were constantly racing across the planet

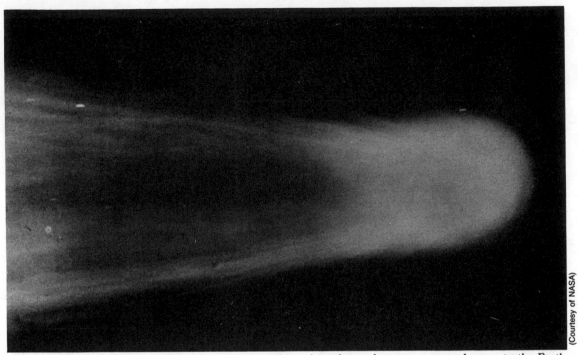

(Courtesy of NASA)

FIG. 2-3. Comets, such as Halley's Comet shown here, brought much water vapor and gases to the Earth.

and were of such violence that their energy output was equivalent to all-out nuclear war 24 hours a day, all year long. Lightning bolts packed such a wallop that they struck the earth with the force of a bomb. Mighty volcanoes, thousands of times more explosive than the greatest eruptions in recorded history, shot ash and gases a hundred miles or more into space. Earthquakes that would have gone off the Richter scale slashed through the Earth, leaving deep scars. The Moon, which was then only about half the distance away, pulled on the Earth and tugged at the infant oceans, causing huge tidal bulges and a great heaving of land and sloshing of water.

This might not seem like an environment that is conducive to life, and it is a wonder that in such utter chaos life could have formed at all. Life has a unique property, however: it is able to meet some of the most rigorous challenges the planet can offer. A certain species of blue-green algae lives in 140-degree hot springs, so it is not inconceivable that life started out on this planet when it was only 1 billion years old and still quite hot.

Evidence for such ancient life forms is found in 3.5 billion-year-old sediments at a desolate place called North Pole in Western Australia. Embedded in the sediments are fossils, called *stromatolites*, of small single-celled organisms. In the earliest periods of the earth, organic molecules already existed in abundance, as shown by a fascinating experiment by the American chemists Stanley Miller and Harold Urey in 1953. They boiled water, ammonia, and methane, which represented the primordial atmosphere and ocean in a special apparatus (FIG. 2-4), in which the gases were passed over an electric spark to simulate lightning and ultraviolet light. After several days, the scientist collected a dark soup containing complex amino acids—the very building blocks of life.

Life also might have started in lumps of clay. Clays attract the antecedents of life, namely protein and DNA molecules, and might have leached them out of the sea during the strong high tides. Clays also have the ability to store energy and release it during times of stress, such as during high and low

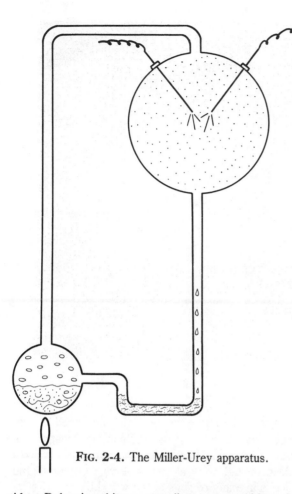

FIG. 2-4. The Miller-Urey apparatus.

tides. Releasing this energy all at once would tend to speed up biological reactions and could be the reason why life started out so quickly after the Earth formed—as though life could hardly wait to get started.

After uncountable random combinations and permutations, a set of organic molecules came together to form a small spheroidal cell that contained all the necessary ingredients for life. It could divide and replicate itself almost perfectly. The cell took its nutrients directly from seawater, which was a soup, bountiful in organic molecules. At this time, the Sun was more stable with less intense solar activity, although it still was not as bright as it is today. The seas were warm and rich in minerals and organic nutrients, allowing the single-celled life form that had

no natural predators to reproduce rapidly in a gigantic population explosion.

As with all species, natural selection tends to favor those who better adapt to their environment. With overpopulation came pollution and famine. Finally, the only species that were able to survive were the ones that had adapted an ability to obtain their energy directly from sunlight through photosynthesis. This early form of blue-green algae, was thus freed from the fierce competition for a scarce food supply, and it quickly became the dominant species.

Photosynthesis also created another great population explosion and a pollution problem of immense proportions because one of the byproducts of photosynthesis is oxygen (FIG. 2-5). At first, oxygen was neutralized by combining with iron to make a form of rust called iron oxide. The early oxygen became locked up in what are today's iron ore deposits and therefore could not endanger the species. When all the iron became oxidized, however, the sea soon became polluted with oxygen, which was poisonous to all forms of life.

Life again seemed doomed until some cells specialized in using oxygen to obtain energy from nutrients in a process called *respiration*. This ability resulted in the perfect symbiosis, whereupon organisms provided each other with a mutual life-support system. This symbiosis paved the way for the evolution of multicellular plants and animals. The animals fed upon the plants and upon each other, and a new predator-prey relationship came into being.

About 0.5 billion years ago, nitrogen became the dominant gas in the atmosphere, and oxygen leaked from the ocean increased dramatically at the expense of carbon dioxide. When oxygen reached a certain level, a tenuous layer of ozone formed in the upper reaches of the atmosphere.

When ultraviolet light strikes a molecule of free oxygen, the diatomic molecule disassociates into two oxygen atoms. They in turn combine with other oxygen molecules to form ozone, a molecule of three oxygen atoms. The ozone layer effectively blocks most of the incoming ultraviolet radiation from the Sun.

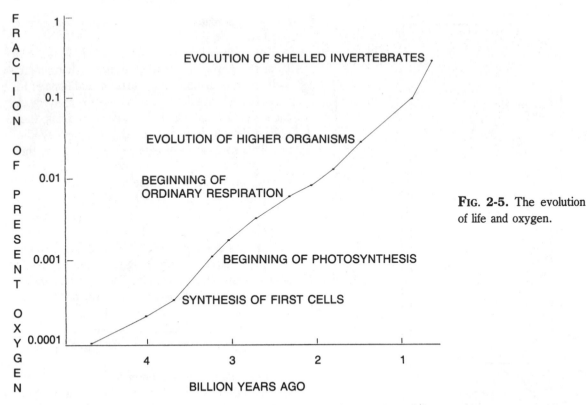

FIG. 2-5. The evolution of life and oxygen.

The layer of ozone signaled the arrival of the land plants because now they could safely leave the ocean, which was their only protection from the deadly ultraviolet rays. The greening of the Earth caused an increased absorption of sunlight, which increased the temperature of the planet, causing more plants to grow, thus producing more atmospheric oxygen.

THE HYDROLOGIC CYCLE

Three-quarters of the Earth's surface is ocean, which averages roughly 3 miles deep. This is a great deal of water, amounting to nearly .5 billion cubic miles. Only about 3 percent of the global supply is freshwater, of which about 75 percent is locked up in the ice caps. The remainder exists in surface and underground reservoirs, rivers, moisture in the soil, and plant and animal tissues.

The atmosphere holds only about .5 percent of the total freshwater supply at any one time. Each day, 1 trillion tons of sea water is evaporated by sunlight and falls to Earth as precipitation, mostly back into the oceans. Uneven distribution of rainfall causes deserts and tropical rain forests, droughts, and floods in many regions of the world. About 15 percent of the moisture in the atmosphere comes from the land by evaporation of standing bodies of water, the evaporation of soil moisture, and transpiration from plants. Plants evaporate a great deal of water through their leaves, both so they can stay cool, and, more importantly, so that water in the soil can bring nutrients up to the limbs by capillary action.

The average journey of a water molecule from the ocean to the atmosphere and back again takes about 10 days and is what is known as the *hydrologic*, or water, *cycle* (FIG. 2-6). The journey is much shorter in the tropical coastal zones, taking only a few hours, and considerably longer in the arctic regions, taking 10,000 years or longer. The quickest route water can take back to the ocean is by runoff in streams and rivers. This is the most ap-

(Courtesy of USGS)

FIG. 2-6. The circulation of water from the ocean to the land and back to the ocean.

parent and perhaps, the most important part of the water cycle.

Rivers provide waterways for commerce and water for irrigation, hydroelectric power, and recreation (FIG. 2-7). Since the dawn of civilization, wars have been fought for the control of rivers. Mighty rivers, like the Colorado, are now only a trickle of their former selves because of overirrigation, leading to long-standing water disputes. Surface runoff transports minerals and nutrients to the ocean and rids the earth of natural pollutants. Unfortunately, man also uses rivers for the disposal of industrial, agricultural, and human wastes, causing a pollution

problem of immense proportions.

The second means by which water is returned to the ocean is by aquifers. Water flows from the recharge area through formations of porous sand and gravel at a rate of only a few inches per year at most. The mistaken belief that groundwaters are bountiful subterranean rivers is painfully being dispelled as one aquifer after another is drying up because of overpumping. Groundwater that does make it to the ocean forms a freshwater-seawater interface near the shore. Excessive groundwater use in this area can cause the loss of hydrostatic head, allowing saltwater intrusion to contaminate the wells.

FIG. 2-7. The Grand Coulee Dam on the Columbia River.

(Courtesy of USGS)

THE CARBON CYCLE

Carbon is the element of life, and although it is speculated that life could be based on other elements such as silicon, most likely if life existed in other parts of the universe, it too would be carbon based. The oceans contain more than 50 times as much carbon as the atmosphere, mostly as dissolved bicarbonate. Most of the carbon is stored in sediments on the continents and on the ocean floor. The amount of carbon in the form of carbon dioxide in the original atmosphere was thousands of times greater than it is today. As the continents grew, however, they took carbon out of the oceans and the atmosphere and locked it up in sediments.

Carbon dioxide is rained out as a weak carbonic acid, which leaches minerals out of the rocks, especially calcium. Streams transport these minerals to the ocean. In the ocean, the calcium minerals are taken up in the shells of marine organisms. When the organisms die, their shells sink to the bottom of the sea, where they slowly build up deposits of limestone.

If this scrubbing of carbon dioxide out of the atmosphere and storing it in limestone continued unchecked, the atmosphere would be depleted of carbon dioxide. Without this important greenhouse gas, the climate would turn cold, bringing on an ice age. It was not until the development of the theory of plate tectonics, with its spreading ridges and subduction zones on the ocean floor, that the mystery was solved.

The ocean crust is relatively young, less than 5 percent of the Earth's age. The ocean floor is continually being created at the midocean ridges and de-

FIG. 2-8. The carbon cycle.

stroyed in the trenches. When the seafloor is forced into the Earth's interior, carbon dioxide is driven out of the limestone by the intense heat. It works its way up through the mantle and eventually ends up in the molten roots of a volcano or a midocean ridge. The eruption of volcanoes and the flow of molten rock from the midocean ridges resupplies the atmosphere with new carbon dioxide, making the Earth one great carbon dioxide recycling plant (FIG. 2-8).

Carbon dioxide plays an important role in regulating the temperature of the Earth, and any changes in the carbon cycle will have profound effects on the climate. As the early Sun heated up and temperatures on Earth rose, more water evaporated from the oceans, which increased rainfall on the land. The increased rainfall speeded up the weathering process, with the consequential loss of atmospheric carbon dioxide, which was converted to limestone on the seafloor. The drop in levels of carbon dioxide in the atmosphere kept the Earth from overheating. If the Earth's temperature began to get too low, less water evaporated from the ocean, chemical and biological reactions became sluggish, and less carbon dioxide was removed from the atmosphere, even though the input from volcanoes and midocean

ridges remain somewhat constant. Thus, the carbon cycle is also the Earth's thermostat, keeping the Earth's temperature within tolerable limits for life.

THE HEAT BUDGET

The atmosphere plays an important part in maintaining the balance of incoming solar radiation and outgoing infrared radiation. The Earth intercepts about one-billionth of the Sun's rays, and about half of this solar energy reaches the surface. About 90 percent of the solar energy that reaches Earth is used to evaporate water to create the weather. The Earth must reradiate back into space exactly the same amount of energy it takes in from the Sun. If it did not emit enough energy, the Earth would get intolerably hot. If it emitted too much energy, the Earth would get intolerably cold. This delicate balancing act is known as the Earth's heat budget (FIG. 2-9).

At the equator, the Sun's rays strike the Earth directly, and more solar radiation is absorbed at the surface than is reflected back into space. In the arctic regions, the Sun's rays strike the Earth at a steep angle, and more solar radiation is reflected back into

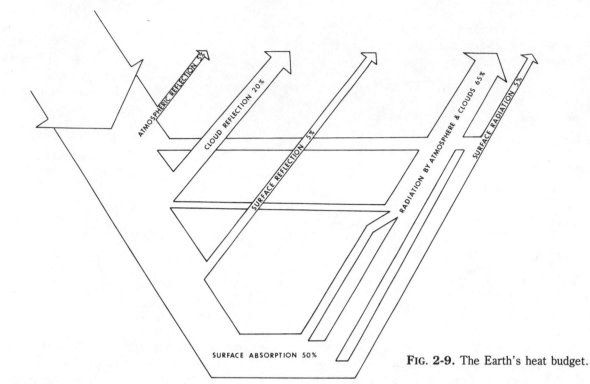

FIG. 2-9. The Earth's heat budget.

Table 2-1. The Wind Scale

BEAUFORT NUMBER	DESCRIPTION	MILES /HOUR	INDICATIONS
0	Calm	< 1	Smoke rises vertically.
1	Light air	1-3	Direction of wind shown by smoke drift, but not by wind vane.
2	Light breeze	4-7	Wind felt on face; leaves rustle.
3	Gentle breeze	8-12	Leaves and small twigs in constant motion; wind extends light flag.
4	Moderate breeze	13-18	Raises dust and loose vapor; small branches are moved.
5	Fresh breeze	19-24	Small trees in leaf begin to sway; crested wavelets form on inland water.
6	Strong breeze	25-31	Large branches in motion; telephone wires whistle.
7	Near gale	32-38	Whole trees in motion; inconvenience felt in walking against the wind.
8	Gale	39-46	Breaks twigs off trees; generally impedes progress.
9	Strong gale	47-54	Slight structural damage occurs.
10	Storm	55-63	Trees are uprooted; considerable structural damage occurs.
11	Violent storm	64-75	Widespread damage.
12-17	Hurricane	> 75	Devastation occurs.

space than is absorbed on the surface. This process should make conditions unlivable at both places because the equator would be unbearably hot, and the arctic would be unbearably cold. This does not happen because of the equalizing effect of the atmosphere. Warm air rises at the equator and travels aloft toward the poles. At the poles, the air cools, sinks, and returns to the equator, where it is warmed again.

This explanation is an oversimplification. The atmosphere is actually broken up into several convection loops, or *Hadley cells* (FIG. 2-10), but the effect of distributing thermal energy around the world is much the same. The warm tropical air makes it only about one-third of the way to the poles before it cools and returns to the equator. Similarly, the cold polar air makes it only about one-third of the way to the equator before it picks up warmth and returns to the poles. The middle latitudes, or temperature zones, then become a battleground between warm, moist tropical air and cold, dry polar air. When these air masses clash, storms are produced.

The distribution of air masses is also responsible for the world's winds (FIG. 2-11), which include, from equator to pole: the westerlies, the trade winds, and the polar easterlies. The Coriolis effect

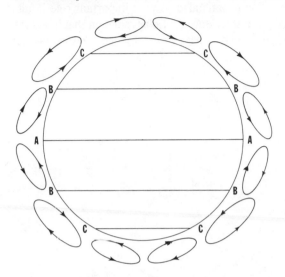

FIG. 2-10. The Hadley cells are responsible for the doldrums (A), the horse latitudes (B), and the polar easterlies (C).

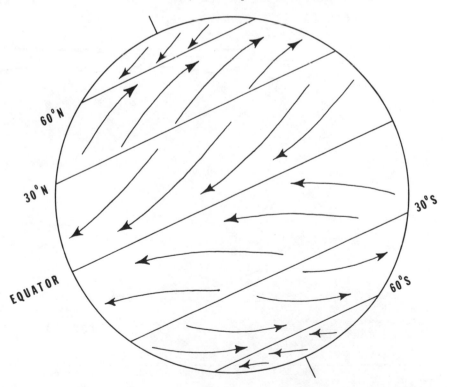

FIG. 2-11. The world's winds.

bends the air currents in response to the Earth's rotation. A point on the ground moves faster at the equator than it does near the poles because it is farther away from the axis of rotation and must travel a greater distance. Air currents moving toward the poles find the ground beneath them slowing down, which deflects them to the east. Air currents moving toward the equator find the ground beneath them speeding up, which deflects them toward the west.

The oceans also play an important role in distributing solar energy. Solar radiation that heats the oceans can be carried away by ocean currents; lost

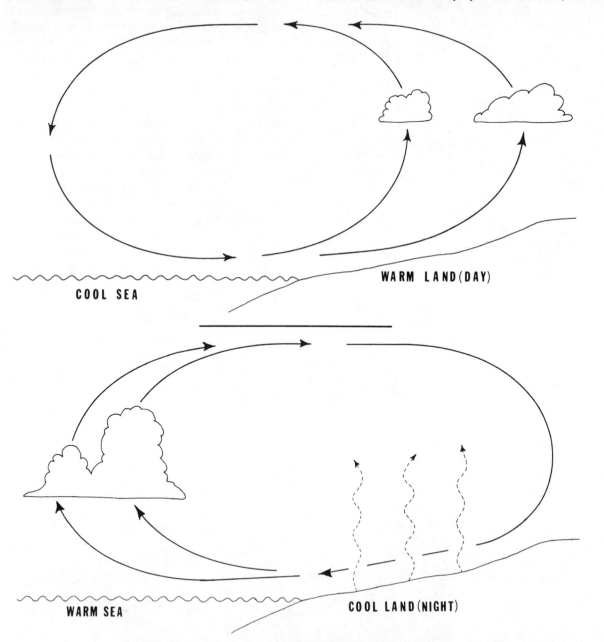

FIG. 2-12. The sea breeze (top) and the shore breeze (bottom).

by conduction, radiation, and evaporation; and regained elsewhere by precipitation. Heat flow between the oceans and atmosphere is responsible for cloud formation. It takes a great deal of thermal energy to evaporate seawater into water vapor. When the clouds move to other parts of the world, they give up this energy as precipitation, effectively distributing the ocean's heat.

The oceans are also responsible for the steady onshore and offshore breezes (FIG. 2-12). During the day, the land is warmer than the sea. Warm air rises from the land and travels aloft to the sea, where it cools and descends to the land again. At night, the land cools below the temperature of the sea. Warm air rises from the sea and travels aloft to the land, where it cools and descends to the sea again.

3

Stormy Weather

COMMON to many legends and religions is an account of a great flood that destroyed the world. In 2000 B.C. the Babylonians wrote of a violent storm with hurricane-force winds, torrential rains, and a disastrous flood, predating the Judeo-Christian version by a thousand years. It is possible that a massive storm surge from a large cyclone in the Persian Gulf could have flooded the Tigris-Euphrates region in what is now Iraq during the fourth millennium B.C.

Evidence of a major flood came from archaeological excavations in the 1930s at Ur. Field workers found a thick layer of water-laid mud between layers of soil laden with mud, brick, ashes, and pottery. According to the Old Testament version, Noah was forewarned about the flood and built an ark to save his family and all species of animals. The boat is reported to have journeyed to Mount Ararat in eastern Turkey, over 600 miles north of Ur. Some proponents claimed that the remains of the ark are buried in a glacier on the 17,000-foot mountain.

EIGHTEEN HUNDRED AND FROZE TO DEATH

The year 1816 went down in the annals as one of the coldest ever. Europeans called it the "year without summer," and rustic Americans called it "eighteen hundred and froze to death." Frost occurred every month that year in a wide area, extending from Ohio to Pennsylvania, New York State, and most of New England.

Farmers in the Northeast grumbled about the unusual lateness of spring, and there were hard frosts even into May. June started out a little better, and crops that had survived the late frosts started to progress. On June 6, the first of three unseasonable cold waves moved into New England and extended into Pennsylvania. The cold and wind lasted until June 11, leaving 3 to 6 inches of snow on the ground. The storm killed all but the hardiest crops from Connecticut to Quebec, and farmers were forced to plow their blackened fields and replant.

As farmers tried to salvage their crops, a second cold wave came on July 9. Although less severe, corn was again killed by frost in all but the best sheltered places. Summer weather did not return again until July 12, and conditions remained reasonably warm until August 20 when the harvest was about to begin. Then the Northeast was hit by a series of unusually early frosts. Ice formed 1 inch thick on tree limbs, and the mountains in Vermont were covered with snow.

A widespread killing frost on September 27 finished off what crops had managed to survive the previous cold spells, and farmers were forced to grind them up for fodder. Some farmers became destitute and had to slaughter their livestock because they could not feed them. There were reports of farmers hanging themselves because of the privations brought on by the cold summer. The shortfalls caused the price of grain to skyrocket, and poorer farmers could not buy grain to feed their families. They decided it was time to move west.

In Canada, conditions were much worse, and wheat that survived reasonably well in the United States perished from the onslaught of cold weather. Canadians, deprived of their major staple, could only look forward to a cold, miserable winter of hunger and starvation.

In Europe, the harsh summer of 1816 followed on the heels of the Napoleonic Wars, which ended with Napoleon's defeat at Waterloo in 1815. The wars left many parts of Europe ravaged and their economies severely disrupted. Attempts to replant wheat that was destroyed by late killing frosts were frustrated because of the lack of seed, and livestock had to be slaughtered for want of fodder. By the end of the year, the shortage of food was critical, especially in the cities where people were forced to eat all manner of things to stay alive.

France was particularly hard hit since all food reserves went to feed Napoleon's army, and none were left to tide the peasants over even in an ordinary bad season. There were food riots and insurrections in many parts of the country, and hungry and enraged citizens fought against soldiers who were stationed to protect the meager supplies of grain.

In Ireland, the potato crop failed, causing widespread famine, which led to a typhus epidemic from 1817 to 1819 that killed 65,000 people. The typhus spread all over Europe, causing more misery and suffering.

The failed harvests in India weakened so many people that an epidemic of cholera broke out and slowly spread to other parts of the world. In New York alone, as many as a hundred people a day died from the disease.

At the time, it was not known that the greatest volcanic eruption from 1600 to the present took place on the island of Sumbawa in Indonesia. In April, 1815, Mount Tambora blew off its upper 4000 feet and ejected some 25 cubic miles of debris into the atmosphere. The volcanic ash completely encircled the Earth and shaded it, dropping average temperatures as much as 7 degrees Fahrenheit in New England (FIG. 3-1) and 5 degrees or more in Europe.

THE BLIZZARD OF 1888

The most talked about snowstorm ever to hit northeastern United States blanketed an area from Maine through Maryland and from Buffalo to Pittsburgh. Snow was 4 feet or deeper, and drifts of 30 to 40 feet literally buried hundreds of towns and villages. The storm affected one-quarter of the country's population and isolated a dozen of its largest cities. The snow began just after midnight on Monday, March 12, 1888, after a pleasant springlike weekend. The snow continued throughout the day accompanied by 10-degree temperatures and 50-mile-per-hour winds.

In New York City, brownstone houses were practically buried under 15- to 20-foot drifts. People trying to go to work on Monday morning found themselves blown off their feet and were forced to crawl through blinding snow on their hands and knees. All traffic came to a standstill as the snow continued to pile up in the streets, and hundreds of people were stranded. Hotels, private homes, public buildings, and bars were soon jammed with people looking for shelter. Overhead telegraph, telephone, and electric wires, strung in unsightly webs, snapped from the weight of the snow, and poles were blown down. By nightfall, the darkened

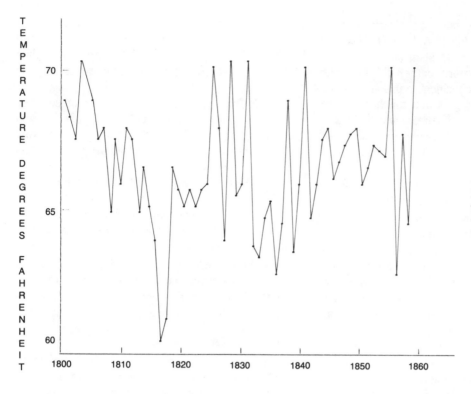

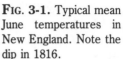

FIG. 3-1. Typical mean June temperatures in New England. Note the dip in 1816.

city looked like an eerie, abandoned arctic landscape, completely cut off from the outside world.

By early Tuesday morning, the snow tapered off to a light fall, and many New Yorkers going to work were faced with snow piled up to the second floor on many streets. Some attempted to climb over the drifts, while others tunneled their way through them. Thousands were hired to shovel the estimated 20 million cubic feet of snow off the streets, and by Friday, the end was still not in sight.

There were shortages of food, especially in the crowded slum areas, because wholesale houses could not make their regular deliveries to the small neighborhood grocery stores. What food that could be gotten went at exorbitant prices. Many of the poor were without food or coal to heat their hovels and had to be taken to safety at nearby police stations.

Over 400 people died, 200 in New York City alone, and thousands more suffered everything from exhaustion to amputation of frostbitten limbs. Some

200 vessels were sunk, grounded, or wrecked, and at least 100 seamen lost their lives.

THE JOHNSTOWN FLOOD

The greatest dam disaster in North America resulted from the failure of a large dam on the south fork of the Little Conemaugh River 15 miles northeast and some 450 feet higher in elevation upstream from Johnstown, Pennsylvania. A population of 55,000 people lived within the narrow river valley, with 30,000 living in Johnstown alone.

The earthen dam was built in 1852 as part of a canal project, which was later abandoned in favor of the railroad, leaving the reservoir unused and neglected. Thirty years after the dam was built, a major break was filled in, and a new lake was formed to promote sport fishing in the area. The dam stood over 70 feet high and 900 feet across, and Conemaugh Lake was about 1 mile wide, 2 miles long, and 70 feet deep. Efforts by opponents to halt construction because the dilapidated dam posed a danger to residents below met with frustration and failure.

In 1888, the foundation was found to be shaky, and many leaks were reported during the spring flood season. Although the townspeople were warned repeatedly of their peril if the dam was not strengthened, the warnings went unheeded.

The following spring brought a record flood. On Friday morning, May 31, 1889, rain had been falling in torrents for 36 hours, with a total accumulation of 8 to 10 inches. The unusual spring runoff sent the Conemaugh River over its banks and flooded the valley.

Swollen mountain streams which fed Conemaugh Lake caused it to rise at a rate of 10 inches an hour. Water spouted out from the dam's foundation, and it poured over the top, greatly weakening the dam. By noon, warnings were sent to residents in the valley below.

For some strange reason, the residents of Johnstown failed to heed the warning of the imminent dam break. Perhaps "Wolf!" was cried too often. Three hours later, the dam was simply pushed aside by the bulging lake, and a wall of water 40 feet high raced down the valley below. One by one, small communities downstream were swept along by the raging waters. By 3:30 P.M. only 15 minutes after the break, the floodwaters reached Johnstown.

The water moved at incredible speed along the narrow confines of the valley. Residents never had a chance to see the wall of water bearing down on them, but only heard a deep, steady rumble that grew louder and louder until its roar was like thunder just before it completely submerged the town. Everything in the water's path was totally obliterated, and people were carried off to certain death. Hundreds of houses and other debris piled up in front of a sturdy stone railway bridge that spanned the river in the center of town.

To add to the terror, the huge jumble of debris, which was people's only source of safety, soon caught fire, and as many as 2000 people still alive and trapped beneath the wreckage burned to death in the blazing inferno, which lasted for several days. The total number of dead within 20 miles downstream of the dam ranged from 7500 to as many as 15,000 people. The tragedy was made even more painful because the disaster could easily have been avoided in the first place.

THE GALVESTON HURRICANE

The most deadly natural disaster in American history occurred on September 8, 1900, in Galveston, Texas. The resort town had a population of about 38,000 and was one of the wealthiest cities in the nation. It was located on the east end of Galveston Island and was connected to the mainland by a single long bridge. It was a city literally built on sand with an average elevation of only 6 feet above sea level.

In late August, a tropical storm born over the mid-Atlantic gathered strength as it moved westward. In early September, it raked several Caribbean islands and entered the Gulf of Mexico. The weather bureau issued severe storm warnings for the Gulf Coast when the hurricane was some 600 miles east of Galveston.

Early on September 8, it began to rain, and swells increased until several city blocks were underwater and several beach houses were destroyed. By noon, it was raining heavily, the wind increased to 40 miles per hour, and 4 feet of water stood in the streets. The seas soon submerged the bridge, and the people of Galveston lost their only way out.

By midafternoon, Galveston Island was almost entirely underwater, and so was half the city. The rain was falling in torrents, and the winds were rising constantly. As night approached, several buildings caved in as waves ate away at their foundations, and the city was plunged into darkness because the generating plants were out.

By early evening, the eye of the hurricane approached the island, and the wind speed was estimated at over 110 miles per hour. A 5-foot tidal wave swept through town, forcing people to take to the upper stories of buildings whose foundations were already weakened by the pounding waves. As the terrible night wore on, building after building crumbled, sending people into the surging waters, where they were taken helplessly out with the tide.

When it was over, thousands of human corpses

Table 3-1. Chronology of Major Hurricanes in the United States

DATE	AREA OR HURRICANE	DAMAGE IN $MILLIONS	DEATH TOLL
1881	Georgia and South Carolina		700
1893	Louisiana		2,000
1893	South Carolina		1,000-2,000
1900	Galveston		10,000
1913	Great Lakes		250
1919	Florida Keys and Texas		600-900
1928	Okeechobee		1,800
1935	Florida Keys		400
1938	New England	$ 300	600
1944	Atlantic Coast		400
1954	Carol	450	60
1955	Diane	800	200
1957	Audrey, Louisiana		400
1960	Donna	400	50
1961	Carla	400	
1965	Betsy	1,400	
1969	Camille	1,400	250
1970	Celia	450	
1972	Agnes	2,100	130
1975	Eloise	500	
1979	Frederic	2,300	5
1979	Claudette	400	
1979	David	300	
1983	Alicia	675	
1985	Elena	550	

and dead animals were strewn along the beach. Burial details loaded the decomposing bodies onto barges for burial at sea in order to keep disease from spreading. The death toll ranged from 10,000 to 12,000 people—6000 in the city alone. The hurricane prompted the construction of a sea wall to protect against any future storm. The project paid off, for almost exactly 15 years later, a similar hurricane bore down on Galveston, this time killing less than a dozen people.

THE GREAT LAKES HURRICANE

On Friday, November 7, 1913, the weather bureau issued storm warnings for all its stations on the Great Lakes, the world's busiest waterway. Normally, shipmasters of cargo carriers tended to ignore the warnings, especially this late in the season. They wanted to make as many trips as possible before laying up for the winter when the lakes were too frozen to navigate. What made most sit up and take notice was that this was not the usual snowstorm or gale warning but a freak hurricane warning in an area where hurricanes have no business being in the first place.

The storm was born in the Canadian wastelands somewhere between Hudson Bay and the Rockies, far from the tropics where normal hurricanes spawn. The storm gathered strength as it grew wide and deep, and it spun into the Great Lakes as though drawn by a magnet.

Ships caught on the lakes had no knowledge of the dangers they faced because hardly any had a radio. The storm was of unprecedented violence, with rapid changes of wind direction and speed. Normally, storms on the lakes blow themselves out in less than 5 hours, but this storm raged for 16 hours with an average wind velocity of 60 miles per hour. Waves were at least 35 feet high and came in quick succession. Often the wind and sea were in conflict with each other, each going in separate directions—a most deadly combination.

Ships were tossed about like toys on an angry sea. A ship would take a dive under a huge wave never to be seen again. Some ships broke in half, some rolled completely over, some were dashed upon the rocky shores and broken to bits, and some were lifted bodily up and left high and dry on the beach. In all, 19 ships were destroyed—12 of them lost with all hands. The storm drove 20 ships onto the rocks. It drowned 250 sailors and caused millions of dollars worth of property damage to various shoreside cities and towns. It was the Great Lakes' ultimate storm with no equal before or since.

THE TRI-STATE TORNADO

The most devastating and incredible tornado outbreak in American history occurred on March 18, 1925. It began about 1:00 P.M. when a huge thunderstorm cloud near Ellington in southeast Missouri developed a vortex, which appeared at the leading edge of the cloud. By 1:15 P.M., without warning, the tornado destroyed its first town: Annapolis, Missouri. From there, it headed northeast in a straight line, traveling at a speed of 60 miles per hour.

The tornado crossed over into Illinois and completely destroyed the town of Gorham. On its way, it grew from one-quarter mile to nearly a mile wide. The enormous funnel assumed a shape like an inverted, truncated cone very close to the ground with lightning darting through it and a constant thundering roar, like a giant freight train.

During its 40-minute stay in southern Illinois, the tornado was its deadliest, severely damaging four towns, killing 540 people, and injuring over 1400

others. The winds were so great that bodies were thrown 1.5 miles out of town.

Leaving rural Illinois in a shambles, the tornado picked up speed and crossed the Wabash River into Indiana, where it completely destroyed the town of Griffin. The storm then veered in a more northerly direction and headed for Princeton. After destroying a quarter of the town, the tornado finally dissipated to the northeast.

The tornado left a 219-mile trail of terror and destruction, and in its 3.5-hour life, it obliterated four towns as though they were hit by an atomic bomb, severely damaged six others, and destroyed 15,000 homes. It killed 695 people—a record for a single tornado—injured over 2000 others, and racked up 50 million of today's dollars in damages. During the same period, five smaller tornadoes touched down in Kentucky and Tennessee, adding nearly 100 more to the death toll and making this the deadliest tornado outbreak in the nation's history.

Next to the Tri-State Tornado in terms of death and destruction was the Great Tornado Outbreak of February 19, 1884. This was also called the Enigma Outbreak (FIG. 3-2), so named because of the controversy over the death toll and the amount of destruction it caused. In a 14-hour period, from 10:00 A.M. until midnight, 60 tornadoes terrorized the South.

As luck would have it, no urban areas were struck by the tornadoes. If they had, the casualties could have been much greater than the estimated 800 dead and 2500 wounded (the reported death toll varies from 400 to 1200). Most of the victims were blacks, freed by the American Civil War, who lived on tenant farms or small plantations. Rough estimates placed property losses between $3 and $4 million. The number of buildings destroyed were estimated at 10,000, leaving 10,000 to 15,000 people homeless. Later that year on August 28, the first known photograph of a tornado was taken 22 miles southwest of Howard, South Dakota (FIG. 3-3).

The granddaddy of them all is the Superoutbreak of April 3 and 4, 1974. It produced the largest number of tornadoes, affected the greatest geographical area, inflicted the most damage, and ranks sixth in the number of deaths of all tornado outbreaks on

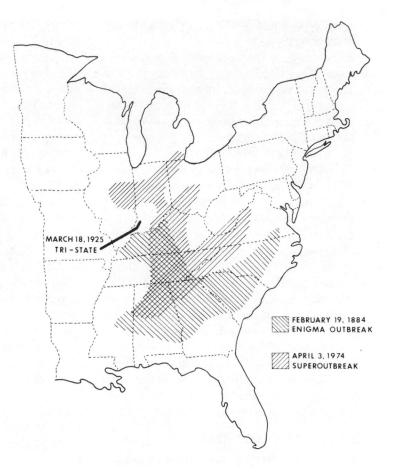

FIG. 3-2. Approximate areas covered by three of the greatest tornado outbreaks. The northeast trending zones also represent the paths of the tornadoes, which are influenced by the jet stream.

MARCH 18, 1925
TRI-STATE

FEBRUARY 19, 1884
ENIGMA OUTBREAK

APRIL 3, 1974
SUPEROUTBREAK

record. Tornadoes were reported in 13 states with deaths occurring in 11 of them. Alabama had the greatest death toll with 77, followed closely by Kentucky with 71.

The outbreak began in Illinois at noon on April 3 and ended in North Carolina at 9:00 A.M. on April 4, between which times 148 twisters were reported. Forty percent of the tornadoes occurred in Tennessee and Kentucky alone.

The total loss of life was 315 people, and there were more than 6,000 serious injuries. Nearly 28,000 families were left homeless, and damages were estimated at $600 million. Had this tornado outbreak taken place 100 years earlier when there was no National Weather Service to give tornado warnings, it could have been one of the most tragic natural disasters in American history.

A HURRICANE NAMED CAMILLE

The most terrifying hurricane in modern American history, and one of the greatest in terms of intensity and destruction, was Hurricane Camille. She was rated as the second strongest hurricane ever to prowl the Atlantic. When Camille entered the Gulf of Mexico, where she gathered even more strength, she made her move at the southern shores of Alabama, Mississippi, and Louisiana, with up to 200-mile-per-hour winds.

Camille made landfall in the Mississippi Delta region at 7:00 P.M. on August 17, 1969, and by dusk, she began whipping at New Orleans. By dark, the longest bridge in the world—the 26-mile Pontchartrain Causeway, which links New Orleans with the outside world—was underwater. Near midnight, Camille struck the Mississippi coast, and a 20-foot

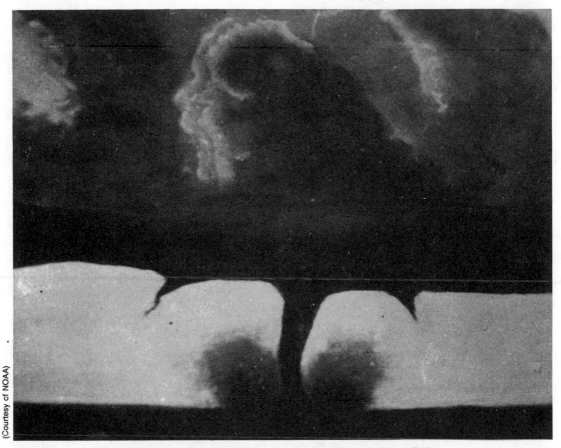

FIG. 3-3. The August 28, 1884, tornado near Howard, South Dakota.

tidal wave slashed at foundations and swept entire buildings, along with their occupants, several blocks landward and piled them up in a chaotic mass of debris. Those buildings which managed to survive the storm surge had their upper stories battered and ripped away by the howling winds. Anyone caught in the open was in danger of being hit by death-dealing missiles flying through the air.

Camille's gusting winds, tornadoes, and surging waves caused a path of destruction along the entire length of the Mississippi coast (FIG. 3-4). The main coastal highway was covered with sand and debris in some places, while in others it was completely washed away. Bridges were severely damaged, and over 500 miles of roads were made impassable because of the 100,000 tons of debris blocking the way.

The tourist industry was all but crippled as expensive resort properties were destroyed or sustained major damages. In the Gulfport area, three large ships suffered heavy damage when they were washed up on the beach.

When Camille had finished her handiwork on the coast, she took a run up the Mississippi River and turned east toward Virginia. Although much of her winds were dissipated, heavy rains fell in the Appalachian Mountains of central Virginia, causing flash flooding in many localities.

Hurricane Camille prompted the largest evacuation on American soil in the history of the country, involving hundreds of thousands of people. If this had not been so, considerably more than the 144 fatalities would have taken place. Nevertheless, she

(Courtesy of NOAA)

(Courtesy of U.S. Navy)

FIG. 3-4. Hurricane Camille as viewed by weather satellite (top), and the destruction she caused (bottom).

FIG. 3-5. Destruction of beachfront property by Hurricane Frederic.

racked up a considerable amount in property damages, which were estimated at $1.4 billion.

Camille was not the costliest hurricane. That distinction goes to Hurricane Frederic. On September 12 and 13, 1979, Frederic hit the United States mainland near the entrance to Mobile Bay, Alabama, close to the Alabama-Mississippi line. Maximum wind speeds registered 144 miles per hour, and maximum prevailing flood elevations were about 11 feet at Mobile and about 14 feet at Gulf Shores, Alabama. Most beachfront homes in the Gulf Shores area were either demolished or severely damaged by high winds and tidal surge (FIG. 3-5).

When Frederic finished his rampage on the coast, he ripped northward to Pennsylvania, New York, and western New England, exiting at northern Maine. In its wake, the hurricane left 13 people dead and an estimated $2.3 billion in property damage, making it the costliest U.S. hurricane ever.

Second only to Frederic in terms of destruction, dollarwise, was Hurricane Agnes. The catastrophic effects of river flooding by a hurricane were made painfully clear by the flood of late June 1972 in the Middle Atlantic States, which resulted from the heavy rains associated with Agnes. The storm originated in the Caribbean in mid-June, crossed the Florida panhandle coastline on June 19, and brought heavy rains from the Carolinas northward to New York (FIG. 3-6). Many streams in the affected area

FIG. 3-6. Track of Hurricane Agnes.

experienced peak flows several times greater than previous record floods, with the worst flooding in New York and Pennsylvania (FIG. 3-7). The widespread flooding claimed 117 lives and caused damages estimated at $2.1 billion.

A Hurricane Named Camille 37

Fig. 3-7. Extensive flooding at Wilkes-Barre, Pennsylvania, caused by Hurricane Agnes.

Hurricane Agnes is a prime example that floods can and do take place anywhere in the country. Floods have been and continue to be not only one of the most destructive natural hazards facing the nation, but also the most expensive. In recent flood annals, 1972 went down as the worst flood year on record, with $4.4 billion in losses and some 550 fatalities.

THE BIG THOMPSON RIVER FLOOD

A classic example of the disastrous nature of flash floods took place in the Big Thompson River Canyon at the foot of the Rocky Mountain National Park, about 50 miles northwest of Denver, Colorado. The trouble began on the eve of Colorado's 100th birthday. Saturday night, July 31, 1976. Stationary thunderstorms dropped 10 inches of rain in 90 minutes in the canyon area. Billions of gallons of water cascaded down the steep slopes overlooking the river and poured into the narrow canyon. The river rose with furious speed, setting in motion a most devastating flood on the Big Thompson River and its tributaries between Estes Park and Loveland, Colorado. For 30 terrifying minutes beginning around 8:30 P.M., thousands of vacationers, mostly campers, became instant amateur mountain climbers as they fled uphill for their lives when a 20-foot wall of water bore down on them.

For almost the entire 25-mile stretch of the canyon, people scampered for the safety of the high ground ahead of the sudden onslaught of water. Automobiles, motorhomes, camp trailers, tents, and assorted camping equipment, along with numerous large trees, houses, barns, and stores, were car-

Table 3-2. Chronology of Major Floods in the United States

Date	Rivers or Basins	Damage In $Millions	Death Toll
1903	Kansas, Missouri and Mississippi	$ 40	100
1913	Ohio	150	470
1913	Texas	10	180
1921	Arkansas River	25	120
1921	Texas	20	220
1927	Mississippi River	280	300
1935	Republican & Kansas	20	110
1936	Northeast U.S.	270	110
1937	Ohio & Mississippi	420	140
1938	New England	40	600
1943	Ohio, Mississippi, and Arkansas	170	60
1948	Columbia	100	75
1951	Kansas & Missouri	900	60
1952	Red River	200	10
1955	Northeast U.S.	700	200
1955	Pacific Coast	150	60
1957	Central U.S.	100	20
1964	Pacific Coast	400	40
1965	Mississippi, Missouri and Red Rivers	180	20
1965	South Platte	400	20
1968	New Jersey	160	—-
1969	California	400	20
1969	Midwest	150	—-
1969	James River	120	150
1971	New Jersey & Pennsylvania	140	—-
1972	Black Hills, S. Dakota	160	240
1972	Eastern U.S.	4,000	100
1973	Mississippi	1,150	30
1975	Red River	270	—-
1975	New York & Pennsylvania	300	10
1976	Big Thompson Canyon	—-	140
1977	Kentucky	400	20
1977	Johnstown, Pennsylvania	200	75
1978	Los Angeles	100	20
1978	Pearl River	1,000	15
1979	Texas	1,250	—-
1980	Arizona & California	500	40
1980	Cowlitz, Washington	2,000	—-
1982	Southern California	500	—-
1982	Utah	300	—-
1983	Southeast U.S.	600	20

FIG. 3-8. Destruction from the Big Thompson Canyon flood in Drake, Colorado.

(Courtesy of USGS)

ried off by the flood. Around 9:00 P.M., the flood crested near the town of Drake (FIG. 3-8) halfway between Estes Park and Loveland. Drake was destroyed, and almost the entire length of Highway 34 through the canyon was washed out, leaving thousands stranded in the mountains.

More than 1000 people were evacuated by Army helicopter, while rescue crews using four-wheel-drive vehicles searched the muddy river banks for other survivors. In many cases, they found the gored remains of those who did not escape the raging waters. Bodies were disfigured almost beyond recognition from the violent action of the water and from being battered against rocks and other objects. At least 139 lives were lost, hundreds of people were injured, and several were reported missing. Several small communities were wiped out, including 323 houses and 96 mobile homes, with over $35 million in damages. Although flash-flood warnings were given well in advance of the torrential rains, this was the height of the tourist season so mostly they went unheeded.

THE GREAT FREEZE OF '83

For three days around Christmas—December 24, 25, and 26—1983, temperatures fell sharply. Unprecedented cold and ice, the worst cold snap in the century, gripped the nation. December was the coldest month on record for most of the United States

(FIG. 3-9). The South, unprepared to deal with extremes of cold, suffered death and destruction out of proportion to the rest of the country. Because of the severity of the freeze and because it occurred during a holiday weekend, a great many people suffered from blackouts, loss of heat, and frozen water pipes, which posed serious problems for fire fighters.

It all started at 9:00 A.M. December 23, when an unusually large arctic air mass spilled across the Canadian border, covering the entire intermountain region from the Rockies to the Appalachians. Extensive snow cover during the month of December allowed the subfreezing air mass to flow southward without warming, as arctic air masses usually do.

The subfreezing air followed the Mississippi River Valley, spreading from the western Gulf of Mexico to Florida. In Florida, the citrus industry was dealt a heavy blow, for not only were fruit and other crops destroyed, but there was also a major loss of citrus trees, which caused roughly a 30 percent reduction in yield from the year before. The freeze caused extensive crop damage (mostly citrus) in Louisiana and south Texas as well.

The agricultural losses alone amounted to several billion dollars. There were extensive losses of marshland wildlife, along with a major fish kill in coastal bays along the Gulf of Mexico. As many as 400 lives were claimed directly by the arctic cold and from indirect causes such as fires and automobile ac-

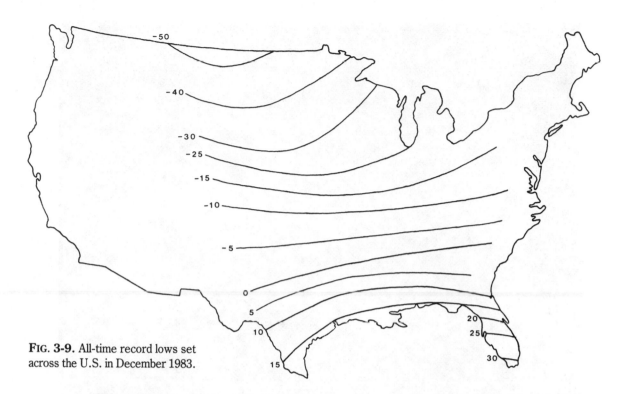

FIG. 3-9. All-time record lows set across the U.S. in December 1983.

cidents on icy roads. In the South, 50 persons died from exposure or hypothermia—fatalities practically unheard of in that region.

THE BAY OF BENGAL CYCLONE

The storms covered in this chapter were among the most violent and destructive in American History. To cover all the major storms worldwide would fill whole volumes. One exceptional area does require attention however, because of the staggering death tolls it has sustained through the ages from destructive cyclones. The cyclones are spawned over the Indian Ocean and are drawn, like a magnet, up the Bay of Bengal.

On May 24, 1985, Bangladesh, with a population of 100 million crammed into a country about the size of Wisconsin, suffered its 60th killer cyclone since 1822, bringing the total death toll to 1.6 million. Although less severe than most, the cyclone whipped up over 100-mile-per-hour winds, which pushed up a 15- to 50-foot tidal wave that swept over a cluster of islands in the shallow bay. Storm warn-

ings were broadcast by the government weather station, but the peasants were too poor to own radios and had no transportation to safety. So they simply rode it out as they usually do.

When it was all over, 15,000 people were dead (some estimates as high as 100,000) and 250,000 were left homeless. The storm left 30,000 cattle dead, 3000 square miles of cropland ravaged, and vital fishing grounds wasted. When rescue workers finally reached the islands, they found whole settlements, along with fishing boats, swamped or washed into the sea; emaciated peasants grubbing for food in the ruins; bloated bodies of people and livestock sprawling in mud-covered fields; and dazed survivors pushing bodies into shallow graves.

The problem is that there is essentially no high ground to retreat to during a tidal surge from a cyclone. Many of the hundreds of islands in the Bay of Bengal are little more than mud flats at high tide, called *chars*, where over 1 million people live. The chars are created when annual floods on the Ganges and Brahmaputra rivers eat away the mainland riverbanks and deposit fertile silt and mud in the shallow

(Courtesy of NOAA)

FIG. 3-10. The 1970 Bay of Bengal cyclone viewed from a satellite.

bay. They grow up in a year or two and then are suddenly washed away.

The bay itself starts broad at the mouth and narrows sharply toward its northern extremity where it is surrounded by low-lying coastal floodplains. Here the danger is made even more acute by the huge concentration of people, who have nowhere to take refuge in a severe storm. The government is incapable of rescuing the people before a cyclone roars through or offer much in aid to the victims. Peasants are also reluctant to leave their homes for fear that squatters will take over their land in their absence. With a high-population density, land is a premium and peasants will settle on the most hazardous ground in order to plant their crops and eke out a meager existence.

The year before Bangladesh achieved its independence from Pakistan, an immense cyclone hit the Bay of Bengal. On November 13, 1970 (FIG. 3-10) the cyclone killed upwards of 1 million people, making it one of the world's worst natural disasters in history.

The people of Bangladesh live in the world's poorest country with a per capita income of only $130, and two-thirds live below the poverty line. With a runaway population growth—estimated at 3.1 percent, or over 3 million each year—the country can hardly sustain itself. If the population of Bangladesh continues to grow at its astounding rate and people are forced to live on low-lying river deltas and cramped tiny islands, a similar cyclone could produce a catastrophe of monumental proportions.

Weather Folklore

MAN is by nature superstitious, especially when it comes to the weather. Primitive man fled for shelter in stark terror as raging thunderstorms bore down on him with their black billowing clouds, lightning bolts darting to and fro, and a deafening thunderous roar. He fought against screaming winds, blinding rain, and deadly icy stones that fell out of the sky. He desperately sought the safety of the high ground as flash floods tore through his village and left his world in ruin. He was caught in the path of a gyrating funnel of a monstrous tornado, the sight of which was an unbelievable horror.

It is no wonder that man named many of his gods after the weather. Jupiter was the Roman god of light, sky, and weather. Uranus was the Greek god of the sky and father of the giant Titans who ruled the world. Thor was the Norse god of thunder, weather, and crops. Today, we are not much different, and even though we have modern technology to help predict the weather, we still believe in certain omens to explain the unexplainable.

ANCIENT WEATHER BELIEFS

Primitive man lived with the elements, and prehistoric hunting and food gathering was closely dependent on the whims of the weather. If the rains failed to come, there would be little to eat because plants died or failed to ripen, and big game migrated to greener pastures. This dependency forced early man to become nomadic, wandering from place to place in response to the changing seasons. People gradually developed an almost intuitive feeling for weather conditions or "weather sense."

Today, this premonition about the weather is still retained by primitive societies and those whose livelihood is dependent on the weather. For today's urban dwellers whose lives are insulated from the natural world by an artificial environment, this weather sense largely has been lost. It takes a disastrous storm that strikes people personally to remind them that they are not so apart from nature after all.

The first thing man noticed about the weather

was that it came in cycles, representing the seasons. There were also celestial cycles, such as the phases of the Moon and the positions of the planets and stars in various constellations. The influence of these celestial events was believed to be responsible for events on earth, such as the weather and human behavior. These observations, known as *astrology*, became the basis for the first calendars. The ancient Egyptian zodiac was an imaginary belt in the heavens that was divided into twelve constellations, or signs. The appearance of special stars in certain constellations foretold droughts, floods, and all sorts of other calamities. When Sirius, the Dog Star, rose just before dawn, this marked the beginning of the new year. It also marked the rising of the Nile because it was the beginning of the flood season—the most important event in the lives of Egyptian farmers.

It was discovered that certain kinds of weather often followed particular types of phenomena, or *signs*. A collection of weather proverbs and folk sayings that were easily committed to memory (since writing had not yet been invented) gradually evolved about various signs, which were regarded as indicators of coming weather. Although much of this weather wisdom was based on superstition and

mythology, some came from actual observations of natural phenomena, such as the changing of the leaves and the migration of birds to mark the coming of winter. There were also observed changes in the color and optical conditions of the sky and how well sound traveled, which are significant effects of atmospheric conditions related to the weather. Our forefathers understood this when they said, "Sound traveling far and wide, a stormy day will betide."

The early weather lore was the collective experience of countless generations of hunters, farmers, and sailors. It became a part of the oral traditions and ceremonies of early societies and cultures and was passed down and modified from one generation to the next. With the invention of writing around 3000 B.C., weather lore was preserved permanently for the benefit of modern society.

The Babylonians developed a literature of epic poems and philosophical writings rich in weather lore around 2000 B.C. They believed that celestial conditions and cycles governed all earthly events. They practiced weather prediction based on omens of many kinds, including observations of planetary motion, optical phenomena, and the appearance of the sky (FIG. 4-1).

(Courtesy of U.S. Navy)

FIG. 4-1. Strange cloud formations over Marseilles, France.

The Babylonian astrologers were particularly interested in solar and lunar halos. They believed that when a dark halo surrounded the Moon (FIG. 4-2), clouds and rain would occur that month; when a halo surrounded the Moon and Mars stood inside, there would be destruction and all sorts of other calamities; and when a small halo surrounded the Sun (FIG. 4-3), rain would fall soon. Actually, they were not that far from the truth. The halos are caused by the refraction of light through tiny ice crystals in the upper atmosphere. This is an indication that moisture is on its way, and it could rain within the next day or so.

The Babylonians looked for recurring cycles in terrestrial phenomena and believed that the harvest could be predicted from thunderclaps heard on specific days. Many of the weather beliefs of the Babylonians were practiced through the medieval period until the advent of the science of meteorology.

Ancient peoples the world over regarded natural phenomena as manifestations of divine power. Nature was personified, and mythological deities represented both its good and evil aspects. Religious rites were performed by high priests to obtain the good will of the gods. Magnificent temples and large

FIG. 4-2. A lunar halo.

(Courtesy of NOAA)

FIG. 4-3. A solar halo.

(Courtesy of NOAA)

statues were built in their honor. If the gods were displeased, pestilence and famine might follow. In times of crop failure, sacrificial offerings, including human flesh, were made to placate the wrath of an angry deity. Religion then became the source of all knowledge about the weather, and any attempts to explain atmospheric phenomena by natural causes was labeled as blasphemy. It was the Greeks, such as Aristotle, who finally broke with tradition and caused a direct conflict between religion and science that was to continue for many centuries.

MEDIEVAL SUPERSTITION

There was no other period in man's history when time practically stood still, and knowledge advanced so little as there was during the Middle Ages, also known as the Dark Ages. For 1000 years after the fall of the Roman Empire (about A.D. 476), scientific investigation about the weather practically came to a halt. The teachings of the Greek philosophers were held to be complete and infallible by medieval scholars and were incorporated into the doctrine of the church, creating an absolute block to further scientific investigations into the weather in the Western world.

After the seat of the civilized world shifted to Islam, knowledge became preserved, fused, and enriched by the work of Muslim philosophers and scientists. There was then a return of weather prediction based on the observation of the motions of heavenly bodies.

A new breed of weather prophets sprang up in the vacuum left by Roman science, which died along with the empire. Many claimed to be able to predict man's destiny, the weather, and other natural events by the motions of the stars, planets, Sun, and Moon; by solar and lunar eclipses; and by the arrival of comets and meteors. The art of astrology, first practiced by the Babylonians 2000 years earlier, was now the accepted form of foretelling the future and was highly respected.

Prognosticators even attempted to make long-range weather predictions, which portended calamities and destruction. One such prophecy attracted much attention and set the Western world in panic. This was the so-called "Toledo Letter" written by

Johannes of Toledo in 1185. He predicted that in September of the following year, the planets would all line up on the same side of the sun and cause treacherous winds that would destroy the cities and bring about famine and other disasters. Frightened people took all sorts of precautions to save themselves from the disaster, which never came. For centuries afterward, similar predictions of disastrous weather events were made by astrologers and failed. These failures would have made the public distrustful if it were not for the fact that people had an unyielding faith in astrological weather predictions.

It is no wonder that, in this climate of fear of the unknown, people developed all sorts of superstitions about nature, and especially about the weather. A lot of false sayings were invented out of ignorance and fear, such as "Lightning never strikes the same place twice."

NAUTICAL WEATHER LORE

Perhaps nobody was more dependent on the weather for their lives and livelihood than sailors. Around 2000 B.C. when sailors first took to the sea in small sailing craft, they stuck closely to the shoreline, never losing sight of it for fear of wandering off into oblivion. When a storm came, they took shelter in some protected cove to wait it out. If they were foolish enough to try and ride out the storm, they might find their tiny ship dashed to bits on the shore.

Commerce flourished up and down the Mediterranean coast, and the seas were crowded with ships of all shapes and sizes. At night, the stars guided the sailors' way; during the day, the position of the Sun in the sky directed them. When the Greeks invented the compass, the sailors could navigate under cloudy skies when the stars and Sun could not be seen, without fear of sailing around aimlessly and falling off the edge of the Earth. As the ships sailed across the seas, far away from land, they were in much danger from sudden storms whose pounding waves could sink even the sturdiest of vessels. Seamen had to develop "weather sense" to survive the vengeance of the seas.

Nautical weather lore was handed down by countless unknown mariners, who based their knowledge on the behavior of the sea and winds, and the state of the sky. "Red sky at morning, sailors take warning. Red sky at night, sailors delight" is an accurate statement. A red sunrise usually indicates a dry air mass to the east, which likely will be replaced with less favorable weather when it moves away. A red sunset is usually a sign of a high-pressure system to the west and fair weather. A red sun also indicates that there is a good deal of dust and moisture in the atmosphere—two essential ingredients for rain.

A gray morning sky indicates a blanket of fog, which presages a clear day. A gray evening sky means the western sky is banked with clouds. This gave rise to the saying, "Evening red and morning gray, help the sailor on his way. Evening gray and morning red, bring down rain upon his head."

As sailors voyaged farther out to distant lands, they learned the geographical differences of wind and weather. They probably used nautical folk sayings such as, "Rainbow to windward, foul falls the day. Rainbow to leeward, damp runs away." or "Rainbow in the morning gives you fair warning." Rainbows are caused by the refraction of sunlight into its various colors by raindrops, which act like tiny prisms. The degree of arc depends on the angle of the Sun: the lower the Sun, the larger the rainbow. Since weather systems generally travel from west to east, a rainbow in the west promises rain, while one to the east indicates rain is moving away.

Another favorite folk saying was, "Mare's tails and mackerel scales make tall ships take in their sails." Mare's tails usually occur after the passing of a cold front, while a mackerel sky, resembling fish scales, precedes a warm front. Both are conditions that in many instances spell out an approaching storm.

During the fifteenth and sixteenth centuries, explorers roamed the world's oceans in tall ships in search of new sea routes and exotic lands. They gained new knowledge about the geographical distribution of winds (FIG. 4-4) and ocean currents, and the general weather conditions around the world. They took with them their ancient nautical lore for guidance about the coming weather. Italian navigator Christopher Columbus set out from Portugal to find a new westward sea route to India in 1492. He must have had a keen weather eye for, had he sailed farther north, his ships would have run into a long line of intense tropical storms, and someone else would have had to discover America. As it was, he safely landed in the West Indies.

THE WEATHER ALMANAC

Since the early days of writing, notes were made of natural phenomena and a variety of weather lore.

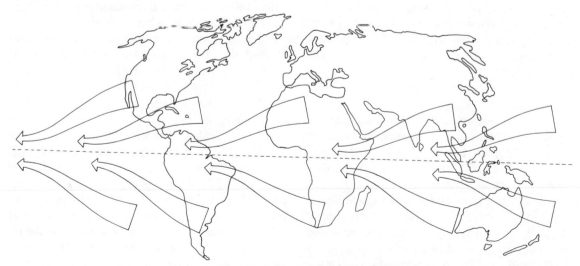

FIG. 4-4. The trade winds.

These became the first almanacs. Around 800 B.C., the Greek poet Hesiod wrote tablets giving advice to sailors about the best time for sailing. Clay tablets were kept on board ships so that captains could consult them in times of impending bad weather. During the fourth century B.C., Greek weather calendars recorded the normal succession of weather events throughout the year. In the first century A.D., the Romans compiled works that included weather signs and predictions. In the Middle Ages, small pamphlets were prepared containing an astrological prediction of the weather for a single year. With the introduction of the printing press in the fifteenth century, large numbers of these books were produced and became the predecessors of modern almanacs.

Because letters predicting disastrous weather events by astrology—such as planetary conjunctions, eclipses, and comets—were not very accurate and only served to scare people, publications about the weather took on a more general view and contained rules for weather predictions that were applicable at any time. Almanacs became a compilation of astrological and meteorological data, along with other miscellaneous information, including folklore. By the eighteenth and nineteenth centuries, pocket-sized, paper-bound almanacs were very popular. They contained information about the tides, astronomical features, and weather predictions based on astrology, and they were always read with great interest. They tended to avoid definite statements concerning the weather, especially about time and place. On occasion, an almanac weather prophet might venture to make a definite and explicit prediction and, by chance, turn out to be right, but this was more the exception than the rule.

When early settlers arrived in America from Europe, they brought along their traditions and weather lore not knowing the climate of this new and strange land (FIG. 4-5). The first settlers froze to death during their first winter because of lack of knowledge about the climate, lack of farming skills, and lack of supplies from Europe. New settlers sought signs of a benign climate, for their very existence depended on it. Their desires to remain and prosper on this new continent overshadowed some of their reports about the climate, to encourage their benefactors to send more supplies and manpower.

Eventually, the colonies grew and so did their weather lore. Not to be outdone by the Europeans, Benjamin Franklin published annually his *Poor Richard's Almanac*, a collection of witty sayings, proverbs, commonsense, folklore, astrology, and long-range weather predictions. His publication ran for 25 years, beginning in 1732, and sold as many as 10,000 copies annually.

Many almanacs based their weather predictions on the Moon and contained phrases like "Clear Moon, frost soon." This saying has some truth in it; for on a cloudless, cold winter night when there is an especially bright, clear Moon, the earth tends to cool rapidly by outgoing radiation, and frost might well form. If the crescent of the new Moon formed a cup that could hold water, then it is said that rain would pour down upon the Earth.

It was believed that the gravitational pull of the Moon exerted a control over the atmosphere. This notion became popular during the nineteenth century and still has some adherents. Long-range weather forecasts were based on the relative positions of the Earth, Moon, and Sun. It was known that the Moon causes tides, and during its 29.5-day orbit around the Earth, its gravitational influence is strongest during new and full moon. Over the course of 19 years, the Moon completes every possible variation in its cycle. Since three-quarters of the Earth is covered by ocean, which is where most of the weather is generated, it seemed not unreasonable to conclude that the same lunar pull that causes the tides also influences the weather.

Other forces also were thought to come into play, including an invisible Moon, Saturn-like rings surrounding the Earth, and an elusive planet called Volcan orbiting between Mercury and the Sun. The so-called Grand Alignment, occurring every 180 years (the last was in 1980), is a time when all the planets are in a line on one side of the Sun. The gravitational pull of the planets, mostly Jupiter, on one side and that of Sun on the other side was thought to cause huge tidal bulges in the Earth. These bulges were held to be responsible for anything from treacherous weather to earthquakes.

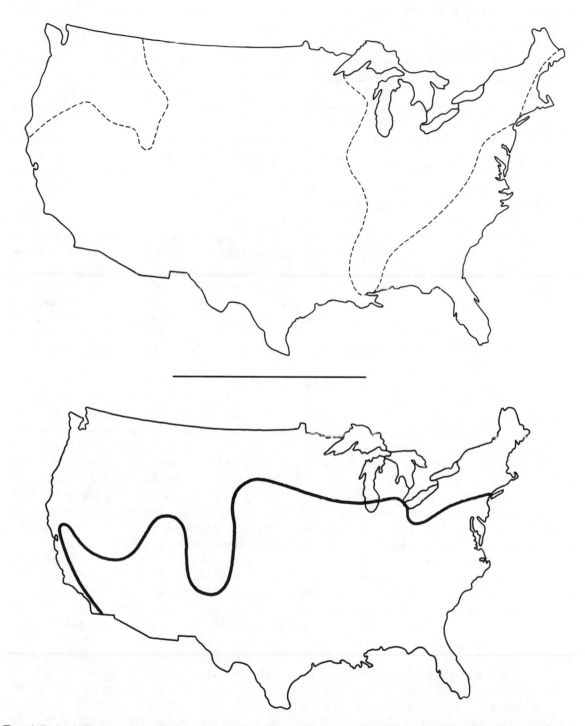

FIG. 4-5. (top) The gloomiest parts of the country where, during winter, possible sunshine is less than 50 percent. (bottom) The summer hot line, below which areas are subject to more than 700 degree-days.

ANIMAL WEATHER FORECASTERS

Through the ages, people have placed a great deal of confidence in the ability of animals to predict the weather. Since the earliest of times, people have looked to animals to guide them in their weather predictions.

The first observation was probably the migration of birds, whose direction of flight foretold the coming of the seasons. The birds themselves are no experts at weather forecasting, but time their migrations in accordance with instinct based on natural cycles, tempered with subtle changes in the weather such as temperature, humidity, air pressure, and density. Geese on the wing choose an altitude where the air is fairly dense and provides the most lift. On fair, high pressure days, the optimal height can be thousands of feet. When a low-pressure air mass moves in, however, the best altitude is close to the ground. Hence the saying, "Goose honks high, weather fair. Goose honks low, weather foul."

The ears of swallows and bats are sensitive to variations in air pressure. Prior to a storm when the barometer falls, the animals drop down closer to the ground to equalize the pressure in their ears. Ducks landing on local ponds have been known for their excessive quacking before a storm. Other birds are also pressure sensitive and tend to stay on the ground or roost in trees, instead of taking to the air, when a storm is imminent.

Fish are also thought to be pressure sensitive, and with the approach of a major thunderstorm, fish become less active and refuse to bite. Hence the saying, "Fish bite least with wind in the east," meaning that the worst storms come from lows with backing winds. Fishermen disagree on what is the best fishing weather, however, and cite good catches in any weather. Dolphins and porpoises seemingly at play on the ocean's surface signal the approach of a storm, and this is why ancient sailors considered them an evil omen.

The croak of a frog is thought to be another indicator of pressure, and when he is particularly noisy, it means the barometer is falling and it will rain soon. Frogs also have a low skin-moisture tolerance, and when the air is dry, they tend to stay in the water, but the high humidity before a storm brings them out in the open, along with their vocal effects. Even today, some people still keep a small tree frog in a jar of water as a sort of homemade barometer. The position of the frog lower down in the water indicates bad weather is at hand, and when the weather is fine, he is often out of the water entirely. Leaches are similarly used, and when the weather is fair, they lie placidly on the bottom of the jar but become restless on the approach of a storm.

The activity of bees and ants is also thought to be an indicator of low pressure. Prior to a storm, bees tend to stay close to their hive, and ants tend to march in straight lines.

The senses of animals are much more acute than those of humans, and they can sense a forthcoming storm long before humans can, although some people do complain of headaches, swollen joints, and aching corns prior to a storm. (This has more to do with gas pressure building up around a sore as the barometer falls.) Teachers also dread an upcoming storm; school children become most unruly and behave badly.

An approaching thunderstorm emits low-frequency sound waves that only animals can perceive. For example, birds can pick up sound waves down to 0.1 Hertz (cycles per second) through their hollow feathers. Many sayings cite the restlessness of animals before a storm. The proverbs indicate that among things to watch for are horses shying, goats butting, cattle and sheep leaving hilltops for lower ground, prairie dogs covering their burrow entrances with clumps of grass, crows cawing more than usual, and donkeys making a ruckus.

Earthquakes also emit a low-frequency sound, and unusual behavior in animals has been used as a method of earthquake prediction especially in China. Earthquakes also can produce an atmospheric phenomenon known as earthquake lights (FIG. 4-6). The air above an earthquake fault becomes ionized prior to rupture and produces an eerie glow, which frightens animals as well as people.

Animals are also sensitive to variations in temperature. Crickets are accurate thermometers, and the warmer the weather, the faster the cricket's metabolism, which produces a subsequent higher fre-

FIG. 4-6. Earthquake lights over Matsushiro, Japan, which lasted from 1965 to 1967.

quency of chirps. To get an idea of the outside temperature, count the number of chirps in one minute, divide by five, and add the remainder to 43. This is accurate to within a degree or two Fahrenheit above 55 degrees. Below this temperature, the cricket ceases his serenade. If it rains in the early evening, the accuracy is thrown off because of evaporative cooling close to the ground.(Although this simple rule applies specifically to Colorado crickets, it should work with other varieties as well.)

Although animals are able to make short-range weather forecasts, such as an impending storm, their ability to predict the weather on a seasonal basis is suspect. If a squirrel seems to be busier than ever gathering nuts, it does not necessarily mean that he is preparing for a long, cold winter, but that the harvest of nuts is better than usual. Also, if his tail is bushier, it does not necessarily mean that winter will be colder. Animals only react to climate change, they cannot predict it.

Much has been made of the dark brown stripes on the woolly bear caterpillar. Some people are convinced that the width of the bands can foretell whether winter will be bitter or mild: the narrower, the colder.

Groundhog Day is observed in one variation or another in just about every country in the Northern Hemisphere. It stems from the Christian feast of Candlemas, which falls on February 2, when winter provisions start to run low. "Candlemas day, Candlemas day, half your wood, half your hay." By then, people look for any sign of the coming spring. Supposedly, if the groundhog sees his shadow on that day, he is frightened back into his burrow and hibernates for six more weeks. (When the sun shines brightly in winter, it is accompanied by a very dry, cold Arctic mass, suggesting prolonged wintery weather.) On the other hand, if the day is overcast, and the groundhog does not see his shadow, it means the approach of warmer, moist conditions, and spring is not far behind.

MODERN WEATHER LORE

We live in a world with all sorts of electronic gadgetry that can tell us everything we want to know about the weather. Meteorology has come a long way from its humble beginnings, but sometimes direct observations by people with some weather sense can be more accurate in their own locality than the weather forecaster. An example would be the smoke rising from a chimney. If it continues to rise high in the sky, then the air is dry and stable—good conditions for fair weather. If the smoke falls toward the ground, however, then there is a great deal of humidity in the air from a low-pressure system, making the smoke moisture laden and heavy.

Most people believe that storms approach from the direction the wind is blowing. Actually, if the wind is coming from the east (a backing wind), it often means the storm is approaching from the southwest—the normal course storms take in the United States. To locate the direction of the low-pressure system, stand with the wind to your back. The low is to your left, and the high is to your right. Also, if the winds are out of the northwest, there is a good chance that a high-pressure system dominates the area and the weather will be fair.

Observation of the sky will probably render the most important clues about the forthcoming weather. Much of the weather lore based on observations of atmospheric conditions is fairly accurate. If wisps of high cirrus clouds are observed, followed by a succession of progressively lower clouds, there is a good chance a warm front with its accompanying rain is on the way. If the skies are covered with high, little puffs of cloud that look like fish scales, a turbulent warm air mass and the precipitation it brings will move quickly through the area. If clouds are retreating to the south or southeast with accompanying rain and lower temperatures, then a cold front has moved in, which will be followed by clear skies.

Observation of jet aircraft contrails can also tell a lot about the moisture content in the upper atmosphere. If the planes leave no contrails or the contrails die out fairly quickly, then the upper atmosphere is dry, indicating stable air and fair skies for awhile. If the aircraft leaves long, lingering contrails, there is a significant amount of moisture in the upper atmosphere, indicating that a warm front

FIG. 4-7. A home-built weather station.

is on the way. A ring around the Moon is another indication of moisture in the upper atmosphere.

A backyard weather station needs to be nothing more than a weathervane and a cup-type wind-speed indicator (FIG. 4-7). The direction and speed of the wind are two of the most important things to watch for when predicting the weather. An outdoor thermometer and an inexpensive barometer are also handy. A rapid drop in temperature and pressure usually indicates a storm is approaching. If you want to keep a record of the rainfall, an inexpensive plastic raingauge will do just fine.

A simple homemade device that can be used to predict the weather by the moisture content in the air is the hygrometer (FIG. 4-8). Human hair, as well as hemp tends to shrink in high humidity, which often precedes a storm. In the hygrometer, this slight shrinkage, or expansion when the air is dry, is transmitted to a lever, which acts as a pointer to indicate rainy or fair skies. Another popular hygrometer is the little Dutch weather house. If it is going to rain, the man of the house stands holding an umbrella in one of two doorways. When the air is dry, the man goes inside, and his wife appears at the other door

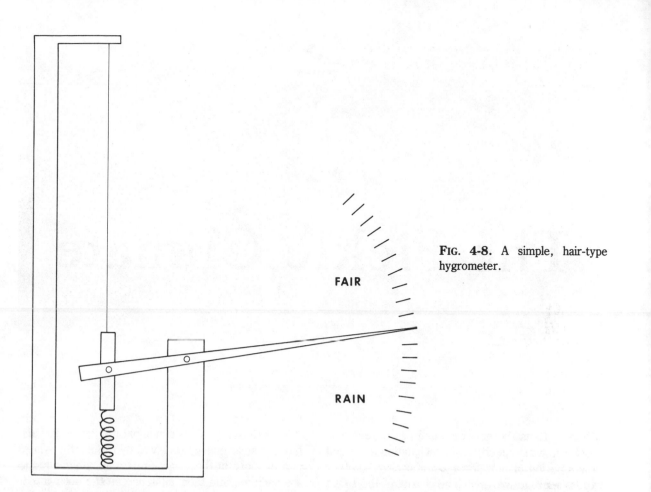

FIG. 4-8. A simple, hair-type hygrometer.

FAIR

RAIN

holding some flowers. It uses a coil of catgut, which twists up tight when the air is dry and uncoils by absorbing moisture when the air is humid. If you pre-fer not to bother with all these contraptions, there is always the weather forecast on the evening news. But that takes all the fun out of it!

5

The Fickle Climate

CLIMATE is the general trend of the temperature, wind speed, and precipitation averaged over a period of time for a given locality; in other words, average weather. The climate of the 1970s was different from the climate of the 1980s. Last century's climate was different from this century's. The climate 18,000 years ago when the Earth was locked in a deep freeze of an ice age was very much different than the climate of today.

Although the Sun is an important factor in influencing the climate, what the Earth does with its supply of solar energy is just as important. Other factors that enter into the climate puzzle are the Earth's orbit and the precession and degree of tilt of its axis. The drifting of the continents throughout geologic time had a large impact on the climate. There might even be extraterrestrial influences, such as the alignment of the planets which causes gravitational effects on the Sun and the Earth. If the Solar System passes through a large dust cloud as it travels around the Galaxy, the amount of sunlight the earth receives might be affected.

All these variables run in natural cycles and affect the solar energy received by the Earth. When two or more of these cycles overlap, their effects are additive, and their influence on the solar input can then be significant and greatly affect the climate of the Earth.

THE SOLAR CYCLE

The total amount of solar energy intercepted by the Earth spread uniformly across the surface and averaged over a year's time is known as the *average solar input*, and is roughly about 30 watts per square foot at any one instant. This means that a football field would receive on the average about 1.5 megawatts (million watts) of solar energy. It would be much less if the football field were located at the poles than at the equator, and if it were located in an area with mostly cloudy skies than one that is mostly sunny. If this energy could be converted into electricity at 100 percent efficiency, there would be enough electricity to run a small community. Many households take advantage of this abundant energy from the sun and use it to supplement their furnaces and water heaters.

For centuries, scientists have talked about a *solar constant*, that is, the amount of solar energy impinging on the Earth remains steady throughout time. The solar constant depends on the Sun's *luminosity*, or brightness, and the Earth's orbit. The Sun's luminosity depends on its size and surface temperature. The Earth receives more radiant energy when its orbit takes it closer to the Sun, and less when it is farther away. A reduction of the solar constant by only a few percent is sufficient to bring on a major ice age.

Although the average solar energy output of the Sun seems fairly steady over the short term, in its entire lifetime the Sun's luminosity has been steadily increasing. About 4 billion years ago, the Sun was some 8.5 percent smaller and its luminosity was 3 to 4 percent less than it is now. These facts imply that the solar constant was as much as 30 percent less than it is today. Over the next 4 billion years, the Sun is not expected to get any hotter, but it will continue to grow in size until it eventually encompasses the orbit of the earth.

The solar luminosity is controlled by the nuclear reactions taking place in the Sun's core, the properties of gases in the outer layers, and the gravitational forces that keep it all from flying apart. The conversion of hydrogen into helium to create energy makes for a constant depletion of hydrogen, with a consequent increase in luminosity over a very long period of time. This long-term rise in luminosity is too small to be detected by Earth-orbiting satellites, but small, short-term fluctuations—which many meteorologists and climatologists believe to be sufficient to produce deviations in the weather—are detected. These small changes in the solar output come in regular intervals of 22 years, which is known as the *solar cycle*.

Coinciding with the solar cycle is the 11-year sunspot cycle (FIG. 5-1). During a sunspot maximum when large numbers of sunspots mar the Sun's surface (FIG. 5-2), it would not be unreasonable to think that the dark spots would cool the Sun's surface,

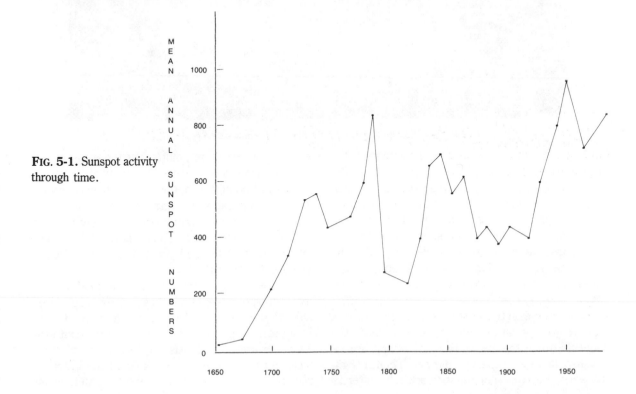

FIG. 5-1. Sunspot activity through time.

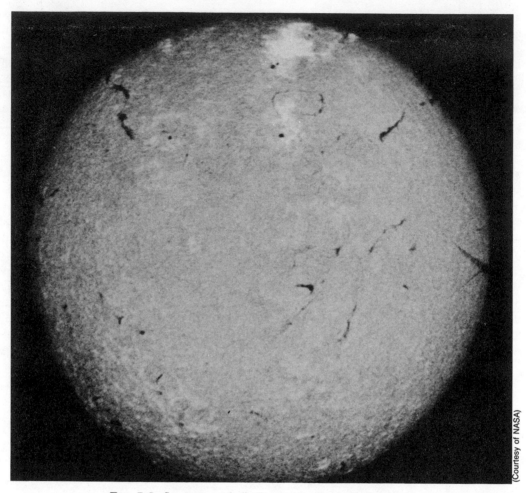

FIG. 5-2. Sunspots periodically mar the Sun's surface.

but that is not the case. Instead, the activity of the Sun increases. It did this by as much as 0.4 percent between 1976 and 1979. It is when there are no sunspots that the Sun can cool by as much as 1 percent.

Sunspots have long been known to the ancient Greek and Chinese astronomers, but Galileo was the first to observe them through a telescope, which he built. This occurred during the Inquisition, so scientists had to take a more cautious view on sunspots.

For more than two centuries, astronomers kept a telescopic eye on the sun, yet nobody made the connection that the appearance and disappearance of sunspots came at specific intervals. Then in 1843, the German astronomer Heinrich Schwabe, after 17 years of observation, pointed out the existence of a pronounced cycle of sunspot activity about every 11 years. Rudolf Wolf of the Zurich Observatory initiated an international program of solar observation that continues today. He searched widely through earlier observation records and concluded that a sunspot cycle, averaging 11 years, had existed for the years 1700 to 1848.

Since the mid 1800s, the accuracy and reliability of sunspot observations has improved considerably. Now it is well established that the sunspot cycle is not strictly periodic, but ranges from about 9 to 14 years in duration. Also, other solar activity—including solar flares, solar cosmic rays, ultraviolet radiation, and X-rays—varies directly with the sunspot cycle. Moreover, the polarity of the Sun's magnetic field reverses from cycle to cycle, producing a double cycle of 22 years.

In the middle of the nineteenth century, the English astronomer Richard Carrington made two important observations about the Sun and its activity. He showed that, in the course of each cycle, sunspots tend initially to appear at high solar latitudes, then progressively nearer the solar equator. This observation led Carrington to discover that the Sun does not rotate as a solid body, but rather the sunspots at the equator rotate faster than those at higher latitudes.

In 1908, scientists demonstrated that sunspots were associated with strong magnetic fields several thousand times stronger than the magnetic field on the Earth's surface. The Sun's magnetic field was thought to be generated on the surface by the difference in rotational speeds between the core and the upper gas layers. This action of converting mechanical energy into magnetic energy has been dubbed the *dynamo effect*. Because a magnetic field generated in this manner would be self-sustaining for long intervals, however, there would be little overall change in solar activity for perhaps billions of years. Also, dynamo theories fail to explain the migration of sunspots toward the Sun's equator.

An interesting alternative explanation involves the Sun's natural magnetically controlled oscillation, which would require a large-scale internal magnetic field that is a remnant of the field the Sun acquired when it first formed. Its intensity would be comparable with that of the sunspots, and it would reverse polarity coincident with their advent.

Near the turn of this century, in 1894, the English astronomer Walter Maunder made the startling discovery of a 70-year cessation of sunspot activity from 1645 to 1715. Known today as the *Maunder Minimum*, it was linked to the coldest part of the *Little Ice Age*, a span of unusual cold weather in Europe and North America from the sixteenth to the early nineteenth centuries. The unusually low level of solar activity is also supported by a gap in East Asian naked-eye sunspot records for the same period.

Recently, Chinese investigators claimed that a new source of records of naked-eye observations proved that sunspots continued unabated during the entire seventeenth century. They believed that the Maunder Minimum was nothing more than the result of insufficient data collection during times of internal turmoil brought on by political chaos. Interestingly, though, another Maunder-type minimum was uncovered during the investigations, which occurred under the Ming dynasty between 1400 and 1600, a period when official records of astronomical phenomena were relatively complete.

Tree rings (FIG. 5-3) are an ideal indicator of past climate: the wider the rings the more hospitable the climate was for that year. Individual rings also can be analyzed for their carbon-14 content. Carbon-14 is generated in the atmosphere when cosmic rays interact with nitrogen atoms (FIG. 5-4) and is an indirect measure of the changing solar activity. Growing plants incorporate radioactive carbon-14, which has a half-life of 5730 years, along with ordinary carbon-12 in their tissues. By measuring the carbon-14 content of the rings of ancient, but well-preserved, trees, investigators have been able to reconstruct the history of carbon-14 in the atmosphere going back more than 7000 years.

Also, by analyzing tree rings of the bristlecone pine, one of the longest living plants on earth, scientists have obtained a drought index for the Western United States dating back to the year 1600. The tree rings showed a drought period every 22 years, which provided a good correlation with the 22-year cycle of the Sun's magnetic polarity, or twice the sunspot cycle. An even better correlation existed between the drought record and the combination of the solar cycle and the 19-year cycle of lunar tides. In those tree rings formed between 1645 and 1715 is an account of a period of very unusual behavior of the sun, matching closely that of the Maunder Minimum.

In South Australia, lake-bed sediments, called *varves*, dating to the Precambrian era some 700 million years ago, show distinct dark bands of varying widths of mud and silt, with numerous lighter bands in between. These bands look almost like tree rings. During the time when these lake-bed sediments were laid down, the Earth was in the grip of a severe ice age, possibly the worst the planet has ever

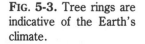

FIG. 5-3. Tree rings are indicative of the Earth's climate.

(Photo by L.E. Jackson, Jr., courtesy of USGS)

endured. Ice sheets covered the Earth almost to the equator, and life did not get a good foothold until the ice sheets had finally disappeared. The atmosphere during this time had only a fraction of today's oxygen content, which might have had an effect on the growth and maintenance of the ice sheets. Increased solar activity caused a corresponding increase in the temperature on Earth, which in turn entailed a greater annual discharge of glacial meltwaters and the deposition of thicker, darker layers of sediment.

The varves have periods of 11 years, as well as periods of 22 years and 90 years: the same as the sunspot rhythms observed in modern times. Also, periods of 145 and 290 years match modern periods in some tree-ring climate records.

This correspondence between sunspot activity and varve thickness provided a strong argument for a link between solar activity and terrestrial climate 700 million years ago. It also implies that the Sun's

activity has not changed much between then and now.

One of the most intriguing correlations made between solar activity and the effects on the atmosphere was between the 11-year sunspot cycle and the jet stream, which appear to influence the intensity of certain weather features. Scientists have analyzed data from the upper troposphere and the lower stratosphere where the jet stream exists, for a period covering 1949 to 1973, or just over two sunspot cycles. The results indicated that, during the winters of this period, the average position and strength of the jet stream have a strong correlation with solar activity. The reasoning is that the direct solar effect on the mesosphere and stratosphere during times of sunspot maximum could cause a 1500-foot rise in the troposphere, thereby affecting the jet stream.

This phenomenon could be useful in making

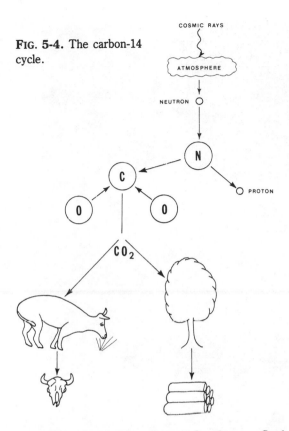

FIG. 5-4. The carbon-14 cycle.

then, to be a one-on-one Earth-Sun relationship, and storms on the Sun seem to affect storms on Earth.

THE MILANKOVITCH MODEL

In the 1920s, the Yugoslav geophysicist Milutin Milankovitch painstakingly calculated the changes of incoming solar radiation, latitude by latitude. There were no computers in his days, so his task was arduous and time consuming. When his labors were over, he had found three cycles that coincided

weather forecasts of 2 to 3 years in advance. Such forecasts could have enormous economic impact, but there is one catch. Solar activity will need to be accurately predicted as well.

The outermost extension of the Sun's atmosphere, the corona, is not gravitationally bound to it; therefore, the coronal layers escape from the Sun and give rise to the solar wind. The solar wind striking the Earth reverses magnetic polarity about four times with each rotation of the Sun, or about once a week. In between reversals, the solar wind dies down, and when it builds to full power again, there is a marked change in the weather, and strong lows march across the country.

One possible cause for this increased weather activity is an increase in electrical activity of the ionosphere. The ionosphere carries one electrical charge, and the Earth carries the opposite charge. Current flow passing from one to the other through thunderclouds create lightning storms (FIG. 5-6), making a global electrical circuit. There appears,

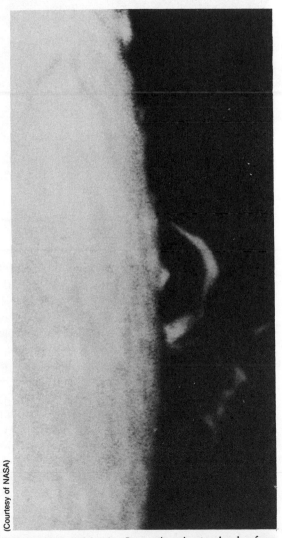

(Courtesy of NASA)

FIG. 5-5. Powerful solar flares give rise to clouds of gas and plasma particles.

FIG. 5-6. Lightning near Kankakee, Illinois.

neatly with the 100,000-, 41,000-, and 22,000-year ice-age cycles.

All possible orbital motions of the Earth can be defined as three elements: the shape of the orbit, the precession of the equinoxes, and the tilt of the axis. None of the orbital elements will affect the total amount of solar radiation reaching the Earth in a year's time. They only alter the amount of solar energy reaching certain latitudes in certain seasons. Thus, one area might have cold winters and hot summers at one time and mild winters and cool summers at another.

In 1941, Milankovitch proposed his theory of orbital variations (FIG. 5-7), in which he stated that cool summers, not severe winters, were all that were necessary to bring on an ice age. However, like his contemporary, Alfred Wegener, who proposed the continental drift theory, his ideas did not gain acceptance by the scientific community until the late 1960s.

The Earth's orbit around the Sun varies from almost a perfect circle to an ellipse. When orbiting the Sun in a circle, the Earth maintains a constant distance of 93 million miles from the Sun at all seasons; therefore, the amount of heat received from the Sun is the same throughout the year. During the ellipse phase, the Earth is closer to the Sun at one season, making it warmer, and farther away at the opposite season, making it cooler.

Today, the Earth is in an elliptical orbit. The point at which the Earth's orbit takes it closest to the Sun within (91.5 million miles) is called the *perihelion* and occurs in early January. The point at which the Earth's orbit takes it farthest from the Sun (94.5 million miles) is called the *aphelion* and occurs in early July. The Earth is 3 million miles closer to the sun in January than it is in July. This means that the sunshine is 7 percent weaker during the northern summer than during the southern summer. In an extremely elliptical orbit, the Earth might vary by as much as 30 percent from its strongest solar input to its weakest during the course of a year.

A complete orbital cycle from near circular orbit to elliptical orbit and back again takes roughly

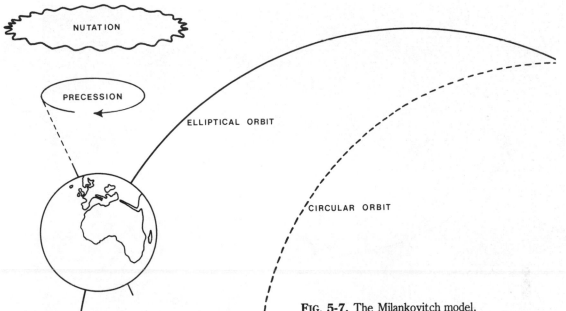

NUTATION

PRECESSION

ELLIPTICAL ORBIT

CIRCULAR ORBIT

FIG. 5-7. The Milankovitch model.

100,000 years. This Milankovitch cycle was used to explain the waxing and waning of the great ice ages every 100,000 years for the last 2 million years.

The Earth is inclined to the *ecliptic*, the plane of the Earth's orbit around the Sun, at an angle of 23.5 degrees. This tilt of the axis of rotation is responsible for the seasons (FIG. 5-8). During the summer solstice on June 22, the days are their longest in the Northern Hemisphere, and everywhere north of the Arctic Circle is in 24-hour daylight, while everywhere south of the Antarctic Circle is in 24-hour darkness. The Sun is directly overhead at the Tropic of Cancer, 23.5 degrees north latitude.

During the fall equinox on September 23, the Sun crosses over the equator into the Southern Hemisphere, where the days become longer than the nights. Both the North and South poles received an equal amount of sunlight with the Sun just breaking over the horizon.

During the winter solstice on December 22, the days are their shortest in the Northern Hemisphere. Everywhere north of the Arctic Circle is in 24-hour darkness, while everywhere south of the Antarctic Circle is in 24-hour daylight. The Sun is directly overhead at the Tropic of Capricorn, 23.5 degrees south latitude.

During the spring equinox on March 21, the Sun crosses over the equator into the Northern Hemisphere, where the days again become longer than the nights. As with the fall equinox, both the North and South poles receive an equal amount of sunlight.

The Earth's axis of rotation presently points toward Polaris, the North Star, but this was not always so. The Sun and Moon exert a force on the spinning Earth, making the Earth's axis wobble, or *precess*, like a toy top. The Earth's axis describes a cone as it precesses in the opposite direction of the Earth's rotation, or in a clockwise direction. The Earth's axis precesses quite slowly, taking about 22,000 years for one complete cycle. This means that around the year 10,000 B.C., Vega was the North Star. Summer and winter would have been the reverse of what they are today, with summer in the Northern Hemisphere between January and April. Those constellations presently seen only in the Southern Hemisphere would then have been seen in the Northern Hemisphere. In about 10,000 years from now, the Earth will again be tilted in the opposite direction.

The incline of the Earth's axis was not always 23.5 degrees, but has varied from 22 to 24.5 degrees. The effect of a change in the axial tilt an-

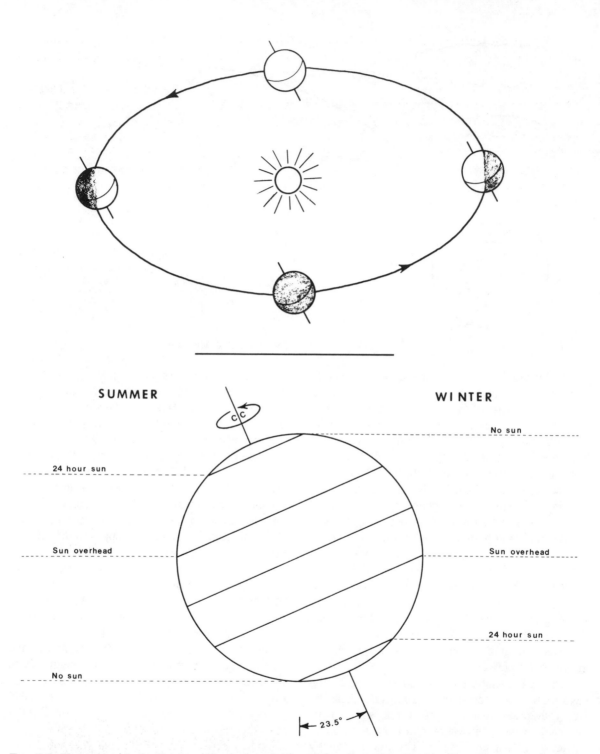

FIG. 5-8. The seasons in the Northern Hemisphere (top), and the effect of the Earth's tilt on the seasons (bottom).

gle is to shift the position where the Sun is overhead during the seasons. The greater is the tilt, the greater the difference between summer and winter temperatures.

If the Earth's axis had no tilt and was perpendicular to the plane of the ecliptic, the Earth would have no seasons; the Sun would remain directly over the equator at all times, the poles would barely see the Sun rise, and all parts of the Earth would receive the same amount of sunlight that they do during the equinoxes, all year long. It would be as though the earth were in a perpetual spring or fall equinox.

On the other hand, if the axis were parallel to the plane of the ecliptic, similar to the planet Neptune, the Sun would be directly over the North Pole during the summer solstice, the Northern Hemisphere would be in 24-hour light, and the Southern Hemisphere would be in 24-hour darkness. During the winter solstice, the Sun would be directly over the South Pole, the Southern Hemisphere would be in 24-hour light, and the Northern Hemisphere would be in 24-hour darkness. During the fall and spring equinoxes, the Sun would be directly over the equator, like it normally is, as it passes quickly from pole to pole.

Luckily for us the Earth is somewhat in between these two extremes, but even slight changes in tilt can cause large climatic effects. The shift of the Earth's axis from maximum to minimum and back to maximum again, as though the Earth was nodding up and down, is called *nutation*. The earth completes one full nutation cycle every 41,000 years. For the past 10,000 years the degree of tilt has been getting less, which should produce cooler summers and warmer winters.

These variations in orbital motions combine to produce the overall changes in the pattern of solar radiation falling on the Earth. They could be combined in such a manner as to bring about the worst possible weather conditions which could cause ice ages in the Northern Hemisphere. If the summer sunshine in the Northern Hemisphere should drop below a certain level, causing cool summers and severe winters, the volume of glaciers and ice sheets (FIG. 5-9) would grow in proportion to the sunlight

(Photo by W.B. Hamilton, courtesy of USGS)

FIG. 5-9. The Antarctic ice sheet.

deficit. Snow that had fallen in the previous winter would not melt appreciably during the summer, and the following winter's snow would fall on top of it. If this should go on unabated for several years, the whole process of changing from an interglacial period, similar to the one we live in today, to a full ice age could take place in a person's lifetime. Once a large area of the Northern Hemisphere became snow covered year round, a lot of heat from the Sun would be reflected away. This reflected heat makes the ice sheets self-perpetuating and is why ice ages linger for as long as they do—90,000 to 100,000 years. It also makes interglacial periods, which last only about 10,000 years, rare events in the Earth's history.

Once an interglacial period is established, it can exist only for as long as the darker, snowfree ground absorbs more warmth from the Sun and helps keep the snow at bay. Unfortunately, it appears that all the orbital variations are presently favoring a cooler Northern Hemisphere.

Dating the ice ages is a difficult task because, since ice melts, it leaves no trace of its existence except for a few mounds of boulders and some scratches on rocks. All the evidence for previous ice ages has been erased by the last one. In order to prove that the Milankovitch Model works, some fairly accurate age dates must be given to the half dozen or so major ice ages in the past 700,000 years.

One means of dating the ice ages is by dating the fluctuations in sea level (FIG. 5-10). During ice ages, a lot of water is locked up in glaciers on the land, and the level of the sea lowers appreciably. Coral grows only at sea level and fluctuations in sea level can leave a staircase of coral growth running up an island called a *coral reef*. The age of the ancient coral is determined by radiometric dating techniques. The ages of the coral terraces tend to be some 20,000 years apart, comparing closely with the cycle of variations in the tilt of the Earth's axis.

The Deep Sea Drilling Project has yielded evidence from ocean-bottom sediments of 400,000-, 100,000-, and 40,000-year cycles through an analysis of the calcium-carbonate content. Climate-related changes in the dissolving power of seawater, in the sea level, in the ocean circulation, and in the rate of erosion of the continents all affect the proportion of calcium carbonate in the sediments. When small,

FIG. 5-10. Relative sea level, through time.

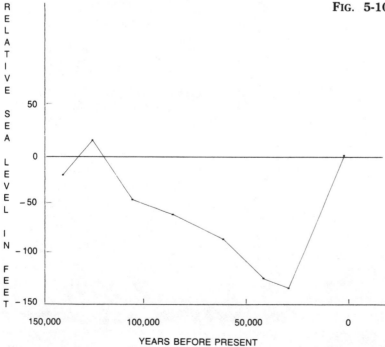

YEARS BEFORE PRESENT

shelled organisms die and are buried in the sediments, they take to their graves an indicator of the climate in which they lived. By comparing the content of the heavy isotope oxygen-18 and ordinary oxygen-16 in the fossilized shells of these creatures, scientists have a direct means of measuring the temperature. When seawater evaporates in a warm climate, water molecules composed of both oxygen isotopes are evaporated and eventually land as snow at the poles. During cooler climates, however, the heavier molecules are harder to lift into the atmosphere and are left behind. Therefore, the more oxygen-18 that is locked up in the shells, the colder the climate.

Chemical analysis of the Greenland and Antarctic ice sheets also has yielded a direct means of temperature measurement by comparing oxygen-18 to oxygen-16. One striking feature of this analysis is how clearly it follows the 41,000-year cycle and strongly supports the Milankovitch Model.

CONTINENTAL DRIFT

During the 1920s, the German meteorologist Alfred Wegener championed his theory of continental drift. Wegener supported his hypothesis with an impressive collection of facts, including the geometric fit of continental margins, matching mountain chains on opposite continents, corresponding rock successions, similar ancient climatic conditions, and identical life-forms on continents now widely separated by ocean. Unfortunately, Wegener died in 1930 at an early age during one of his Arctic explorations. Without his ardent support, continental drift, for over three decades, was unaccepted.

More recently, Wegener's theories on drifting continents have been accepted and were used to explain periods of glaciation. Land existing near the poles is often the cause of extended periods of glaciation. High-latitude land has a higher albedo and lower heat capacity than the surrounding ocean, which encourages the accumulation of snow and ice. The more land area in the higher latitudes, the colder and more persistent is the ice, especially when much of that land is at higher elevations where glaciers can be nurtured. Taking land away from the tropics and replacing it with ocean also has a net cooling ef-

fect because land in the tropics absorbs more of the Sun's heat, while the oceans reflect it back into space. Also, if the land area above a certain latitude is increased, and if snow falls steadily on this increasing area, a permanent polar glacial climate is produced. Once the glaciers are in place, the high reflectivity of snow and ice tends to perpetuate them and sustain a glaciation even if the once high land were to sink to the level of the sea from the weight of the overlying layers of ice.

Some scientists believed that this increasing weight of ice actually squeezes magma out of the Earth, like toothpaste squeezed out of a tube, and causes an increase in volcanic activity. The greater the volcanic activity, the greater the amount of ash that is cast up into the atmosphere, further cooling the Earth, which increases the glaciers.

By the time of the initial breakup of the continents, the climate of the Earth in the Cretaceous period was extremely warm, with a global average temperature 10 to 25 degrees warmer than it is today. There were no large variations in temperature between the tropics and the poles, and there is no evidence of any permanent ice in the polar regions. Coral reefs, for which warm water is essential, ranged as much as 1000 miles closer to the poles than they do today (FIG. 5-11). Alligators and crocodiles roamed in latitudes as far north as Labrador, and the dinosaur was the king of beasts. Continents bunched together near the equator during the Cretaceous allowed warm ocean currents to carry heat poleward. High-latitude oceans were less reflective than land and absorbed heat, which further moderated the climate.

When the continents drifted toward the poles, they disrupted poleward oceanic heat transport and substituted reflective, easily chilled land for absorptive, heat-retaining water. As the cooling progressed, land accumulated snow and ice, creating an even greater reflective surface.

At the end of the Cretaceous, polar forests existed at latitudes up to 85 degrees, well beyond the present-day tree line (FIG. 5-12). The most remarkable example is a well-preserved fossil forest on Alexander Island, Antarctica. This highly unlikely location for a forest could have been a result of a de-

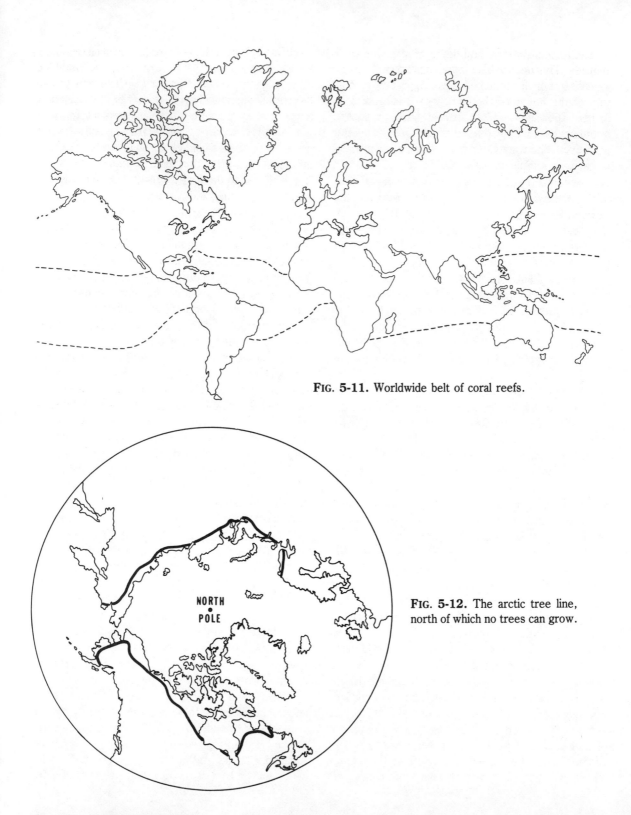

FIG. 5-11. Worldwide belt of coral reefs.

FIG. 5-12. The arctic tree line, north of which no trees can grow.

crease in the Earth's tilt, down to as little as 5 degrees. This decreased tilt would sharply diminish the difference in seasons, allowing more evenly spaced sunlight throughout the year. Even though such a decrease in the Earth's tilt would spread sunlight more evenly, however, it would also reduce the amount of mean annual heat, and plants are more sensitive to lack of heat than light. The trees could have developed a protective mechanism against the cold, but it is more likely that the tilt was not too much different than it is today, and that the trees adapted mechanisms for intercepting the maximum amount of sunlight during a time when global temperatures were warmer than they are today.

About 15 million years ago, most of the continents had just about completed their journey to their present positions. Antarctica moved to the South Pole and acquired a permanent sheet of ice. This was not the first time a continent had moved to a pole. During the late Paleozoic era some 280 million years ago, the entire supercontinent of Gondwanaland was across the South Pole. This brought on extensive glaciation over much of the land surface, while the North Pole, which was covered by ocean, was completely ice free.

Having land in the polar regions where the Sun's heat is feeble allows ice to grow and maintain itself all year round because of the low heat capacity of the land as compared with the ocean. When the land loses its heat, the snow sticks, while it simply melts when it lands on the warmer ocean. Increased snow cover increases the land's albedo, and the land has no chance to heat up and melt the snow. This situation makes for permanent ice that extends into the surrounding ocean and remains until the land finally moves away from the polar region.

The congregation of land in one area also affects the shapes of the ocean basins. The ocean bottom influences how much heat is carried by the ocean currents from the tropics to the poles. When Antarctica separated from South America and, later, Australia some 40 million years ago and moved to the South Pole, a circumpolar Antarctic Ocean current was formed. This current isolated the frozen continent and prevented it from being warmed by poleward-flowing waters. Since the demise of the dinosaurs 65 million years ago, the ocean bottom grew steadily colder so that now it is near freezing (FIG. 5-13).

The Arctic Ocean is the only ocean in the world

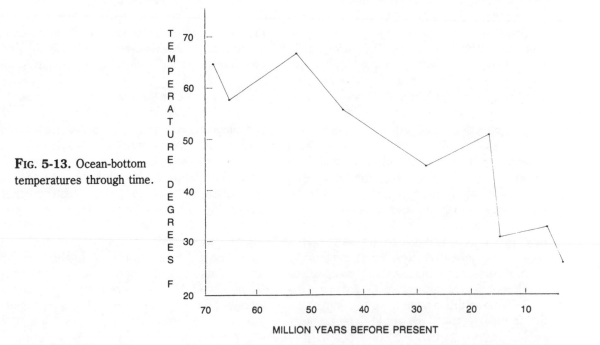

FIG. 5-13. Ocean-bottom temperatures through time.

that is practically landlocked. The land blocks warm currents from the tropics from getting to the North Pole and allowing the polar ice cap to melt completely. If the Bering Strait were to become blocked with ice, the warm Pacific current would effectively be kept from entering the Arctic Ocean, which could keep it frozen and unnavigable year round.

Changes in ocean water salinity also affects the formation of sea ice. If the Soviets were to divert water for irrigation from two major rivers that empty into the Arctic Ocean, as planned, the loss of fresh water into the ocean could increase its salinity. The saltier, heavier water would sink to the bottom, causing the ocean to overturn. Colder, less salty water would then be forced to the surface where it would freeze much easier than the salty water it replaced. Pack ice in the Arctic now varies from over 3 million square miles in the summer to nearly twice that amount in the winter. If none of the ice were allowed to melt in the short warm season, it could continue its expansion onto the continents, bringing with it the full force on an ice age.

The polar ice caps act as major heat sinks. They help drive the large-scale atmospheric and oceanic circulation systems, which have a large effect on the climate the world over. The moisture-laden hot air rising from the tropics is forced to move northward or southward by cooler, heavier air masses that are indirectly cooled by the polar ice. The polar regions, therefore, play a significant role in major long-range alterations in global climate patterns and have a considerable impact on mid-latitude climate.

As the ice cover fluctuates from year to year, so does its effect on the weather. If the ice cover is reduced, the amount of open ocean is increased as is the subsequent evaporation, which increases the cloud cover. The cloud cover in turn decreases the temperature and allows the ice cover to increase, which reduces evaporation and cloud cover.

Thus, a feedback mechanism moderates the Earth's temperature, much like a thermostat moderates the temperature of a house. If the ice caps were to suddenly disappear, the Earth's climate would change dramatically because of the breakdown in the circulation system that transfers heat away from the tropics to other parts of the world. Ice-free poles

could not last very long anyway since they would no longer receive warmth from the tropics, and would soon be covered in ice again.

EXTRATERRESTRIAL EFFECTS

The Sun and the Moon produce a gravitational tug on the Earth which is responsible for tidal bulges on land, sea, and air. The Moon is like a small planet, about three-quarters the diameter of Mercury and a little more than one-fourth the diameter of Earth, making the Earth and Moon a double planet system, with the Earth having roughly ten times more mass. The Moon exerts tremendous tidal forces on the Earth, enough to deform the crust by 3 to 6 inches, lift the ocean several tens of feet, and pull the atmosphere upward several hundred feet.

The Moon's orbit is inclined to the ecliptic by about 5 degrees, crossing the Earth's equator twice during one complete orbit. The Moon does not orbit the Earth in a perfect circle, but has an elliptical orbit. Its *perigee*, or closest approach, is roughly 221,000 miles, and its *apogee*, or farthest recession, is roughly 253,000 miles. The orbital time from perigee to perigee is about 27.5 days.

When the Moon's orbit brings it closest to the Earth, the tidal pull is greater. During a new moon and full moon, the Sun, Moon, and Earth are aligned so that the Sun and Moon pull together on the Earth. This synodic period from full to new moon is about 29.5 days.

When a new or full moon is within a day or two of perigee and within a couple of days of crossing the ecliptic, there seems to be an increase in precipitation in those areas where the Moon passes the zenith (directly overhead) than on other days of the month. It might be that the extra pull of the Sun and Moon on the atmosphere triggers weather systems into producing more precipitation.

It has been speculated that the solar cycle is regulated by the gravitational forces of the planets, particularly the inner planets and Jupiter. Throughout this century, the alignment of the inner planets on one side of the Sun seemed to produce different sunspot numbers than when the planets were merely scattered. Jupiter's orbit around the Sun is also roughly the same as the 11-year sunspot cycle, and since Jupiter is the largest planet, it has the most effect on the Sun.

When the planets line up on the same side of the Sun, their gravitational pull raises tides on the Sun, just as the Moon raises tides on Earth. The tides are probably small because of the distance of the planets from the Sun and the smaller gravitational forces involved, but the years of sunspot maximums and minimums since 1800 coincide closely with the Sun's tidal maximum and minimum. This information could have far-reaching implications for the prediction of sunspots and in turn long-range weather forecasts.

The alignment of the planets also has been thought to have a direct influence on the weather. The ancient Chinese astronomers were the first to recognize this alignment of the planets, or synod. Recently, Chinese researchers have found that the planetary alignments have affected the weather for the past 3000 years. The 179-year synods also coincide with the ups and downs in the temperature rec-ord of the Greenland ice cores and match the roughly 180-year cycle of solar activity (FIG. 5-14).

The planets rotate around the Sun at different rates; the inner planets complete their orbital cycles several times faster than the outer planets. There are nine separate and independent orbital cycles, so it takes about 180 years for the Earth to be on one side of the Sun with the rest of the planets on the opposite side. This occurrence displaces the center of gravity of the Solar System and stretches the Earth's orbit by nearly 1 million miles. Being farther from the Sun, the Earth then cools by a small amount for several years. The last synod occurred in October 1982, and Chinese astronomers predicted that it might have initiated a cold spell that could last up to one-half century.

One of the most fascinating theories for sudden mass extinctions, which occurred roughly every 26 million years for the past 600 million years, deals with a hypothetical companion star of the Sun. Most stars in our Galaxy have one or more companion stars, which are bound by a common center of

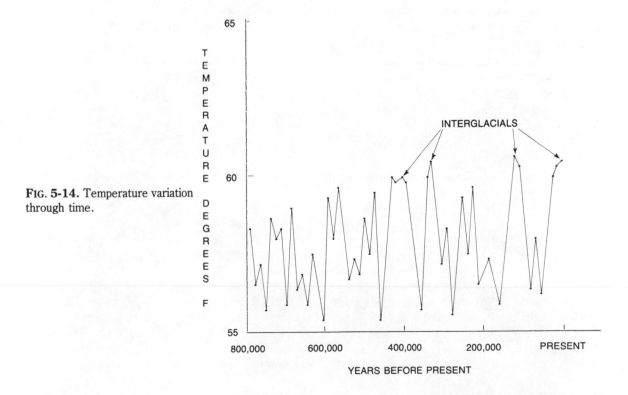

FIG. 5-14. Temperature variation through time.

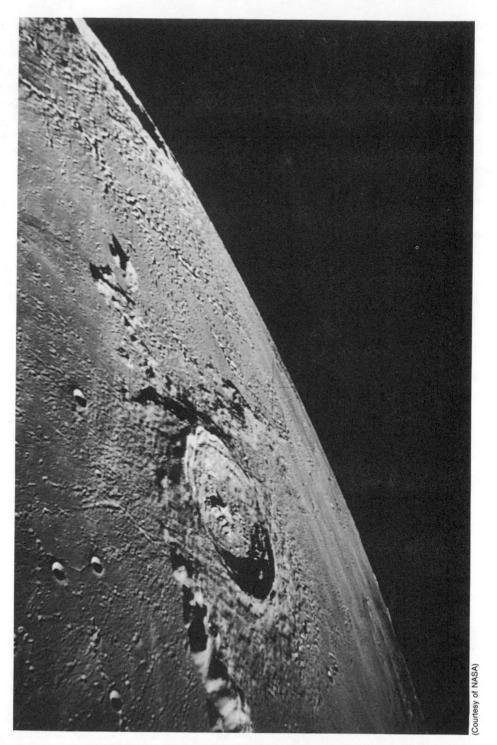

FIG. **5-15.** A large lunar crater viewed by Apollo 17.

gravity, making them orbit each other. The theory envisions that a small dark companion star, too far away for astronomers to see, orbits the Sun in a highly elliptical orbit. Every 26 million years or so, the Sun's companion star swoops out of the heavens and passes close enough to disrupt the Oort Cloud. This disruption scatters a large number of comets in all directions, many of which shower down on the Earth. The impacts made by the comets greatly disrupt the Earth's climate, causing a great extinction of species.

A search for the meteor craters on Earth is a difficult task because erosion has long since erased them. On the Moon and Mercury, the impacts are quite evident and numerous (FIG. 5-15). Unfortunately, because the craters tend to overlap each other, any regular pattern is probably lost.

There are still a few remnants of the ancient craters left on Earth. For example, the Manicouagan River and its tributaries in Quebec create a reservoir around a roughly circular structure 38 miles across. The structure is composed of Precambrian rocks that have been reworked by *shock metamorphism*, or impact by a celestial body. The impact crater was formed about 210 million years ago, exactly eight cycles of the death star, named Nemesis in honor of the Greek goddess who dishes out punishment over the Earth.

The Earth rotates along with the Galaxy, completing one revolution every 200 million years at a speed that would take it the distance to the Moon in half an hour (the Apollo astronauts took three days). Two or three times every century there is a supernova explosion somewhere in one of the spiral arms of the Galaxy. A supernova injects large amounts of dust and debris into the Galaxy. If the Solar System passed through relatively dense regions of this intergalactic dust cloud, the amount of sunlight the Earth receives could be altered every 100 million years or so.

The passage through such a dust cloud could take 1 million years or more and might have been responsible for some of the earlier glacial periods, which lasted for a similar length of time. This would be too much time to explain the relatively short ice ages of the past few million years, however. It is also doubtful that the Solar System's passing through a dusty arm of the Galaxy would have caused the continuous temperature decrease from the Cretaceous period to the present.

The Global Greenhouse

THE world lives in a greenhouse wrapped in a canopy of air. In that air are certain gases, aerosols, and dust particles, some of which are natural and some of which are man-made. They trap incoming heat from the Sun, and warm the Earth. If there were too many of these substances, the Earth could have a runaway greenhouse effect similar to the one on Venus, the Earth's sister planet. The surface temperature on Venus averages 750 degrees Fahrenheit, and it is not all a result of the planet being closer to the Sun, for it is about the same temperature as Mercury, which is much closer.

If there were not enough greenhouse gases or too much particulate matter, in the atmosphere, the Earth would become as cold as Mars, whose surface temperature averages − 63 degrees Fahrenheit. Fortunately for the Earth, the atmosphere maintains itself at just the right balance. Should this balance be disturbed by the meddling of man, then future generations might need to consider moving to the poles if the Earth became too hot, or to the tropics if it became too cold.

THE ORIGINAL GREENHOUSE

By the time the Earth cooled down, allowing the ocean to form, the atmosphere had evolved from the outgassing of volcanoes and degassing of meteorites into a mixture of water vapor, carbon dioxide, methane, unstable ammonia (which broke down into nitrogen), and traces of other gases. The original atmosphere probably contained as much as 25 percent carbon dioxide (Venus presently has 98 percent).

Carbon dioxide is transparent to incoming sunlight, but absorbs outgoing infrared radiation. The early Earth retained a good portion of the Sun's energy (FIG. 6-1), which was important because the Sun's output was then only about 70 percent of what it is today. If the Earth had our present atmosphere then, the average temperature would be below zero and the ocean would be a solid block of ice. Because of the large quantity of carbon dioxide, however, the Earth was actually a lot warmer than it is now.

Eventually, as the Sun became progressively

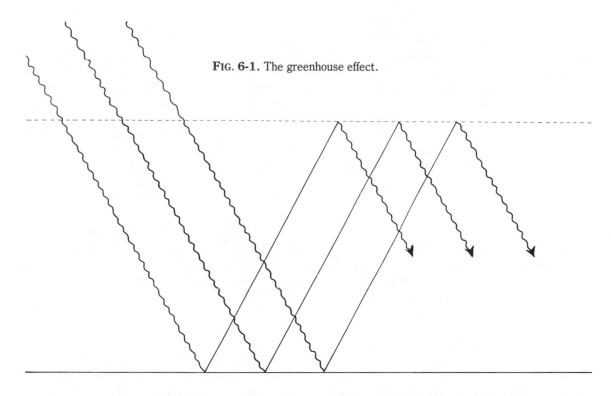

FIG. 6-1. The greenhouse effect.

hotter, carbon dioxide was taken out of the atmosphere and stored on the ocean floor and on the continents as carbonate rocks, or limestone. If carbon dioxide were allowed to increase without these moderating factors, the Earth would have gotten so hot that the oceans would have boiled away, and life would not have come into existence. On the other hand, if the oceans and continents continued to remove carbon dioxide from the atmosphere without it being replaced, the Earth would still be in trouble. The temperatures would plummet, and the planet would be encased in ice. Luckily, the primary source of carbon dioxide—volcanoes—replenished the gas at just the rate it was being removed, setting the global thermostat at a comfortable temperature.

As time progressed, green plants dominated the planet, removing carbon dioxide, combining it with sunlight, and storing it in their tissues as carbohydrates. The Earth probably cooled somewhat with the evolution of surface plants, but it was still much warmer than today. In the great swamps of the Carboniferous period 350 to 280 million years ago, plant growth was highly prolific and new plants practically grew on top of the old, forming thick layers of vegetable matter that was later buried and metamorphosed into coal.

During the Cretaceous period 125 to 65 million years ago, animals were abundant and roamed practically from pole to pole, attesting to a warm climate the world over. Volcanoes were particularly active during this time. They injected large amounts of carbon dioxide into the atmosphere, heating up the planet significantly. When animals, both large and small, were buried under thick layers of sediment, their tissues were metamorphosed into oil and natural gas. When fossil fuels (coal, oil, and natural gas) are burned, they return to the atmosphere their stored sunlight and carbon.

THE INDUSTRIAL AGE

Man discovered fire sometime before the last ice age. It was a good thing, too, because he would have been very cold and uncomfortable during the long, winter nights. For thousands of years, man did not do much with fire except use it to cook his meals, to keep himself warm, and to hunt game by setting brush fires. Then about 6000 years ago, he began to use it to forge bronze to make tools and weapons. The Bronze Age gave way to the Iron Age, about 1000 B.C., which gave way to the Middle Ages, about A.D. 500 to 1500.

All this time, man's use of fire was still rudimentary until the introduction of the steam engine by the Scottish inventor James Watt in 1781. The steam engine ushered in the industrial age, and for the first time, man was freed from muscle, wind, and water. Textile industries, which ran on water power, were converted over to steam, and steam engines drove the billows of mighty blast furnaces to produce vast quantities of iron for machinery.

Before the Industrial Revolution, the small fires of civilization had virtually no effect on the atmosphere. The fuel was mostly wood. It was coal that fueled the engines of the early industrial age, however.

The science of geology evolved out of coal exploration during the 1700s, and geologists mapped coal seams throughout Britain and Europe. In order to locate the coal, a geologist had to identify a certain rock strata of a certain age. Once he did this, then excavation commenced, and the coal was used to feed the furnaces of the factories and foundries, which were often located near the coal mines. The work in the mines was backbreaking and dangerous, and gained poor wages. In America, families settled in company-owned mining towns, where the prices for rent and supplies were often higher than the wages.

Although the Industrial Revolution began in Great Britain and Europe in the 1750s, it did not take hold in the United States for another 100 years. During this time, there was a proliferation of inventions, including the steam locomotive and the steamship, whose tracks and sea lanes spread all over the world to feed the hungry giant of heavy industry. In every major city, coal smoke belched out of a profusion of chimneys.

Although the public generally benefited from the prosperity, it also suffered serious health problems. Smoke was so heavy in some major cities that people were dying in unusually high numbers with lung ailments. Ash and soot covered everything. Buildings, trees, and other objects were painted black from the smoke. The smoke stung the eyes, and everywhere was the sulfurous stench of burning coal. Some days the smoke was so thick, people could not even see the Sun. Yet, farmers dropped their pitchforks and went in droves into the cities to find factory jobs. By the mid-nineteenth century, the populations of major industrialized countries were becoming more urban than rural.

The Industrial Revolution had been made through the exploitation of coal, steam, and iron. In the United States, coal gave way for the most part to oil and natural gas following the discovery of oil in Titusville, Pennsylvania, in 1859. The search for oil even rivaled the California gold rush a decade earlier, and the landscape became dotted with oil derricks.

Oil and natural gas used in industrial plants were much handier fuels than coal because not only were they easier to utilize and more efficient, but they were also less polluting. Electricity generated by fossil fuels and water became a new source of energy, which revolutionized industry and transportation, as well as lighting and heating. Steam engines were replaced by internal combustion engines, and America's love for the automobile was born.

CARBON DIOXIDE

The concentration of carbon dioxide in the atmosphere increased from 265 parts per million (ppm) in preindustrial times to 315 ppm in 1958, 335 ppm in 1978, and 345 ppm in 1986. If present trends continue, by the year 2020 the amount of carbon dioxide in the atmosphere could be twice the current amount, and the global mean surface temperature could increase by about 5 degrees Fahrenheit (FIG. 6-2).

The carbon dioxide content of the atmosphere also fluctuates with the seasons, rising to a peak in late winter and falling to a minimum at the end of summer in the Northern Hemisphere. This fluctuation occurs because plants, which require carbon dioxide are dormant in winter and grow in summer.

The human activities that are increasing the carbon-dioxide content of the atmosphere promise

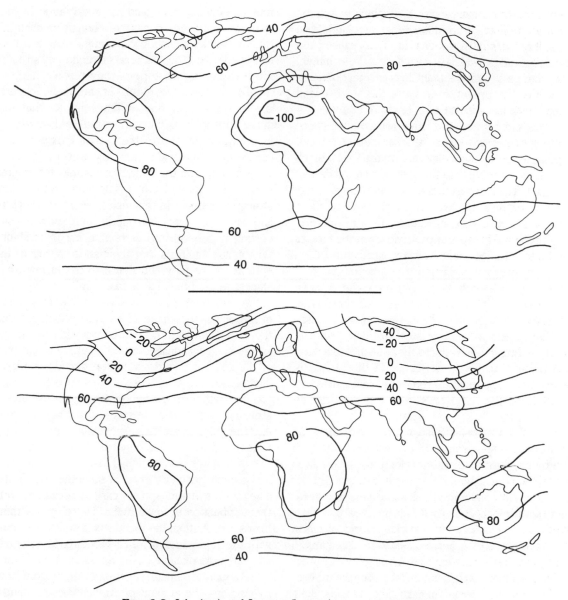

Fig. 6-2. July (top) and January (bottom) mean temperatures.

to bring a general warming of the climate over the next several decades. Although the mechanisms involved are not well understood, the results of a steady rise in carbon dioxide in the atmosphere probably will be catastrophic if other moderating factors do not come into play. An increase in the average world temperature could enlarge the area of arid zones and significantly affect agriculture. On the other hand, an increase in atmospheric carbon dioxide also could encourage the growth of green plants and cause a greening of the earth. Which way the Earth will go still remains an unsolved puzzle.

The world's great forests have a pronounced influence on the carbon-dioxide content of the atmosphere. The seasonal variation in the atmospheric concentration of carbon dioxide is correlated with a "pulse" of photosynthesis in the forests of the middle latitudes, which occurs during the summer. The change is substantially less in the Southern Hemisphere, apparently because the smaller land mass limits the area of forests.

The forests are extensive and conduct more photosynthesis worldwide than any other type of vegetation. Forests incorporate from 10 to 20 times more carbon per unit area than does cropland or pasture land. They also have the potential of storing carbon in quantities that are sufficiently large to affect the content of carbon dioxide in the atmosphere.

The world is presently cutting down the forests for timber and to make way for agriculture at an alarming rate, particularly in the Amazon Basin of South America. Half of the forests in the civilized world are now gone, and the rest are being hastily laid waste by mechanized timber harvests and slash-and-burn agriculture. The stores of carbon in the trees are being released into the atmosphere as carbon dioxide, while the reduction of the forests is weakening their ability to remove excess carbon dioxide from the atmosphere, as well as produce oxygen.

The long-term increase in carbon dioxide in the atmosphere—as much as 15 percent since 1850—is the result of an accelerated release of carbon dioxide by the combustion of fossil fuels on a grand scale. The present consumption of fossil fuels is equivalent to 1 ton of carbon that ends up as carbon dioxide in the atmosphere for each of the world's 5 billion people each year. Americans alone release some 6 tons per person per year. The atmosphere at present holds about 700 billion tons of carbon; therefore, the amount of increase in carbon by humans alone is approximately 0.7 percent annually. Some carbon is taken out of the atmosphere by biologic, hydrologic, and geologic processes, so that the average annual increases of atmospheric carbon dioxide by man's activity is a little less than 0.5 percent.

Several times the amount of carbon in the atmosphere is held in the biota (all living things) on the surface of the earth and humus (dead organic matter) in the soil. The harvest of forests, the extension of agriculture, and the destruction of wetlands speed the decay of humus, which is transformed into carbon dioxide and enters the atmosphere. Also, agricultural lands do not store as much carbon as the forests they replace.

By far, the largest store of carbon dioxide is in the oceans—as much as 60 times greater than that in the atmosphere. The carbon dioxide is dissolved in seawater, much like the carbon dioxide in soft drinks. Carbon dioxide enters the ocean by surface-wave action, and the concentration of carbon dioxide in the topmost 250 feet is as much as the entire atmosphere itself. In this mixed layer, microorganisms use the carbon dioxide in their growth, converting it into calcium carbonate for their shells. When these animals die, their shells settle to the bottom where they contribute to the formation of limestone, or if they fall deep enough, are dissolved in the cold, deep waters of the abyssal. This region of the ocean, by virtue of its great volume, holds the vast majority of free carbon dioxide that is not locked up in carbonaceous sediments. The capacity of the abyssal to absorb carbon dioxide is almost limitless.

Nevertheless, carbon dioxide moves from the atmosphere through the mixed layer of the ocean into the oceanic depths very slowly and at nearly a constant rate, which is only half the rate it is being released by the combustion of fossil fuels. The problem is even more exacerbated since the biota is also a net source of atmospheric carbon dioxide equal to the combustion of fossil fuels. Therefore, without man's contribution, the Earth would be in equilibrium with the same amount of carbon dioxide being absorbed in the ocean as is being naturally produced.

An increase in surface temperature brought on by doubling the amount of atmospheric carbon dioxide could have a worldwide effect on precipitation (FIG. 6-3). Areas between 20 and 50 degrees north latitude and 10 to 30 degrees south latitude would experience a marked decrease in precipitation, encouraging the spread of deserts. These changes would have profound effects on the distribution of the water resources in those areas where they are desperately needed for irrigation of agricultural lands. Not only would rainfall be diminished, but the

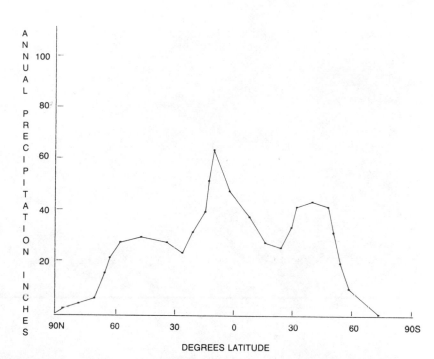

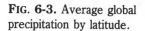

FIG. 6-3. Average global precipitation by latitude.

higher temperature would augment evaporation and the flow of rivers could decline by 50 percent or more. Major groundwater supplies would also be adversely affected, and deep water wells needed for irrigation would go dry. Other areas would receive a large increase in precipitation, causing extensive flooding that could be destructive to prime agricultural lands (FIG. 6-4).

Another consequence of a warmer earth would be the melting of the ice caps, which could raise the sea level by several tens of feet, inundating the coastal regions and agriculturally rich deltas and generally changing the shape of the continents. For every foot of rise in the sea level, 100 to 1000 feet of shoreline would be submerged so that whole areas would disappear. It would, therefore, be of no benefit to mankind to have the global temperature increase, causing agricultural lands to decrease, while the human population doubles every 30 to 35 years.

AIR POLLUTION

Foreign chemicals and particulate matter injected into the atmosphere, either by natural or man-made causes, is air pollution. Natural pollutants include salt particles from breaking waves, pollen and spores released by plants, smoke from forest fires, and wind-blown dust. In the Great Smoky Mountains of eastern Tennessee, pine sap reacts naturally with sunlight and the damp surface air to produce a hydrocarbon-type photochemical haze similar to the smog in big cities. Volcanoes are also big polluters, but much of their ejecta is beneficial to the environment. Man is by far the greatest offender and, since the Industrial Revolution, he has rivaled nature for the amount of toxic wastes and particulates disposed of in the atmosphere.

Air pollution is particularly hazardous to the immediate area if it is not diluted by the atmosphere. If the air is unstable with turbulent winds, smoke and exhaust fumes are carried upward by air currents, mixed with cleaner air, and dispersed by the winds aloft. High-pollution days do not necessarily indicate an increase in the output of pollution. They could mean that the air into which the pollution is released is not dispersed by the wind, making the air more toxic. With stagnant air under a zone of high pressure there is little vertical mixing of the pollutants with the cleaner air above, and air quality goes down considerably. This is what happens during a

FIG. 6-4. A flooded farmstead in the Red River Valley, North Dakota.

temperature inversion, when warm air overlies cooler air and acts like a lid, preventing upward movement and leaving the pollutants trapped below.

Geography also plays an effective part in increasing pollution. In areas like Los Angeles, polluted air can get trapped in the valley during an inversion with no hope of escape. Perhaps, the worst air-pollution disaster occurred during the London smog of 1952. Four thousand deaths have been attributed to the 5-day-old smog, the worst the city, and perhaps the world, has ever known.

Once the pollutants are well mixed with the air, they chemically react with other chemical substances in the atmosphere, including oxygen and water, to produce a secondary type of pollution. This results in the production of photochemical substances, corrosive acids, and deadly poisons such as ozone, which is beneficial in the stratosphere but highly toxic near the ground.

For the past couple of decades, the release of cancer-causing chemicals into the atmosphere has been on the upswing. Thousands of tons of dangerous chemicals are released by factories around the world each year. One of these chemicals is the very same methyl isocyanate that killed nearly 3000 people living around the Union Carbide chemical plant at Bhopal, India in late 1984. Many of these substances are rained out of the atmosphere and end up in rivers, lakes, and soils, where they are concentrated by chemical and biological factors.

The amount of particulate matter that enters the atmosphere has been increasing steadily. Slash-and-burn agriculture deposits large amounts of smoke into the troposphere. Dust blown up into the atmosphere from newly plowed or abandoned fields has been on the increase. Factories belch huge quantities of soot and aerosols into the air. The transportation industry alone accounts for half of the particulates and aerosols.

The amount of soot and dust suspended in the atmosphere at any one time as the result of human activity is estimated at 15 million tons. This activity has been called the "human volcano," referring to the fact that volcanoes also send aloft large quantities of particulate matter in the form of volcanic ash and aerosols. The final outcome of all these pollutants clogging the skies is a decrease in sunlight reaching the ground and a subsequent cooling of the surface. It could be that the reason an increased level of carbon dioxide in the atmosphere has yet to show an upward trend in world temperatures is that it is offset by the cooling effect of the particulate matter in the atmosphere.

ACID RAIN

In parts of the Eastern United States, Southeastern Canada, and Western Europe, measurements of the acidity levels of rain and snow reveal that precipitation has changed from a nearly neutral solution 200 years ago to a diluted solution of sulfuric and nitric acids today. The most extreme case was a storm in Pitlochry, Scotland, on April 10, 1974, where the rain had an acidity equal to that of vinegar (pH 2.4). In that same month, similar pH values were reported on the west coast of Norway and at a remote location in Ireland.

The pH factor is a scale ranging from 0 (the most acidic) to 14 (the most alkaline); a pH of 7 is neutral. The scale is logarithmic, meaning that a pH of 4 is 10 times more acidic than a pH of 5, and 100 times more acidic than a pH of 6. Normal rainwater is slightly acidic (pH 5.6) because of the combination of atmospheric carbon dioxide and water, forming a weak carbonic acid which, among other things, helps break down rock into soil.

Acid rain is principally a result of an increase in the burning of fossil fuels, accompanied by a rise in the emission of sulfur and nitrogen oxides into the atmosphere. The oxides mix with water and form an acid, which precipitates out of the clouds and produces a variety of harmful effects on plant and animal life (FIG. 6-5).

The Industrial Revolution brought with it the burning of large quantities of high sulfur coal and oil, and the smelting of large quantities of sulfide ores, particularly in the heavily industrialized and urbanized temperate regions of the Northern Hemisphere. Human activity accounts for more than 90 percent of all sulfur emissions throughout the world. At the huge Sudbury copper-nickel smelter complex in Ontario, Canada, annual emissions of sulfur from a quarter-mile-high smokestack have about equaled the amount thought to have been emitted annually by all the volcanoes in the world.

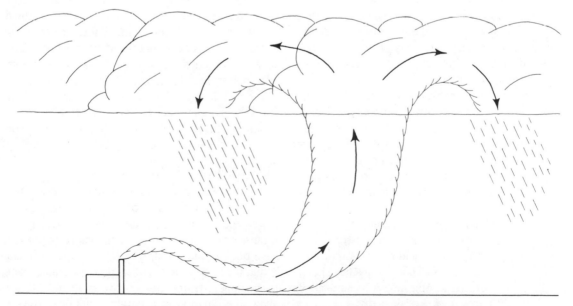

FIG. 6-5. Acid rain produced by cloud scavaging of air pollutants.

The combustion of sulfur produces sulfur dioxide (one sulfur atom, two oxygen atoms) which enters the atmosphere and combines with oxygen, yielding sulfur trioxide (one sulfur atom, three oxygen atoms). Sulfur trioxide combines with atmospheric moisture to produce sulfuric acid by the formula $H_2O + SO_3 = H_2SO_4$. Sulfuric acid is highly corrosive, and a strong solution is used as an electrolite in automobile batteries. Large quantities of sulfuric acid are also used in industry, such as for the milling and refining of metallic ores.

Acid rain has been known to exist for many decades in the vicinity of large cities and industrial plants. Very tall smokestacks were constructed to disperse the offending emissions high into the atmosphere and away from the cities, but all this did was relieve the local pollution problems by turning them into regional ones. The pollutants travel long distances, even crossing international borders and causing a host of political problems. Nations such as Sweden and Norway, which are not large polluters, are constantly being bombarded with acid rain produced by heavy industrialized areas, such as those in Great Britain and West Germany.

Annually, rain and snow over large regions of the world are now up to 50 times more acidic than the lowest expected value for unpolluted atmospheres. Some individual storms can produce rain several hundred to several thousand times its natural acidic value. In large sections of the industrialized world, the average annual pH of precipitation ranges from 4 to 4.5.

The acid deposits consist of roughly 70 percent sulfuric and 30 percent nitric compounds, which come in both wet (acid) and dry (aerosol) varieties. They deface statues and buildings by dissolving marble stone. Metal structures such as bridges become corroded and weakened. The Statue of Liberty in New York harbor had to have a face lift prior to its 100th birthday celebration in 1986 because acids had pitted and tarnished its copper plating.

Streams and lakes in many parts of the world have become so acidic from acid rain runoff or polluted by toxic wastes that fish populations have been virtually wiped out. In the Adirondack Mountains of New York, 90 percent of the lakes that have acid levels of pH 5 and below are completely devoid of fish. In Sweden, it is estimated that more than 15,000 lakes are without fish because of acid rain. Some soils have become so acidic they can no longer grow crops.

Plants are damaged by adverse affects on foliage and fine root systems. Acid precipitation is resulting in the destruction of the great forests of North America, Europe, China, and Brazil. There are widespread reductions in tree-ring width and increased mortality of red spruce in the Eastern United States. Resorts and wilderness areas, like those in the Western United States, Norway, and particularly West Germany's Black Forest, which are dependent on their trees for the tourist trade, are losing much of their beauty.

It is unlikely that the combustion of fossil fuels will decline in the industrial countries over the next 30 years; in fact, it is more likely to increase. Third-world nations, too, will want to industrialize to improve their standard of living. Also, it is estimated that by the middle of the next century, most, if not all, of the petroleum reserves will be gone. Unless some other safe alternative, such as fission, fusion, and geothermal energy is developed and rapidly exploited on a grand scale, industrial plants will have to convert to coal, whose resources are barely touched. Unfortunately, as experience has shown, coal is a particularly dirty fuel. There are efforts to reduce acid precipitation caused by coal-fired plants by installation of scrubbers on smokestacks to eliminate sulfur dioxide along with the burning of low-sulfur coal. Many older plants, however, and plants in other countries, are not required to make these expensive investments, and sulfurous smoke continues to cloud the skies.

THE OZONE LAYER

Every spring since the decade of the 1970s, a giant hole about the size of the continental United States appears in the ozone layer over Antarctica. A number of explanations for the cause of the hole have been put forward. The most plausible reason is that there is some chemical process taking place. In the upper stratosphere between 20 and 30 miles above the Earth's surface, ultraviolet light splits diatomic oxygen molecules into single oxygen atoms, which in turn combine with other oxygen molecules to form ozone, a molecule of three oxygen atoms. This unstable molecular arrangement slowly decays back into oxygen within the ozone layer, and an equilibrium is therefore maintained between oxygen and ozone. The variation of ozone concentration in the ozone layer is affected by the seasons, latitude, and strong weather systems that can penetrate into the stratosphere. If ozone finds its way to the lower levels of the atmosphere, it is destroyed before reaching the ground. This is fortunate because ozone is highly toxic, causing irritation to the eyes and lungs if it is present in the lower air.

Ozone plays a very important role in shielding the Earth from the harmful ultraviolet radiation of the Sun. Without this shield, life could not exist on the Earth's surface. Even a slight increase in ultraviolet radiation can increase the incidence of cancer, possibly harm plant life, and cause a number of other adverse effects. The ultraviolet wavelength is above the blue spectrum of visible light; therefore, it is invisible to humans. Ultraviolet radiation that reaches the surface in small quantities is beneficial to man and helps the body generate vitamin D, a vital nutrient. It also tans the skin, which is the body's defensive mechanism against too much ultraviolet light. Even with this type of protection, however, the incidence of skin cancer is on the rise.

Laboratory experiments have shown that certain chemical substances, particularly chlorofluorocarbons and nitrous oxides, destroy ozone. Chlorofluorocarbons, more popularly known by the trade name Freon, are used as refrigerants in refrigerators and air conditioners, and escape into the atmosphere when the units are first manufactured or later damaged. They are used as propellants in spray cans, and although in 1978 the United States banned such sprays, they are still being used extensively in other countries. The chemical is used in the manufacture of foam plastics, such as Styrofoam coffee cups. Freon is also used as an industrial solvent and evaporation and spillage send much of the chemical into the atmosphere.

Nitrous oxides are produced by the combustion of fossil fuels, especially under conditions of high temperatures and pressures, like those found in automobile engines. The tall chimneys of coal-fired plants send huge amounts of nitrous-oxides high into the atmosphere, where some is mixed with water and rains out as nitric acid. The remainder finds its way into the upper stratosphere and breaks down ozone. Nuclear weapons in addition to other dangerous side effects, also produce massive quantities of nitrous oxides, which can poke holes in the ozone layer.

7

The World of Volcan

VOLCANOES have greatly influenced the atmosphere ever since the Earth was formed. They replenish the vital substances in the air by spewing out large quantities of water vapor, carbon dioxide, nitrogen, and other important gases (FIG. 7-1). Volcanoes are responsible for most of the dust in the air, which scatters sunlight. If it were not for air molecules, dust, and aerosols, the sky would be black instead of blue and there would be no beautiful red sunsets. Volcanoes are some of nature's most majestic mountains, rising tall among the surrounding terrain. Volcanic ash makes a rich soil, and villagers farm the flanks of active volcanoes, sometimes to their own peril.

Through the ages, volcanoes have threatened the lives of those who settled in their domain, and when an eruption destroys an entire city, more than likely it is rebuilt again on the same spot. Luckily, great eruptions only occur once or twice a century. If we had many more Mount St. Helens eruptions over a short time span, there would be so much dust in the atmosphere that the climate could get cool enough to bring on a new ice age.

HISTORIC VOLCANOES

The volcanoes of Indonesia (FIG. 7-2) are among the most explosive in the world and have produced more violent blasts in historic times than those of any other area. Three great volcanoes in this region have made their presence known over the last two centuries: Mounts Tambora, Krakatoa, and Agung. On April 11 and 12, 1815, the island of Sumbawa witnessed what was possibly the most explosive volcanic eruption in the last 10,000 years. Tambora sent more dust into the upper atmosphere and obscured more sunlight than any other volcano in the past 400 years. The volcano took the lives of nearly 60,000 people in the surrounding area and caused climatic havoc, starvation, and disease in other parts of the world.

The island of Krakatoa, located between Java and Sumatra, was nearly totally destroyed on August 27, 1883, by an eruption that was equal to the force of 3000 Hiroshima-size atomic bombs going off all at once. The sound of the explosion was heard as far as Madagascar, 3000 miles away, and the pressure wave was recorded on barographs all

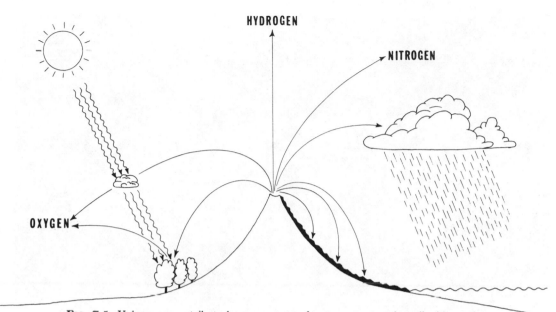

FIG. 7-1. Volcanoes contribute large amounts of water vapor, carbon dioxide, and other important gases to the atmosphere, as well as contribute to the growth of continents.

around the world—it was the loudest noise known to mankind. The explosion produced giant tsunamis (tidal waves) over 100 feet high, which drowned 36,000 people throughout the area.

More recently, Mount Agung on the island of Bali put in its appearance on March 17, 1963, and again two months later on May 16. The eruptions produced destructive, glowing avalanches that devastated many villages, killing 1900 and leaving 85,000 homeless. It was thought that the volcano caused a 1 degree Fahrenheit global cooling. It was discovered, however, that half of the temperature drop was a result of a large number of atomic bomb tests that were conducted during this time, which also lofted huge amounts of debris into the atmosphere.

The largest volcanic eruption in the continental United States in several centuries took place in a remote part of southwestern Washington on May 18, 1980. Mount St. Helens (FIG. 7-3) is associated with 15 major active volcanoes in the Cascade Range, running from northern California to southern British Columbia. The eruption was the equivalent of 400 megatons of nuclear explosions spread over a nine-hour period or 32,000 Hiroshima-size

atomic bombs: one going off every second. The explosion blew off the top one-third of the mountain, lofted a cubic mile of debris into the atmosphere, produced one of the largest avalanches in recorded history, and created a massive mudflow (FIG. 7-4). The northward-directed blast devastated 200 square miles of forestland, and enough timber to build a fair size city lay toppled, like toothpicks. Within three days, the ash cloud crossed the United States, dropping ash as far east as Denver, Colorado (FIG. 7-5).

This century's answer to Krakatoa, almost a hundred years later, were the three big eruptions of El Chichon in the state of Chiapas, in southernmost Mexico beginning on March 28, 1982. It was one of the world's dirtiest volcanoes in recent history. The gigantic dust cloud (FIG. 7-6) blocked the Sun in nearby areas until there was near total darkness, and visibility was less than 15 feet. Ten miles to the northeast, 20 inches of ash was measured on the ground. In the town of Palenque, 75 miles east of the volcano, the ash measured 16 inches. The volcano killed 187 people and left 60,000 homeless. The ash cloud obtained an altitude of 16 miles, far above the weather that cleanses out the dust. It completely circled and spread over the en-

(Courtesy of NASA)

FIG. 7-2. An active Indonesian volcano (center) on Anonoara Island. Note the 30-mile-long ash plume trailing off.

tire globe in three weeks, and did not dissipate in the higher atmosphere for months after the eruption.

The cloud caused a 5-degree warming in the stratosphere, the warmest it has ever been since records were first kept in 1958. This caused a substantial cooling, as much as 1 degree, near the surface. In many parts of the Northern Hemisphere, summer was cooler and wetter than normal, and winter was colder. The eruption might have also trig-

gered a coincidental appearance of the El Niño current in the Pacific, which practically destroyed the fishing industry off the coast of Peru.

THE RING OF FIRE

There are almost 400 active volcanoes in a near continuous ring that surrounds the Pacific Ocean (FIG. 7-7). These are associated with subduction

Table 7-1. Chronology of Major Volcanic Eruptions

DATE	VOLCANO	AREA	DEATH TOLL
A.D. 79	Vesuvius	Pompeii, Italy	16,000
1169	Etna	Sicily	15,000
1631	Vesuvius	Pompeii, Italy	18,000
1669	Etna	Sicily	20,000
1701	Fujiyama	Japan	——-
1772	Papandayan	Java, Indonesia	3,000
1783	Laki	Iceland	——-
1790	Kilauea	Hawaii	——-
1815	Tambora	Sumbawa, Indonesia	12,000
1822	Galung Gung	Java, Indonesia	4,000
1845	Hekla	Iceland	——-
1853	Niuafou	Samoa	70
1857	St. Helens	Washington	——-
1873	Mauna Loa	Hawaii	——-
1877	Cotopaxi	Ecuador	1,000
1883	Krakatoa	Java, Indonesia	36,000
1888	Bandai-san	Japan	460
1897	Mayon	Philippines	——-
1902	La Soufriere	St. Vincent, Martinique	15,000
1902	Pelee	Pierre, Martinique	28,000
1902	Santa Maria	Guatemala	6,000
1903	Colima	Jalisco, Mexico	——-
1911	Taal	Philippines	1,300
1912	Katmai	Alaska	——-
1914	Lassen Peak	California	——-
1917	San Salvador	El Salvador	——-
1919	Keluit	Java, Indonesia	5,500
1932	Volcano del Fuego	Guatemala	——-
1935	Cosequina	Nicaragua	——-
1943	Paracutin	Michoacan, Mexico	——-
1957	Capelinkos	Azores	——-
1963	Surtsey	Iceland	——-
1973	Helgafell	Iceland	——-
1980	St. Helens	Washington	62
1983	El Chichon	Chipas, Mexico	187
1985	Nevado del Ruiz	Armero, Columbia	20,000
1986	Augustine	Alaska	——-
1986	Kilauea	Hawaii	——-

zones along the rim of the Pacific Basin. Tectonic plates are subducted into the mantle by the collision of a continental plate with an oceanic plate, or an oceanic plate with another oceanic plate (FIG. 7-8).

The lithospheric plate melts during its dive into the mantle, and the lighter rocks work their way back up into the crust to resupply the volcanic reservoirs with new magma.

The Ring of Fire **85**

FIG. 7-3. The 1980 eruption of Mount St. Helens.

FIG. 7-4. Mudflow resulting from the eruption of Mount St. Helens.

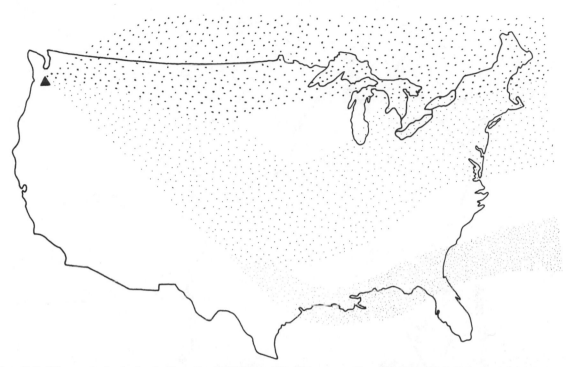

FIG. 7-5. Dispersal of ash clouds from the 1980 Mount St. Helens eruption. The upper band represents the coarsest material below 10,000 feet altitude.   The middle band, between 20,000 and 40,000 feet, circled the entire world in 17 days. The lower band represents the finest material, carried to an altitude of 50,000 feet and over.

FIG. 7-6. The eruption cloud (lower center) from El Chichon, Mexico, viewed from space.

(Courtesy of NOAA)

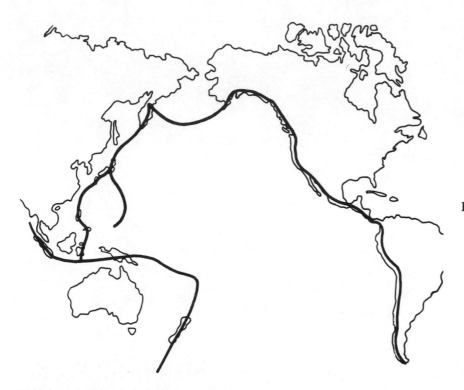

FIG. 7-7. The ring of fire.

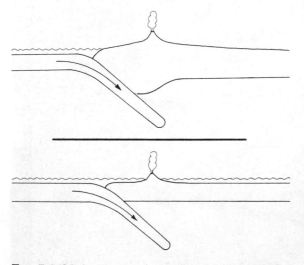

FIG. 7-8. Most volcanoes are produced by a collision of continental and oceanic plates (top) or a collision of two oceanic plates (bottom).

The rate at which the plates are thrusted into the mantle seems to control the level of volcanic activity. In Indonesia and Japan where the annual subduction rate is about 2.5 inches, there is usually at least one volcanic eruption a year. The composition of the magma also controls the type of eruption. Explosive eruptions occur when a viscous magma containing trapped gases is kept from reaching the surface by a plug in the volcano's vent. As pressure increases, the obstruction is finally blown away along with the upper peak.

A large proportion of the volcanoes occur in *island arcs* which are a series of volcanic islands, mostly in the Pacific, that describe a graceful curve. The longest island arc is the Aleutian Islands, extending more than 3000 miles from Alaska to Asia. The Kurile Islands south of the Kamchatka Peninsula form another long arc. The islands of Japan, the Philippines, Indonesia, New Hebrides, Tonga, and the arc from Timor to Sumatra are all island arcs. They have similar curves and are associated with deep ocean trenches.

One explanation for the arcs is that the Pacific plate is slowly rotating clockwise, completing one turn in 3 billion years. Volcanic islands pop up in an arc as a result of the circular motion of the plate away from the volcanic source. This motion would also set up stress fractures on the rim of the plate where it comes in contact with other plates and might account for why two-thirds of the world's active volcanoes, along with most earthquakes, exist on the edges of the Pacific plate.

In the Atlantic Ocean, volcanic activity is far less extensive and generally occurs in two localities: the mid-ocean ridges and the West Indies. Many islands in the Atlantic are part of the Mid-Atlantic Ridge, which extends above the water. Rift volcanoes account for only about 15 percent of the world's known active volcanoes and most are in Iceland and East Africa. Also, it is estimated that there are about 20 eruptions of deep submarine rift volcanoes every year. Shallow-water volcanoes off Iceland are explosive because of the rapid boiling of seawater when it comes in contact with the magma chamber. Once the volcanoes rise above sea level, their eruptions are relatively quiet. Rift volcanoes on continents such as in East Africa can be very explosive and produce a greater variety of volcanic rocks than their oceanic counterparts.

Scattered around the world are more than 100 small regions of isolated volcanic activity known as *hot spots*. Unlike most of the world's active volcanoes which are usually found at plate boundaries, these lie deep in the interior of a lithospheric plate. Hot spots could be the result of plumes of hot material rising up from deep within the mantle, creating a domelike structure in the crust. The crust eventually weakens and cracks, allowing the magma to reach the surface.

(Courtesy of U.S. Navy)

FIG. 7-9. The birth of a new Icelandic volcano.

The most prominent and most easily recognizable hot-spot volcanoes created the Hawaiian Islands. The volcanic islands popped out on the ocean floor, conveyor-belt fashion, with the oldest being the farthest away from the hot spot northwest of the main island of Hawaii. More than half of the hot spots are on the continents, with the greatest concentration on the African, the Antarctic, and the Eurasian plates. This could indicate why these regions are moving very slowly since on rapidly moving continental plates, such as North and South America, hot-spot volcanism is rare.

The output of pyroclastics (ejected material) and lava for a single volcanic eruption ranges from a few cubic yards to as much as 5 cubic miles or more. Together, the volcanoes of the world's subduction zones produce about 1 billion cubic yards of new, mostly pyroclastic, volcanic material per year. Rift volcanoes generate about 2.5 billion cubic yards per year, mainly as submarine flows of basalt. Hot-spot volcanoes produce about 0.5 billion cubic yards per year, mostly as basalt flows in the oceans and pyroclastics and lava flows on the continents. This brings the Earth's average yearly total output of new volcanic rock to about 4 billion cubic yards, or nearly 1 cubic mile. Many years might go by without a large volcanic eruption, however, until a volcano, like Tambora or Krakatoa comes along to even out the score.

VOLCANIC PRODUCTS

Ejecta from volcanoes have a wide range of chemical, mineral, and physical properties. Nearly all volcanic products are silicate rocks, composed mainly of oxygen, silicon, and aluminum, with lesser amounts of iron, calcium, magnesium, sodium, potassium, and other elements. Basalts are relatively low in silica and high in calcium, magnesium, and iron. Magmas that are more siliceous have more sodium and potassium and less magnesium and iron.

Magmas of different composition are indicative of their source materials and their depth within the mantle. Degrees of partial melting of mantle rocks, partial crystallization which enriches the melt with silica, and assimilation of a variety of crustal rocks in the mantle affect the composition of the magma.

When the erupting magma rises toward the surface, it incorporates a variety of rock types along its way, and the magma changes its composition, which can have a dramatic effect on the type of eruption: be it be mild or explosive.

When the magma reaches the surface, the volcano erupts with gases, liquids, and solids. Volcanic gases are composed of steam, carbon dioxide, sulfur dioxide, and hydrochloric acid. The gases are dissolved in the magma and are released as the magma rises to the surface and the pressure decreases.

The composition of the magma determines its viscosity and whether a volcano erupts in a mild or explosive state. If the magma is highly fluid and contains little dissolved gas when it reaches the surface, it flows from a volcanic vent or fissure as basaltic lava. On the other hand, if magma rising to the surface contains a large quantity of dissolved gases, it suddenly separates into liquid and bubbles. With decreasing pressure, the bubbles expand explosively and burst the surrounding liquid, which fractures the magma into fragments. The fragments are driven upward by the force of their own expansion, like pellets from a shotgun, and are hurled far above the volcano. The fragments cool and solidify during their flight through the air and can range in size from fine dust to large blocks weighing several tons. The finer material is caught by the wind blowing across the eruption cloud and carried for thousands of miles.

The eruption cloud contains particles called *tephra*, ranging in size from coarse ash to dust. Only the tephra that remains airborne for long periods affects the climate. The effect of dust in the atmosphere on the climate depends on the nature of the dust and its location in the atmosphere. Eruptions that toss dust into the atmosphere are divided into two categories: those that create dust layers in the troposphere and lower stratosphere up to about 20 miles altitude and those that reach altitudes of about 30 miles or more. It is the first group that has the greatest influence on the climate because such eruptions produce dense, long-lived dust clouds.

Atmospheric scientists agree that it might not be the dust alone which blocks out heat from the Sun. Volcanoes also produce vast quantities of water vapor and gases, including sulfur dioxide which reacts with water to produce sulfuric acid. These aerosols also might penetrate the stratosphere like a fine mist and obscure sunlight. Aerosols block incoming solar radiation, and also are transparent to outgoing infrared radiation, which would further cool the Earth. With the combination of both dust and aerosols being expelled into the atmosphere, the large volcanic eruptions make the most important impact on the climate.

CLIMATIC EFFECTS OF ERUPTIONS

Many of the coldest, wettest summers, like those of 1784 and 1816, have been termed *volcanic dust years*. Volcanic dust probably played some part in all the very worst summers and some of the coldest winters from the seventeenth to the twentieth century. With over 200 years of observations of volcanoes and weather (since 1784), the correlation is quite close, although volcanoes alone do not explain all the ups and downs of the climate record. The English meteorologist Hubert Lamb carried out an extensive historical survey of all volcanic eruptions from 1500 to 1970. He related their impact on the atmosphere to a standard scale called the *dust veil index*, using the 1883 eruption of Krakatoa as 1000 units. Actually, the 1815 eruption of Tambora blasted three times as much dust into the upper atmosphere as did Krakatoa, so its dust veil index would be 3000. Tambora was preceded and followed by other eruptions around the world between 1811 and 1818, which taken together, produced a total veil of 4200, the largest in modern history.

One of Lamb's students, the meteorologist P.M. Kelly, and his colleagues at the University of East Anglia in England looked for regular variations in the dust veil index and the climate, and found that both show a 7- to 8-year cycle. It is highly unlikely that the two cycles kept in step from 1725 to 1950 by coincidence. This discovery supports the idea that changing volcanic activity alone influences the climate. The volcanic cycle also could be related to a similar known fluctuation in the Earth's rotation, over which the length of day first increases and then decreases by a fraction of a second. These slight wobbles in the Earth could trigger volcanic erup-

tions, thereby affecting the weather.

The scientists made an even more startling discovery of a 180-year rhythm in volcanic activity resulting from changing tidal stresses acting on the Earth. This cycle is similar to a 180-year weather cycle and a 180-year rhythm in solar activity. The changes in tidal stresses are related to the gravitational forces caused by the alignment of the planets.

The 1883 eruption of Krakatoa and its effects on the climate were better observed than any other volcano up to that time. Scientists marveled over the changes in the atmosphere produced by the eruption. People of all walks of life could not help but notice the spectacular green-tinged sunsets and the appearance of a blue Moon. It was estimated that 5 cubic miles of rock, ash, and dust, were blown upward into the atmosphere, much of which reached more than 50 miles into the stratosphere, where it spread throughout the world and lingered for years. Scientists at the Montellier Observatory in southern France noticed with astonishment a drop in the direct solar radiation from 30 percent above normal for that time of year to 20 percent below normal, and it remained 10 percent below normal for 3 years after the eruption.

Only part of the incoming solar radiation that is lost is reflected back into space by the volcanic dust. Some of the radiation goes to warm the dust itself, and some is scattered sideways, so it still reaches the ground but at an indirect angle. This sideways scattering of sunlight is partly responsible for making the sky blue and is the reason for spectacular sunrises and sunsets. Therefore, scattered solar radiation does not reach the surface directly from the Sun's disk, which is what measurements of direct solar radiation record. If the total output of the Sun actually did fluctuate by as much as 10 percent, as it might have done in its early history, it would play havoc with life on Earth since surface temperatures would reflect much larger fluctuations. A decrease in direct solar radiation of 5 percent would not cause the surface to cool by 10 degrees, which is enough to bring on a new ice age, but rather less than 1 degree because the decrease in direct radiation is matched by an increase in indirect radiation, scattered sideways by the volcanic dust.

The effects on the climate from volcanic eruptions in the higher latitudes, such as those of Mounts St. Helens in 1980 and Augustine, Alaska, in 1986, are not near as great as those in the lower latitudes. Volcanic dust blasted into the stratosphere in the temperate zones tends to spread less and thereby has a lesser effect than dust injected by volcanoes in the tropics. The dust from volcanic eruptions in the tropics is carried poleward by a high-altitude flow of air originating from the tropics and concentrated in the higher latitudes, where sunlight strikes the Earth from a steep angle and therefore has a longer path through the dust.

Apart from the spectacular sunsets, blue Moons, and milky cast to the sky, the influence of one or more Krakatoa-size eruptions could certainly have pronounced effects on weather and climate that might persist for several years. The American meteorologist Harry Wexler made the connection between volcanoes and climate in the early 1950s. He noted that, following a major eruption, there was a marked change in the weather patterns over North America, and July's weather map might resemble that of mid-May. Wexler also made the striking discovery that for 50 years since 1912, no major volcanic eruptions have occurred in the Northern Hemisphere. During this period, the winters have grown steadily warmer, making present-day climate conditions comparatively warmer than those of the last century. The most conspicuous change in the weather patterns is that for 150 years prior to 1912, volcanoes have erupted in the Northern Hemisphere in one great explosion after another, whereas since 1912, they have been comparatively quiet.

GLOBAL COOLING

The *albedo* is a measurement of the amount of sunlight reflected back into space. The greater the albedo, the colder the Earth becomes. The albedo is influenced by the amount of atmospheric dust, cloud cover, snow and ice cover, and other light-colored areas on the ground.

The climatic effects of volcanic dust are dependent on the type of particles being released into the atmosphere, including the size of the dust particles and where they are concentrated in the atmosphere.

Large dust particles in the troposphere could actually trap heat from the ground that would otherwise escape into space and could thereby warm the Earth. It is the smaller particles, or aerosols, that tend to allow the heat from the ground to escape into space, while stopping the Sun's heat from reaching the ground. If the dust overlies light-colored surfaces, such as snow-packed areas, it absorbs more incoming solar heat than the surface would be able to, so there is less albedo and a net warming of the earth. If instead, the dust overlies a dark-colored surface, such as a forest, it absorbs less heat than the surface would be able to, so there is more albedo and a net cooling of the surface.

By blocking out the heat from the Sun, volcanic dust could have caused the glacial ice cover to increase, bringing on the "Little Ice Age" that occurred between 125 and 550 years ago. The longer a volcano remains quiet, the more explosive is its eruption. There are at present several dozen candidate volcanoes, including some in the Cascade Range, that can be expected to erupt any time.

Some climatologists argue that many volcanic eruptions occurring around the world in a short space of time throw so much dust into the upper atmosphere to alone cause the onset of an ice age. Their argument is supported by geological evidence of thin layers of volcanic dust buried in sediments that correlate reasonably well with times of increased ice cover.

In cores taken from the Greenland ice sheet are found detectable traces of volcanic eruptions dating back 10,000 years, near the end of the last ice age. Direct temperature measurements are made by comparing the changing proportions of oxygen isotopes in the ice. Because volcanic eruptions eject huge quantities of acid gases into the atmosphere, periods of great volcanic activity are followed by periods of acid rainfall or acid snowfall. The traces of acid in the ice conduct electricity more easily than does ice made from pure water, so they can be detected by observing the drop in electrical current through the ice core at various points along its length. A comparison of the top layers of the ice with the historic record of volcanic eruptions shows that this acid test is a good indicator of volcanic activity.

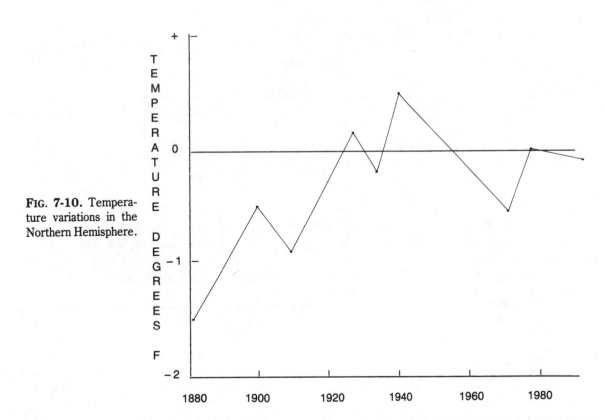

FIG. 7-10. Temperature variations in the Northern Hemisphere.

The acidity changes also match up well with other indicators, such as tree rings, where narrow bands of growth indicate colder seasons and records of historic climate.

Since the end of the nineteenth century, the Earth first warmed up slightly by about 1 degree, and then it cooled down after 1940 (FIG. 7-10). By the 1970s, the cooling reached over 1 degree below the peak low of the early 1940s. To some extent this pattern might be related to changes in solar activity. However, another factor that must have played some part is the changing pattern of volcanic activity, in which the middle of the twentieth century was relatively free from the cooling effects of volcanic dust. After several eruptions in the late nineteenth and early twentieth centuries, there were relatively few great volcanic outbursts for several decades. It could be that the gradual warming of the Earth up to the 1940s corresponded to the time it took for volcanic dust to settle out of the stratosphere. In the second half of the twentieth century, volcanic activity has been on the rise.

8

Polar Flip-Flops

MAGNETIC fields are responsible for most of the violent activity in the universe, from auroral displays in the Earth's atmosphere to stellar flares and X-ray emission, and the massing of clouds of interstellar gas in the galaxies. Most stars generate magnetic fields, and some, called *pulsars*, have fields a trillion times stronger than the Earth's magnetic field.

Before space exploration by unmanned probes, all planets in the Solar System, with the exception of Mercury, were thought to have magnetic poles similar to those on Earth. It was believed that Mercury could not generate a magnetic field because it was too small, having a radius of about one-third that of Earth, and its rotation rate was too slow, rotating only 1.5 times for every orbit around the Sun. Its high density indicates, however, that Mercury has a relatively large metallic core, with a radius about half the radius of the Earth's core, giving it a small magnetic field. Only Venus and Mars were found not to generate magnetic fields. Venus, roughly the size of Earth, generates no magnetic

field because its rotation is too slow, rotating on its axis about once for each revolution around the Sun. Mars, however, about half the size of Earth, rotates essentially at the same rate as Earth. The low density of Mars suggests that if it has a metal core, it is a small one. Also, Mars is tectonically dead, meaning that convection currents in its interior, which are important for generating magnetic fields and other geologic processes, have stopped.

THE DISCOVERY OF MAGNETISM

Nature produces a natural magnetic rock, called *magnetite* or *lodestone*. It is formed when magma from below penetrates the crust and deposits an iron-rich, metallic mineral. As the rock cools and solidifies, its iron atoms, like miniature bar magnets, line up in the same direction as the Earth's magnetic field, producing magnetism in the rock. After some time, the surface above the ore body is eroded away, exposing the lodestone.

It was probably during the early Iron Age, about 2000 years B.C., that magnetite was first discovered as an iron-rich ore. Its strange magnetic properties must have fascinated its discoverers. The rocks had an unusual attraction toward or repulsion against each other. The early Greeks and the Chinese studied this strange behavior of the lodestone.

At one time a sliver of the rock was either suspended from a string or floated on a piece of wood in a bowl of water. In either case, the rock always swung around to the same direction and pointed north. It was thought that the North Star exerted a pull on the rock, causing it to turn in its direction. This must have given early scientists an insight, and by the Middle Ages, the crude compasses were refined to help navigators find their way on the high seas in time to explore new continents.

It was commonly believed that the reason the compass needle always pointed north was because of the existence of a huge lodestone deposit at the North Pole. The idea that the Earth itself was a huge magnet was first proposed by the English physician and physicist William Gilbert in 1600. He studied the interaction of magnetized needles with spheres made of magnetite he called *terrellas*, or little earths. Gilbert took his ideas from the English compass maker Robert Norman, who a few decades earlier discovered that if a magnetized needle is allowed to pivot freely in the vertical north-south plane, the north-seeking end of the needle dipped downward toward the earth. In London, for example, the angle of inclination from the horizontal was approximately 70 degrees.

Gilbert explained the inclination as an effect of the geometry of the Earth's magnetism. He explored this geometry by measuring the orientation of magnetized needles placed near the surface of a terrella. He found that the magnetic field lines of the magnetized sphere were vertical at the poles, horizontal at the equator, and in between were inclined at an angle that increased with latitude. The same effect can be accomplished by placing a piece of paper over a bar magnet and sprinkling iron filings over it. The iron filings line up with the magnetic field, parallel to the magnet in the middle and pointing inward toward the poles.

The Danish physicist Hans Christian Oersted tried to prove that magnetism and electricity were related phenomena. It was known that during severe thunderstorms, compass needles reacted to close flashes of lightning by vibrating vigorously or even being deflected in the wrong direction. In 1820, Oersted stretched a platinum wire aligned in a north-south direction over a compass needle. He passed a high electrical current from a battery through the wire until it started to glow. Oersted then noticed that the north pole of the compass needle was deflected to the west. When the current was shut off, the needle returned to its original north-south position. If the compass was suspended above the wire and the current switched on, the needle was again deflected, but this time the north pole of the needle pointed east. Once again when the current was shut off, the needle returned to its normal position.

Ten years after Oersted proved that a current flowing through a wire produces a magnetic field, the English physicist Michael Faraday set out to prove that the opposite was also true: that an electrical current could be produced by means of a magnetic field. Faraday constructed a simple dynamo (FIG. 8-1), consisting of a metal disk that rotated over a coil of wire. The coil was electrically connected to the disk and its shaft by brushes. As the disk rotated, a current was passed through the coil, which induced a magnetic field aligned with the axis of the coil. The electrons in the disk moving through this field were forced to flow from the axis to the periphery of the disk. The current thus generated then flowed from the disk through the brushes to the coil, amplifying the magnetic field generated by the coil, which in turn amplified the current flowing through the disk. As long as the disk kept rotating, the magnetic field could be maintained indefinitely. Today, the Earth's magnetic field is thought to be generated in the metallic core in much the same manner as the Faraday dynamo.

THE EARTH'S CORE

The Earth's core is 4320 miles in diameter, or a little over half the diameter of the Earth. The core is about one-sixth of the Earth's volume and about one-third of its mass. The density of the core varies

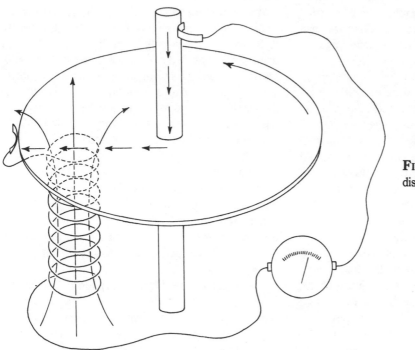

FIG. 8-1. The Faraday disk dynamo.

from a minimum of about 9 times the density of water at the top of the outer core to about 12 times the density of water at the center. The temperature at the top of the outer core is about 4500 degrees Fahrenheit and increases to 5300 degrees at the top of the inner core, with no appreciable increase toward the center. The pressure at the top of the outer core is 1.5 million atmospheres and increases to 3.5 million atmospheres at the top of the inner core with only a slight increase in pressure toward the center.

The inner core is composed of iron-nickel silicates and is roughly 1500 miles in diameter. The liquid outer core is composed mostly of iron with some nickel. The Earth's core is not permanently magnetized, and any residual magnetism would have been lost from the intense heat during its differentiation into a liquid outer core and solid inner core. The same situation occurs when a magnet is heated above a certain temperature, called its Curie point: its iron atoms vibrate wildly and lose their north-south alignment, and they remain disoriented after cooling.

THE GEOMAGNETIC FIELD

In the early 1950s, the British physicist P.M.S. Blakett invented the magnetometer, which can detect extremely weak magnetic fields in rocks. When the new instruments were first taken to the field, scientists in England obtained strange results. Rocks formed 200 million years ago showed a magnetic inclination of 30 degrees north. The inclination is almost 0 degrees at the equator and 90 degrees at the poles. What bothered the scientists was that England's present inclination was about 70 degrees north. The only conclusion that could be drawn from this was that England must have at once been farther south.

At this time, skeptics refused to acknowledge the shifting of the continents and pointed out that the same phenomenon could be caused by the shifting of the Earth's magnetic poles. Such polar wandering (FIG. 8-2) would have altered the direction of the Earth's magnetic field, and records of these changes would be permanently locked up in the rocks. Therefore, rocks formed at different times

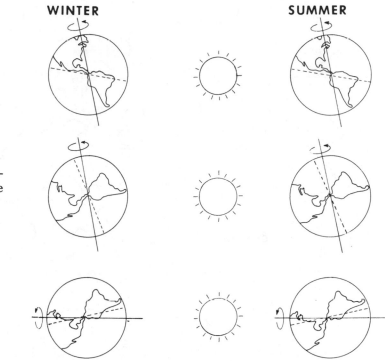

WINTER SUMMER

FIG. 8-2. Varieties of polar wandering and their effects on the seasons.

in England could have been imprinted with different inclinations without moving an inch.

The evidence for the drifting land masses was then turned against itself to prove it was the North Pole that had wandered around on top of the world over millions of years. However, this theory backfired when similar experiments with magnetometers were conducted in North America. Although the polar paths derived from data on both continents were much the same shape and had a common point of origin, the curves gradually veered away from each other. Only by hypothetically joining the continents together would the two curves overlap.

The strength of the Earth's magnetic field measured at the poles is several hundred times smaller than the ends of a toy horseshoe magnet, and the magnetic field near the core is about ten times stronger than it is at the surface. The magnetic poles do not coincide with the axis of rotation, but are tilted at an angle of 11 degrees. The poles are not stationary but slowly wander around the polar regions (FIG. 8-3).

Since the seventeenth century, navigation charts have been made indicating the strength and direction of the magnetic field at points all over the Earth. Over the past four centuries, the charts revealed two major trends in variations in the magnetic field. The first is a slow, steady decrease in the intensity of the field at such a rate that if it continued, the field would vanish altogether in 3000 years. The second variation is a slow westerly drift in irregular eddies in the field, amounting to 1 degree of longitude every 5 years. The drift suggests that the fluid in the core is moving at a rate of about 100 yards a day.

The self-sustaining dynamo theory best describes the generation of the magnetic field in the core (FIG. 8-4). A dynamo is a machine that converts mechanical energy into electrical or magnetic energy. The liquid core is an excellent thermal and electrical conductor, much better than copper, and it probably has a viscosity about the same as water. Convective motions in the core fluid might be driven by gravitational energy liberated by the migration

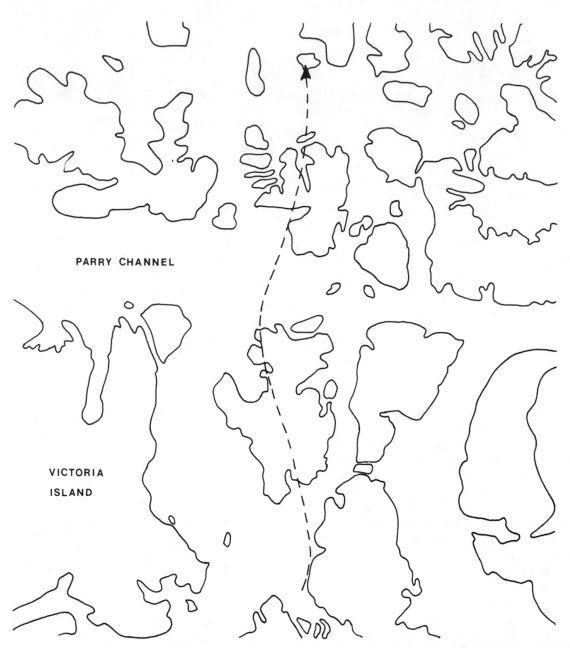

Fig. 8-3. In 150 years, the north magnetic pole wandered from the Boothia Peninsula to Ellef Ringness Island in the Canadian Arctic, a distance of approximately 450 miles.

of heavy materials to the center of the core and of light materials to the outside of the core. The Earth's rotation plays a fundamental role in the origin of the magnetic field by the Coriolis effect on the core fluid, which is similar to its effect on the at-mosphere and the ocean: it is responsible for large-scale cyclonic motions of air and sea currents.

As in the Faraday dynamo, rotation by itself is not enough to start the magnetic field; some out-side magnetism must be supplied. Since there is no

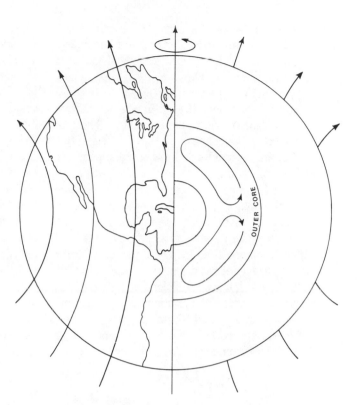

FIG. 8-4. The Earth's magnetic field is generated by the slow rotation of the solid, metallic inner core with respect to the liquid outer core.

OUTER CORE

permanent magnetic fields in the core or the mantle above because of the intense heat, the field must be supplied from outside the Earth. The Earth's dynamo could have been initially activated by the small magnetic field that permeates the entire galaxy. The dynamo mechanism would then take over and generate a much stronger field of its own. The generated electric currents in the core serve to reinforce the magnetic field so that no external field is needed beyond that which originally triggered the dynamo. The electrical currents in the core can last for about 10,000 years before decaying away. Failure to regenerate the electrical currents, either from a short circuit or some physical force, such as the shock from an impact of a large meteorite, would result in a total collapse of the magnetic field, which would then be regenerated with the poles being reversed.

Energy sources for the core might be gravitational, chemical, and radiogenic heat. The heat ultimately flows into the mantle, so it cannot be so great that it melts it. Radioactivity would not be expected to play as important a role in heating the core as it does in heating the mantle. A more promising source is the energy liberated by the latent heat of the core liquid as it freezes to form the solid inner core. The thermal capacity of the core is so great that a steady drop in temperature of 200 degrees over the past 3 billion years would provide the required energy. As the inner core grows at the expense of the outer core, gravitational energy is released because of the large contrast in density. In order for heat to drive the dynamo, there must be a difference in temperature between the inside and outside of the core; therefore, convection currents in the mantle must carry away the excess heat in order to keep the core's engine running.

THE MAGNETOSPHERE

The Earth's magnetic field protects the planet from the solar wind, which is a plasma of charged subatomic particles flowing continually from the Sun. It also protects from cosmic rays originating from space. The invisible lines of force of the Earth's magnetic field loop from one magnetic pole to the other. The solar wind stretches the magnetic field lines into a cylindrical, wind-socklike region, extending into space way beyond the orbit of the Moon.

The magnetosphere (FIG. 8-5) was not discovered until the beginning of the space age. The Explorer I satellite, launched in early 1958, registered on its onboard radiation counters charged particles some 1500 miles altitude in an area that was once thought to be empty space. When the satellite crossed the equator, the readings often dropped to zero, indicating that the intense radiation was jamming the instruments and causing them to fail.

Like the ozone layer protects the Earth from the Sun's ultraviolet radiation, the magnetosphere protects the Earth from deadly ionizing radiation. Infrequently, some of this radiation does sneak into the atmosphere, especially during periods of strong solar flares. It is responsible for disrupting long-distance radio communications and magnetic com-

passes, along with dazzling eruptions of the northern and southern auroras (FIG. 8-6). This testifies to the devastation that would be wrought should, at any time, the Earth let down its magnetic shield.

The solar wind and the magnetosphere form a vast electrical generator in which the interaction of magnetic fields and solar wind particles converts the energy of the solar wind's motion into electricity. The magnetic field is split into two narrow belts centered above the equator, called *Van Allen* belts after their discoverer, the American physicist James Van Allen. The first band lies between 600 and 3000 miles altitude, and the second and larger belt from 6000 to 40,000 miles altitude. Some of the high-energy particles of the solar wind enter these belts, and their charges interact with the magnetic lines of force. They become trapped as they spiral along the lines of magnetic force, ricocheting back and forth from pole to pole. At the periphery of the Van Allen belts where the magnetic lines of force descend toward the magnetic poles, charged particles from

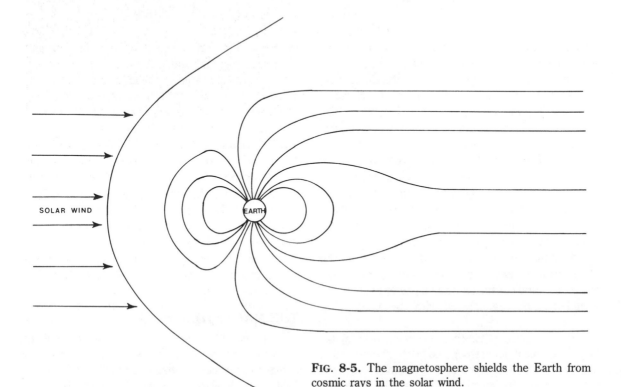

FIG. 8-5. The magnetosphere shields the Earth from cosmic rays in the solar wind.

Fig. 8-6. The aurora borealis, or northern lights.

(Courtesy of NOAA)

the solar wind smash into the ionosphere and light the northern or southern sky with an aurora.

The plasma particles trapped in the Van Allen belts along with those that cause the auroras are only a small fraction of the particles that stream earthward from the Sun. The rest are deflected by the edge of the magnetosphere, called the *magnetopause*. This deflection produces a bow wave more than 40,000 miles sunward from the Earth where the solar wind compresses the Earth's magnetic field.

MAGNETIC POLE REVERSAL

Reverse magnetism was first discovered in lava flows from the Massif Central Mountains of France in 1906 by the French geophysicist Bernard Bruhnes. Lava is normally iron rich, and when it cools and passes through the Curie point, the iron atoms line up in whatever direction the North Pole happens to be at the time. This forms weak magnetic fields in the rock called *remnant magnetism*, like miniature fossilized compasses.

On the ocean floor on either side of a spreading ridge, lava is laid out in parallel, alternating bands of magnetic rocks, somewhat like tree rings, which allows them to be dated. In Eastern Ireland, some 900 separate lava flows dating back 20 million years were found to have 60 complete changes of magnetic polarity, or on the average of about 3 every 1 million years, with the last reversal occurring some 700,000 years ago.

Reversals also have occurred during Precambrian time (over 570 million years ago) and have been observed in all subsequent periods. There is no evidence that one polarity was favored over the other for long durations, except for the Cretaceous period between 135 and 65 million years ago, when there appeared to be no reversals for more than 20 million years.

The Earth's magnetic field reverses in a highly irregular fashion and the reversal appears to be a random process. The reversals could arise because of interactions of the various parts of the dynamo's electric circuit. The action would be similar to having three pendulums attached to a common support (FIG. 8-7). When one of them is set swinging, eventually the other two will start to swing. At certain times, one of the pendulums will stop for a short period as energy sloshes back and forth among the three of them.

Although the motions of the pendulums appear to be random, they can be determined mathematically. By the same token, disk dynamos give rise to reversals that appear to be random, but can actually be determined. It would not be unexpected, therefore, that reversal of the Earth's dynamo can be mathematically determined, although it would be much more complicated.

Reversals in the Earth's dipole field occur along with reversals of convective currents in the core. The reversals might result from fluctuations in the level of turbulence in the Earth's core, caused by two competing energy sources such as heat loss at the mantle-core boundary and progressive growth of the inner core. The growth of the inner core opposes and destabilizes the effect of the heat loss at the mantle-core boundary. The presence of opposing energy sources at the two boundaries of the outer core could provide the triggering mechanism for reversals in polarity through changes in boundary conditions.

Core pressure changes brought on by tectonic events, ice ages, and meteorites also could cause fluctuations in the core's turbulence. After several hundred thousand to millions of years, the strength of the field gradually decays over a period of 10,000 years and then suddenly (in geologic terms) reverses itself and slowly builds back to normal strength.

EFFECT ON THE CLIMATE

It has long been thought that there is a correlation between changes in the Earth's magnetic field, whose origin is deep within the Earth, and events at the surface. Using geological techniques, Earth scientists can determine the age of rocks and the strength and direction of the Earth's magnetic field when the rocks were first laid down. Conversely, knowing the ages of the magnetic reversals gives scientists a method of dating rocks, since no two sequences of magnetic reversals are exactly alike.

Rock cores provide a continuous sequence, layer upon layer, of magnetic reversals dating back millions of years. Comparison of the reversals with known ups and downs in the climate in many cases shows a striking agreement. During a geomagnetic reversal when there is no magnetic field, the Earth is colder. The effect is similar to intense bursts of solar activity, which also tend to cool the Earth.

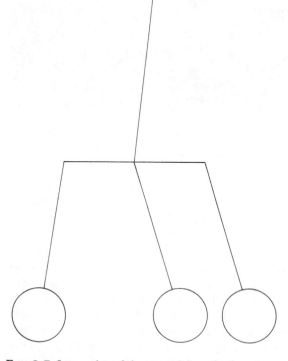

FIG. 8-7. Interaction of three pendulums having a common pivotal point.

FIG. 8-8. The March 27, 1964, Alaskan earthquake was one of the largest ever recorded. Shown here is a suburb of Anchorage.

(Courtesy of USGS)

When the field is weaker, the Earth is warmer because, when the Earth's magnetic field is weak, more cosmic rays can penetrate into the lower atmosphere and warm it.

Another means by which magnetic reversals could affect the climate is by lowering the protective shield of the magnetosphere. When the strength of the magnetic field is down, the atmosphere is exposed to the solar wind and high-intensity cosmic radiation. The increased bombardment could influence the composition of the upper atmosphere by making more nitrogen oxides, which would block out more of the Sun's heat and thereby alter the climate. During times of intense solar activity, weather is affected on Earth; therefore, any reduction in the magnetic shield would have a similar effect. Those latitudes that are particularly sensitive to changes in the Sun's activity would be similarly affected by a decrease in the Earth's magnetic field. Because magnetic reversals coincide with the extinction of species, there is a possible link between the magnetic shield, atmospheric composition, and even the evolution of life.

Although changes in the magnetic field do sometimes agree with changes in global ice volume, short-term rapid glaciations, and climatic cooling, there has yet to be decisive proof that the relationship is anything but coincidental. Yet, internal turmoil in the core that upsets the dynamo and causes it to reverse itself could be the result of excess heat, which produces erupting plumes in the mantle. This translates on the Earth's surface as an increase in seafloor spreading rate from a larger amount of volcanism both on the ocean floor and on the continents. As mentioned in Chapter 7, volcanoes have a direct impact on the climate by expelling large quantities of ash and gas into the atmosphere, and a number of large volcanic eruptions could effectively bring on an ice age.

Very high magnitude earthquakes (FIG. 8-8) actually set the globe ringing, like a large bell, lasting for weeks. Large meteor impacts can produce a sudden jolt to the Earth. The gravitational pull of the Sun, Moon, and planets might generate tides in the fluid core. There are variations in the Earth's orbital elements such as eccentricity of the orbit, precession of the equinoxes, and tilt of the axis. There are cyclic variations in solar activity. All these factors might combine to have some effect on the Earth's magnetic field. Therefore, variations in the geomagnetic field could be just another expression of the same phenomena.

9

Streams in the Sea

THE Earth is the only planet known to have oceans. The oceans cover over 70 percent of the Earth's surface, and 60 percent of the Earth's surface is covered by water over 1 mile deep. In the Pacific Basin, the ocean is as much as 7 miles deep, and if Mount Everest, the tallest mountain in the world, were placed there, the water would still extend over a mile above it (FIG. 9-1). If the Earth were as round and smooth as a billiard ball and completely covered by ocean, the water would be 2 miles deep. Even this depth, however, compared to the overall size of the Earth, makes the ocean almost insignificant—equivalent to the thin outer skin of an onion.

The ocean floor is crisscrossed by vast mountain ranges greater than any found on land. Some of these mountains break the water's surface, and their peaks become islands. Underwater volcanoes rise tens of thousands of feet from the ocean floor to create new volcanic islands. There are canyons in the ocean floor that rival even the Grand Canyon.

Currents in the atmosphere distribute heat from the tropics to other parts of the world. Similarly, oceans have currents that work effectively in the same manner (FIG. 9-2). The ocean's ability to store and move about vast quantities of heat, much more than the atmosphere, has a profound effect on the climate. The oceans retain the summer's heat and slowly give it up in the winter, moderating the Earth's temperature between the seasons. Furthermore, to change significantly the temperature of the upper 1000 feet of the ocean would take about a decade; to change the temperature of the abyss would take a thousand years or more. The oceans are a vast chemical factory, taking toxic substances from the continents and the atmosphere, and giving back life-supporting ingredients.

MAKING A WET PLANET

Of the four inner terrestrial, or rocky planets, only Earth has such a large quantity of water. Sometime after the formation of the Sun and its planets,

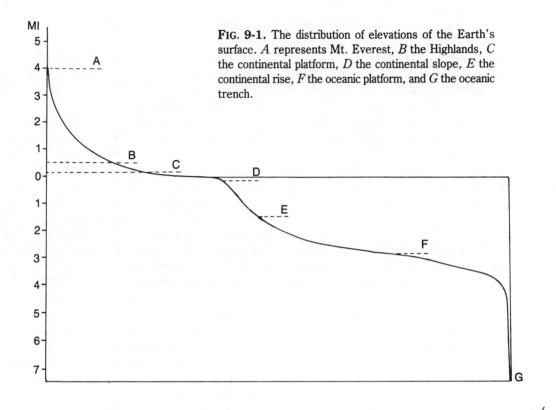

FIG. 9-1. The distribution of elevations of the Earth's surface. *A* represents Mt. Everest, *B* the Highlands, *C* the continental platform, *D* the continental slope, *E* the continental rise, *F* the oceanic platform, and *G* the oceanic trench.

FIG. 9-2. Turbulence in the upper layers of the ocean induces mixing of temperature and nutrients.

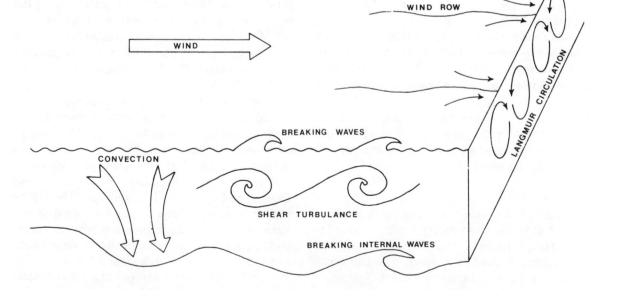

the Sun spouted giant solar flares that swept across the surface of the closer planets, stripping them of their atmospheres and water vapor. The strong solar wind sent the gases out into space, where they were deposited on the larger gaseous planets. After the Sun settled down, the Earth, as well as the other planets, began producing large quantities of water vapor and gases through volcanic vents in the crust, in what geologists term the "big burp."

Magma contains a large quantity of water, which is an important volatile, allowing it to flow easily. When the magma reaches the surface, the water is released, sometimes explosively, as volcanic steam into the atmosphere. In the Earth's early history, there were a large number of volcanic eruptions going on all at once, and a single volcano produced several times more water vapor and gases than the largest volcano does today. Some of the water also came from icy meteorites during a great bombardment early in the Earth's history.

The present position of the Earth's orbit around the Sun has a lot to do with the planet's ability to hold onto its water and maintain it in a mostly liquid state. A few million miles farther away from or closer to the Sun, and the Earth could either be encased in ice, or like Venus, its oceans could have boiled away due to a run-away greenhouse effect. The Earth is also tectonically active, and important greenhouse gases, like carbon dioxide, are constantly being recycled. There are also other orbital features, such as the tilt of the axis, which help distribute the Sun's energy more equitably. Finally, life itself modified its own environment by reducing the amount of carbon dioxide and creating oxygen, thereby helping to cool the Earth, while the Sun progressively became hotter. Life might have been sparked on the other planets, but it was soon snuffed out because climatic conditions radically changed and early life had no chance for survival.

THE ICE CAPS

Until within the last few million years, the Earth never had two permanent ice caps in its long history. The presence of even just one polar ice cap was a rare and short-lived event. This has mostly to do with the way the Earth was constructed. In

the Earth's early life, continents were confined to a region around the equator, which allowed warm ocean currents free access to the polar regions, keeping them ice free year round.

Within the last 200 million years, the continents shifted their positions so that the South Pole is now covered by a continent, and the North Pole is now covered by a nearly land-locked sea. Most of the continental land mass moved north of the equator, leaving little land in the Southern Hemisphere, where there is 90 percent ocean. This radically changed the pattern of ocean currents, whose access to the poles was almost entirely blocked. Without warm ocean currents from the tropics to keep the polar regions ice free, ice, which has a very high albedo anyway, was allowed to stay permanently.

Antarctica became a continent of ice when it broke off from Gondwanaland and drifted into the South Pole. As long as it was connected to a larger land mass, Antarctica was fed warm ocean currents from the tropics, which kept it relatively ice free. When it separated, a new ocean current was established. Easterly blowing south polar winds circled the Earth, pushing upon the water as they blew across its surface. The friction between wind and wave set a permanent ocean current in motion. This current completely circumnavigated the globe, like a snake chasing its tail, circling around Antarctica. It isolated the frozen continent from the rest of the ocean, preventing warmer currents from reaching it. About 30 million years ago, Antarctica was covered by a thick layer of ice, which dwarfed the present ice sheet. The highest mountains were buried under 1500 feet of ice, which extended across the water onto the tip of South America.

About 3 percent of the Earth's water is now locked up in the ice caps (FIG. 9-3). The ice caps cover on the average about 7 percent of the Earth's surface area. The Arctic is a sea of pack ice whose boundary is considered to be the 10-degree Celsius (50-degree Fahrenheit) July isotherm. The sea ice covers an average area of about 4 million square miles and its average thickness is several tens of feet. If the entire pack ice in the Arctic should melt, it would only raise the sea level a few feet.

By far, the greatest amount of ice is in Antarc-

(Courtesy of U.S. Navy)

FIG. 9-3. A giant iceberg at Hallett Station, Antarctica.

tica, the coldest place on Earth, where entire mountain ranges are covered by a sheet of ice 3 miles thick in spots and averaging about 1 mile thick. Since the average surface area of Antarctic ice is about 6 million square miles, the total amount of ice is approximately 6 million cubic miles.

The oceans cover about 140 million square miles of the Earth's surface. If all the ice in the Arctic and Antarctic should melt, it would raise the level of the sea by about 300 feet, which would move the shoreline anywhere up to 70 miles inland in most places, even more at low-lying deltas, and radically change the shape of the continents (FIG. 9-4). Mississippi, Louisiana, east Texas, and major parts of Alabama and Arkansas would practically disappear. All of Florida, along with south Georgia and the eastern Carolinas, would be gone. The isthmus separating North and South America at Panama would sink out of sight, and ships would have free passage without the need of a canal. The Dutch who worked so hard to reclaim their country from the sea would find most of it underwater. Many islands would be skeletons of their former selves, with only their mountainous backbones showing above water. Most of the major cities of the world, since they are either located on the coasts or along inland waterways, would drown, with only the tallest skyscrapers showing above the water line.

THE OCEAN CURRENTS

During the colonizing of North America, ship captains noticed that the trip from England to the Colonies sometimes took longer, depending upon the sea route. Sometime before the Revolutionary War, Benjamin Franklin was working as the deputy postmaster general in London for the American Colonies. Franklin puzzled over why British mail packets sailing to New England took two weeks longer to cross the Atlantic than American merchant ships. Whaling ship captains were apparently aware of a large ocean current, like some vast river in the sea, that flowed about 3 miles per hour. The whales generally kept to the edges of the current and did

FIG. 9-4. Areas of Europe that would be flooded should the polar ice caps melt. It would drown nearly 20 of Europe's greatest cities.

not try to swim against it. British captains, unaware of the stream, kept in the middle of it. Sometimes when the winds were weak, they were actually carried backwards.

Franklin had the Gulf Stream charted in 1769, believing that it was generated in part by the trade winds. He also thought that a thermometer would be a useful instrument for navigators because currents coming from the northern to the southern seas would be colder, and conversely, the currents from the southern seas into the northern seas would be warmer.

A century passed before any serious investigations into the Gulf Stream were ever conducted. The United States Coast Survey had ships crisscross the stream several times, measuring the depth and temperature. A well-equipped research ship was com-

missioned to study the current. Ship captains were requested to send in their log books from their voyages across the Atlantic. This allowed the Navy to update its charts, showing the exact position of the 13,000-mile-long current that circles the rim of the Atlantic Ocean like a giant wheel.

Recognition of the Gulf Stream led to the discovery of other ocean currents (FIG. 9-5). The north Pacific has a strong current, called the Japan or Black current, which is much like the Gulf Stream. It bears warm water up from the tropics, sweeps against Japan, crosses the Pacific, and warms the coast of California. The German naturalist Alexander von Humboldt discovered an important northward-flowing current in the Pacific Ocean, called the Humboldt or Peru current, which flows along the west coast of South America.

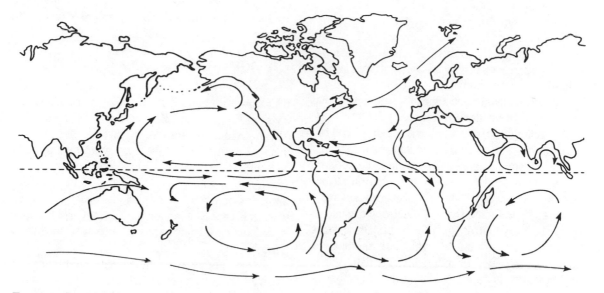

FIG. 9-5. The major ocean currents. The Gulf Stream is a warm current that originates in the Caribbean, passes the eastern coast of North America, and crosses the North Atlantic. The Pacific Humbolt current originates in the South Pacific and passes up the west coast of South America.

All ocean currents are driven by the winds, whose momentum is imparted to the ocean's surface. The currents would seem to flow in the same direction of the wind, but this is not the case. The Coriolis effect deflects the ocean currents to the right of the wind direction, or to the northwest, in the Northern Hemisphere and to the left of the wind direction, or to the southwest, in the Southern Hemisphere. The currents pick up warm water from the tropics, distribute it to the higher latitudes, and return with colder water. This process moderates the temperatures of coastal regions and makes Japan and the British Isles much warmer than they otherwise would be at their latitudes.

The Gulf Stream is also unstable, and like the jet stream in the upper atmosphere, it snakes its way around the North Atlantic basin, surrounded by eddies or rings of swirling warm and cold water, like enormous underwater tornadoes as much as 100 miles or so across. Marine animals and other sea life caught in these eddies are kidnapped to more hostile environments, such as waters that are too warm, where they can survive only as long as the eddies and the food supply holds out, which can be

upwards of several months. When the eddies die, so do the animals.

Deep ocean currents are driven by thermal forces combined with those of chemical origin, taking cold water from the poles and distributing it in the tropics. If this were not so, heat from the Earth's interior would make the ocean bottom warmer than the surface. This situation could cause the entire ocean to overturn, with disastrous consequences to sea life.

When warm currents from the tropics flow northward or southward, they encounter cold Arctic or Antarctic water, which is saltier. Salt makes water more dense and less buoyant, and determines at what temperature the surface water sinks. Salty water sinks at warmer temperatures than fresher water. The sinking water hits the ocean bottom and spreads out horizontally.

The sinking of water in one place is matched with the rising of water in another. The cold waters that sank in the polar seas rise in upwelling zones in the tropics, creating an efficient heat transport system. The tropical seas are heated from above and cooled by upwelling water from below, giving rise to an equator-to-pole transport of heat from the oceans into the atmosphere.

The current moves very slowly. Surface currents can complete a journey around the ocean basin in 10 years or so, but the vertical overturning of deep water takes up to 1000 years. It involves the entire ocean waters in a gigantic heat engine that transports a great deal of heat.

Upwelling currents along with offshore and onshore winds (FIG. 9-6) are also important in transporting bottom nutrients and oxygen to the surface. Simple, microscopic plant life, or phytoplankton, thrive near the surface where sunlight can penetrate the water for photosynthesis. These tiny organisms are at the very bottom of the food chain and are eaten by larger predators, which are themselves eaten by even larger predators on up to fish. As sea life flourishes, it depletes the water of important nutrients, such as nitrates and phosphates. This nutrient depletion then limits further growth of marine plant and animal populations.

Fortunately, scattered around the world are numerous upwelling zones of colder water that support prolific booms of phytoplankton and other sea life on up the food chain. These areas are of great economic importance to the commercial fishing industry; therefore, ship captains search for upwelling waters. There are, however, fluctuations in the atmospheric and oceanic circulation systems that can cause periodic shifts of the coastal upwelling zones with potentially disastrous consequences to the world's protein supply.

THE SOUTHERN OSCILLATION

Near the end of every year, a weak ocean current flows southward from the equator along the coast of Ecuador and Peru and warms the surface water. Ordinarily, the ocean surface there is cool and is kept that way by the northward-moving Peru current, which brings with it cold, nutrient-rich waters upon which large schools of fish feed. For hundreds of years, local residents called this backwards current El Niño for the Christ Child because it made its appearance around Christmas and left by Easter.

Every few years, a much larger and more extensive than usual ocean warming breaks out in the same area at about the same time and lingers for more than a year. These major warming episodes are associated with heavy rainfall in otherwise arid coastal regions. They are not confined just to the South American coastal region, but extend westward along the equator for a quarter of the distance around the world. Their perturbations on the climate are a global event, affecting the weather in many scattered parts of the world. The physical processes responsible for the warming trends are quite different from those of the weaker annual events, so the term *El Niño* has been applied to these major events, which occur on the average every seven years.

When a major El Niño ocean warming occurs, the barometric pressure over vast reaches of the southeast Pacific falls, while the pressure in Indonesia and northern Australia rises. When El Niño ends, the pressure difference between these two areas swings in the opposite direction, creating a massive seesawing of atmospheric pressure. This phenomenon, called the *Southern Oscillation*, is related to large-scale changes in atmospheric circulation over the tropical Pacific and Indian oceans. When the Southern Oscillation index is low, summer monsoon rains in India fail, and when it is high, the rains are plentiful. The appearance of El Niño is also associated with a low index. The 1972-73 El Niño that

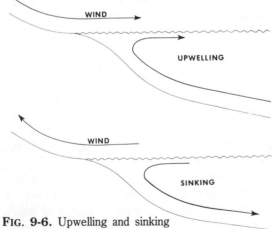

FIG. 9-6. Upwelling and sinking ocean currents are driven by offshore and onshore winds.

devastated the Peruvian anchovy fishery came at a time when the index had fallen to one of its lowest values ever, and it was accompanied by a severe drought in India (FIG. 9-7).

Normally, the trade winds over the northeast and southeast Pacific converge just north of the equator, along a line called the Intertropical Convergence Zone (ITCZ). The flow of air moves westward near the equator, dragging the surface water with it. The water piles up in the western Pacific, with a consequential lowering of the sea level in the eastern Pacific. The shallowing of the warm surface layer in the east allows the upwelling of deep, cold water, which is rich in nutrients. This supports a large fishing industry off the coasts of Ecuador and Peru.

During El Niño years, the equatorial easterly winds reverse and blow from the west. The wind then drags on the ocean surface in the opposite direction, resulting in major changes in the equatorial current system. Underwater waves, called *Kelvin waves*, are initiated in the western Pacific and are like a great sloshing of water in the Pacific Basin. They travel eastward along the equator at speeds of about 10 miles per hour, reaching the North and South American coasts several weeks later. The arrival of the slowly moving subsurface waves results in a thickening of the warm surface water layer and chokes off the upwelling of deeper, colder water. With their supply of nutrients brought from below cut off, sea life in an already overfished area dwindle to the point that it takes years for their recovery. Meanwhile, poor Latin American countries which depend much on their fishing industry to feed a starving populace is deprived of a major food source.

At the same time that the elevated ocean temperatures persist, enormous amounts of additional heat and moisture are pumped into the atmosphere by evaporation. This additional heat and moisture add extra fuel to the global atmospheric heat engine, speeding up the tropical jet stream winds and providing the raw materials for additional storminess and rainfall, mainly over the Western Hemisphere. This situation sets up a host of weather anomalies, from too much precipitation in one area to too little in another.

Because large-scale atmospheric pressure variations affect the atmosphere the world over, there is virtually no place on Earth that the weather is not influenced by the atmospheric and oceanic conditions in the tropical Pacific. The Southern Oscillation and El Niño events associated with it can then be expected to have a significant effect on the state of weather and climate almost everywhere (FIG. 9-8). El Niño might also have been responsible for numerous weather-related disasters down through the ages, spawning hurricanes, floods, and droughts.

THE 1982-83 EL NIÑO

The spring of 1982 was remarkable for the large degree of pressure variations in the Southern Oscillation. The easterly winds in the equatorial Pacific collapsed between May and June. By July, the average flow over the area changed to a westerly direction and remained so until December.

The strength of the westerly winds far exceeded those recorded over the previous decade and was associated with a dramatic shift in the large-scale precipitation in the tropical Pacific. Dry areas in the central and eastern equatorial Pacific received copious amounts of rainfall, while much of Indonesia and eastern Australia suffered severe, record-breaking droughts. In Indonesia, 340 people died from starvation. The nearly year-long drought in Australia cut grain production by roughly half that of the previous year. Thousands of hungry, thirsty cattle and sheep had to be shot and buried in mass graves, bringing the total agricultural losses to $2.5 billion. More than 1 million people faced possible famine as a result of drought-related crop losses. Southern Africa suffered one of is worse droughts in this century, leading to severe water shortages, major crop failures, and widespread hunger.

At the other extreme, in the Gilbert and Line islands to the east of Indonesia, there was day after day of drenching rain, which disrupted the economy and ecology of these equatorial islands. Nearly the entire marine bird population on Christmas Island, some 17 million birds in all, disappeared never to be seen again.

The central equatorial and southeast tropical

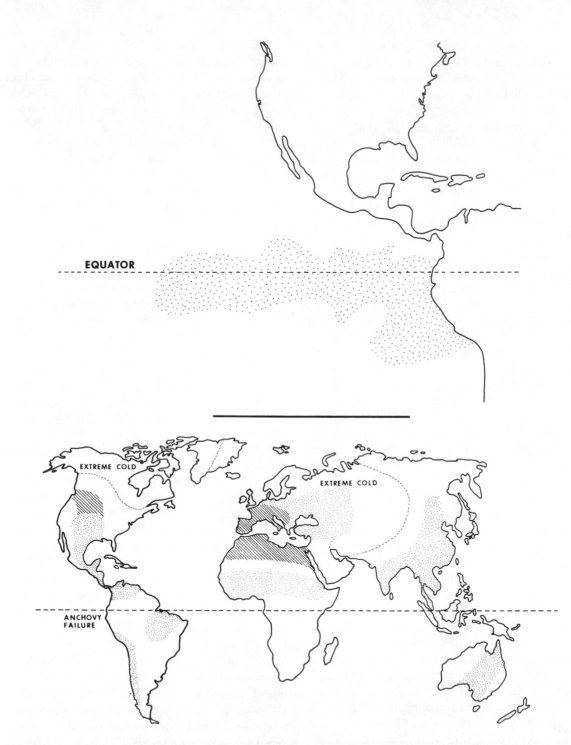

EQUATOR

EXTREME COLD

EXTREME COLD

ANCHOVY
FAILURE

FIG. 9-7. (top) Areas affected by increased sea-surface temperature during the 1972 El Niño. (bottom) The strange weather of 1972. Stippled areas represent areas affected by extreme drought. Hatched areas represent areas affected by unusually wet weather.

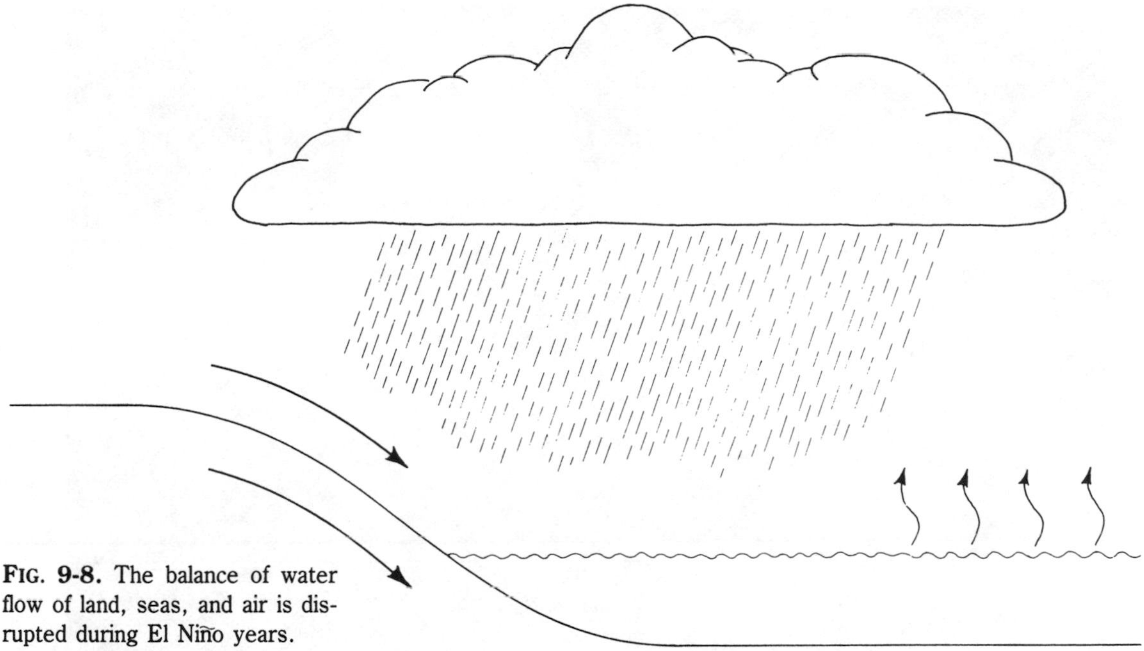

FIG. 9-8. The balance of water flow of land, seas, and air is disrupted during El Niño years.

areas of the Pacific were also plagued with excessive rainfall (FIG. 9-9). The unusually large eastward shift of the South Pacific Convergence Zone (SPCZ) was associated with a similar eastward shift in the region of the Pacific, where tropical storms are born. As a result, French Polynesia, which normally only gets about one typhoon in 3 years, was devastated by a series of six major typhoons between December 1982 and April 1983. One of these typhoons, called Veena, was the most severe typhoon to strike Tahiti in modern times. A freak northward-moving typhoon, named Iwa, struck the Hawaiian Islands in November and caused $200 million in damages. While typhoons stalked the south Pacific, the hurricane season in the Atlantic was unusually quiet, with the fewest (two) hurricanes in 50 years.

By September 2, 3 months after the collapse of the equatorial easterlies, there followed a rapid development of warmer water in the eastern equatorial Pacific. This followed a readjustment of sea level with a rise in the east and a lowering in the west.

These developments led to the onset of strong El Niño conditions along the South American coast in October. The ITCZ shifted southward, bringing an early rainy season to Ecuador. The record rains and flooding during the next nine months were part of the most catastrophic and prolonged El Niño visitation ever recorded in Ecuador and northern Peru. The floods and mudslides cut roads, washed away crops, and took hundreds of lives. In December, the warm coastal waters were 7 degrees above normal and reached as much as 11 degrees above normal in places. The high sea-surface temperatures persisted in the extreme eastern equatorial Pacific, and the unseasonally heavy rainfall continued along the South American coast.

During the winter of 1982-83, the intensification of the Pacific jet stream reached record proportions. The mean monthly sea-level barometric pressure in the Gulf of Alaska was lower in February 1983 than at any time in this century. The tracks of storms entering North America from the Pacific were at times displaced hundreds of miles eastward, bringing destructive winds, tides, flooding, and landslides to the California coast, causing more than $300 million in property damages, and forcing 10,000 people to evacuate their homes.

Unusually wet weather beset the Sunbelt of western United States in the winter and spring.

FIG. 9-9. A squall line at sea.

Storms marched across America's southland, putting portions of Mississippi, Louisiana, and Florida (FIG. 9-10) under water and forcing the evacuation of tens of thousands from their homes. A huge mountain snowpack in the Colorado Rockies brought the Colorado River to flood stage. There were severe dislocations of aquatic life along the west coast of the Americas. This resulted in a drastic decrease in the populations of fish eggs and larvae, and sharp drops in the catches of commercial fish.

From the standpoint of economic costs and the amount of human misery it caused, this El Niño will go down in the record books as the worst weather event of this century, if not in modern history.

FORECASTING EL NIÑO

The weather-related damage around the Pacific rim from the 1982-83 El Niño was estimated at more than $6.5 billion. Therefore, there is a strong incentive to be able to forecast these events, although many related phenomena are still not well understood. In February 1986, meteorologists eyeing the latest observations from the tropical Pacific saw the ocean warming in much the way it does in the earliest stages of an El Niño. These early signs prompted the National Weather Service's Climate Analysis Center in Washington, DC, to issue an El Niño watch on February 11 and an advisory on March 13. By mid-June, however, the watch had been dropped because by that time, there was no longer anything particularly unusual going on in the Pacific. The warming had not progressed southward along the Peruvian coast, heavy rains over the desert regions had not appeared, and the east Pacific warming seemed unusually shallow. This does not make El Niños inherently unpredictable, just that some situations are more predictable than others.

The failure to predict El Niño underscores the

FIG. 9-10. A frontal cloud formation over Pensacola, Florida.

current lack of understanding of how it develops. No two El Niños are exactly alike, but fortunately, they do share enough similarities and precursory signs to possibly make them recognizable early on. Stronger than normal trade winds are a reliable predictor of El Niños, as well as a rise in the Southern Oscillation index. By averaging observations for all El Niños between 1949 and 1973 (the 1982 El Niño might have been triggered by the 1982 erup-

tion of the El Chichon Volcano in Mexico), common precursory signals could be made to stand out. Unfortunately, summer droughts in India and above-normal rainfall in the central Pacific, which are regarded as hallmarks of El Niño, also occur in non-Niño years. If fairly reliable predictions of El Niño are not developed soon, the next El Niño could mean economic chaos and human suffering of unprecedented proportions in many parts of the world.

10

Weather or Not

WEATHER forecasting is an art as ancient and respected as any other means of seeing into the future. Early weather prognosticators were aware of certain signs in nature that foretold of the upcoming weather. Gradually this art changed from its obscure beginnings immersed in mythology and astrology to its basis on scientific methods using modern technology. As a science, meteorology is relatively young compared with its sister sciences of mathematics, physics, and astronomy, yet no other single field has touched the lives of so many people.

DEVELOPMENT OF METEOROLOGY

Meteorology owes its beginning to Galileo, the scientist for all seasons. Around 1600, Galileo constructed the first thermometer, a device he created out of his vacuum experiments. It consisted of a long, vertical glass tube with a bulb at its upper end. The bottom end was placed in a beaker of water, and a water column was drawn up inside the tube. The water in the tube was forced down as the air in the bulb warmed and expanded. Conversely, the water rose as the air became cooler and contracted. The instrument was not very accurate and could only indicate the relative change in temperature and not the temperature itself, but it became the forerunner of the thermometers used today.

One of the things that greatly puzzled Galileo was why water could be suspended in a column no more than 34 feet. Galileo posed this problem to his student Evangelista Torricelli in late 1641, just before he died at the age of 77. Torricelli scaled down the apparatus by using the heavier liquid mercury, which weighs 14 times greater than water. A 3-foot glass tube was filled with mercury and submerged upside down in a bowl of mercury. The mercury column descended to a level of 30 inches, leaving a vacuum at the top of the tube. Torricelli correctly interpreted the level of the mercury, not to its being pulled up by the vacuum at the top, but rather by its being pushed up by the weight of the atmosphere.

To prove that air had weight and that air pressure decreased with height, the French mathematician Blaise Pascal had Torricelli's barometer taken up a 5,000-foot mountain in southern France in 1648. At the base of the mountain, the barometer had a reading of 28 inches of mercury, and at the summit, it read a little under 25 inches, indicating to Pascal's satisfaction that air was an elastic substance whose weight decreases with altitude.

It was soon recognized that variations in the height of the liquid column were usually followed by certain changes in the weather. The barometer, or *weather glass* as it was called, became the most important tool in weather forecasting. The English chemist Robert Boyle, who invented the first practical anemometer, was the first to introduce the term *barometer*. He used a cumbersome apparatus similar to the barometer built by Galileo, which consisted of a long pipe set in a cistern of water. At the upper end of the pipe, the air was pumped out until the water level was raised to its maximum of 34 feet. From a lofty rooftop, Boyle could then observe the effects of atmospheric pressure as the water level in the barometer rose or fell.

One of the first to use the barometer to forecast the weather was the German scientist Otto von Guericke. He predicted severe storms by observing a large drop in the water level of his barometer.

The first attempt to establish an international network of meteorological observation stations was made in 1653, and standardized instruments were constructed and sent to locations throughout Europe. A uniform reporting procedure was devised for observations of temperature, pressure, and humidity, as well as the state of the sky.

From an investigation of these reports, the eighteenth century English meteorologist George Hadley recognized that pressure changes did not always occur simultaneously at different places. The French physicist J. de Borda found that pressure changes were propagated with a certain direction and speed which opened up a new concept of traveling pressure systems, or cyclones and anticyclones.

The first weather map was drawn in 1820, based on observations collected from observatories all over Europe. Because the information had to be gathered by mail, however, the storm systems would already have run their course, so it was of little value for weather forecasts. It was not until the invention of the telegraph in 1843, which provided instant communication, that the modern era of weather forecasting began.

EARLY DAYS OF FORECASTING

In 1849, over 200 weather observers across the United States telegraphed daily weather reports to the Smithsonian Institution in Washington, DC, where for interested observers, the collected observations were displayed on a large weather map. Americans also looked forward to reading the weather reports in their daily newspapers. Between 1861 and 1865, however, these activities were temporarily halted by the American Civil War. Shortly after the war, President Ulysses S. Grant ordered the Army to begin making meteorological observations to give warnings of storms that threatened the sea coasts and the Great Lakes. The United States Weather Bureau was established by an act of Congress in early 1871 to provide the nation with an early-warning system against severe storms. Its successes were modest because of the archaic tools of the trade and poor understanding of atmospheric dynamics.

Accuracy was greatly improved when weather instruments were carried aloft by kites or balloons in the 1890s. The high-altitude observations gave a better understanding of the vertical structure of weather systems in the troposphere and eventually led to the discovery of the stratosphere. A new kind of weather chart (FIG. 10-1) was introduced, which connected areas of equal pressure with lines called *isobars*, vastly improving the understanding and the forecasting of the weather.

During World War I, weather forecasts were considered classified information, and neutral Norway was cut off from weather reports, which it desperately needed for its fishing fleet. The resourceful Norwegians were forced to set up their own weather forecasting system, using a network of hundreds of observation stations. Detailed reports of cloud formations were used to make up for the lack of upper-air soundings. At the Bergen Geophysical Institute, the Norwegian meteorologist Vilhelm Bjerknes used this data to analyze the

Table 10-1. Significant Events in Meteorology

400 BC	Hippocrates writes on the influence of climate on health.
350 BC	Aristotle writes on weather science.
300 BC	Theophrastus writes on winds.
1593	Galileo invents the thermometer.
1643	Torricelli invents the barometer.
1661	Boyle proposes his law on gases.
1664	Formal weather observations begin in Paris, France.
1668	Edmund Halley draws first map of the trade winds.
1714	The Fahrenheit scale is introduced.
1735	George Halley's treatise on earth's rotation effect on wind.
1736	The Centigrade scale is introduced.
1779	Formal weather observations begin in New Haven, Connecticut.
1783	The hair hygrometer is invented.
1802	Lamark and Howard suggest cloud classification scheme.
1817	Humboldt draws first map of global mean annual temperature.
1825	August invents the psychrometer.
1827	Dove develops the laws of storms.
1831	Redfield makes the first weather map of the U.S.
1837	The pyrheliometer is invented.
1841	Espy develops theory on storm movement.
1844	Coriolis describes the ''Coriolis Effect.''
1845	Berghaus makes first world map of precipitation.
1848	Dove publishes first maps of mean monthly temperature.
1862	Renou makes first map showing mean pressure in Europe.
1879	Supan publishes map of world temperature regions.
1892	Beginning of systematic use of weather balloons.
1902	The stratosphere is discovered.
1913	The ozone layer is discovered.
1918	Bjerknes develops polar front theory.
1925	Beginning of systematic data collection by aircraft.
1928	Radiosondes are first used on weather balloons.
1940	Investigation into the nature of jet streams.
1960	The U.S. launches Tiros I, the first weather satellite.

properties of air masses, based on his theory that air is a fluid, subject to the laws of physics; therefore, forecasting was more of a problem of mechanics.

Bjerknes and his colleagues must have been aware of the combat tactics used in trench warfare, in which masses of soldiers made frontal attacks against concentrated machine-gun fire. The meteorologists envisioned warm and cold air masses marching in fronts across the surface of the Earth (FIG. 10-2). Their observation that cyclonic storms are born in the contrasting zones between warm and cold air masses set in motion a revolution in synoptic meteorology.

Prior to World War II, balloon-borne radiosonde instruments were developed that could transmit accurate measurements of temperature, pressure, and humidity directly to a receiving station on the

C-1. Solar halo. (NOAA)

C-2. Hurricane storm surge. (NOAA)

C-3. Lightning. (NOAA)

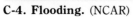

C-4. Flooding. (NCAR)

C-5. Tornado. (NOAA)

C-6. Heavy snow. (USAF)

C-7. Windshear. (NCAR)

C-8. Mudslide. (USGS)

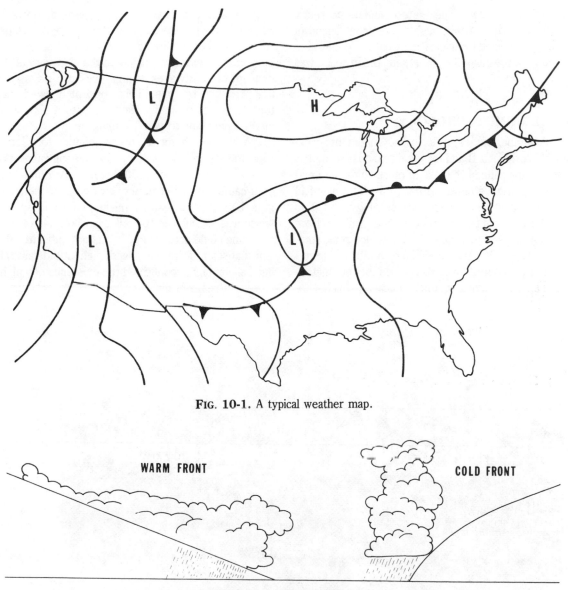

FIG. 10-1. A typical weather map.

WARM FRONT

COLD FRONT

FIG. 10-2. Storm fronts.

ground. A network of upper-air stations scattered across the country vastly improved the understanding of frontal systems, using upper-level weather charts.

A classic example of the importance of accurate weather forecasting for the military was during the Normandy invasion in early June 1944. Never in the history of warfare had there been anything like it in terms of manpower and military equipment. More than any other factor, the weather held the key to success, and it had to be near perfect. Unfortunately, one spring storm after another held back the invasion, which had to begin between June 5 and 7 when the Moon and tides were just right or be postponed for several more weeks. As luck would have it, a wedge of high pressure was located over the Atlantic Ocean. The meteorologists correctly predicted that it would push a cold front ahead of it into France and bring clearing weather in its wake. On June 6, the balloon went up, and the invasion was on.

MODERN METEOROLOGY

A number of meteorological advancements came out of World War II and for good reasons: some Pacific storms caused the loss of more ships than major battle engagements. (FIG. 10-3). The war had a major impact on advancing meteorology, and at no time before was there so much data available from so many parts of the world. The first electronic computer, called ENIAC (Electronic Numeral Integrator And Computer), was developed for the military in hopes of improving weather forecasts, which were

of great strategic importance. A method known as *differential analysis* allowed meteorologists to estimate weather conditions over vast open oceans and over enemy territory, leading to the discovery of the concept of long waves of high-pressure ridges and low-pressure troughs. This concept allowed meteorologists to make five-day forecasts, which were vitally important to war planning.

American bomber pilots bound for Japan reported struggling against a fast-moving current of air at an altitude of about 30,000 feet. At times, aircraft caught in this stream of air overshot their targets because navigators misjudged their speed, which was as much as 100 miles per hour faster than the plane could actually fly. It was not until after the war that scientific probings with high-altitude aircraft and balloon flights confirmed the existence of a high-altitude stream of air.

(Courtesy of U.S. Navy)

FIG. 10-3. An aircraft carrier's flight deck, which was buckled in a Pacific typhoon during World War II.

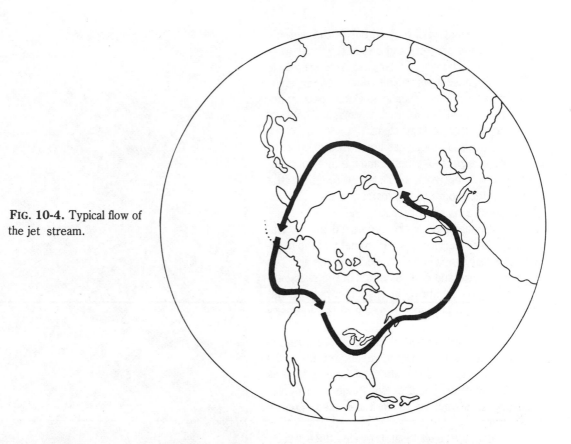

FIG. 10-4. Typical flow of the jet stream.

The *jet stream* (FIG. 10-4) is a ribbon of rapidly moving air normally 180 to 300 miles wide and up to 2 miles thick. It meanders around the Earth from west to east at altitudes between 30,000 and 45,000 feet, with an average speed between 60 and 115 miles per hour. Speeds of 300 miles per hour have also been recorded. Like their sea-going predecessors who rode the Gulf Stream, transcontinental flights from North American to Europe took advantage of the jet stream to save both time and fuel. Of course, they tried to avoid it on the return flight.

The importance of the jet streams and their effects on the weather was not made clear until the 1950s. Jet streams play an important role in transferring heat from the tropics to the poles. They control the development and movement of low- and high-pressure regions in the lower atmosphere. They steer convective storms such as tornadoes and squall lines. Jet streams also can block the advancement of low-pressure systems, causing stagnation, which can result in severe winters or scorching summers in the middle and high latitudes.

The two most important jet streams are the polar front and the subtropical jet streams. The first is located in the upper reaches of the troposphere between the temperate and polar air masses. The abrupt drop in temperature in the vicinity of the polar front creates a steep pressure gradient aloft near the tropopause. At the edge of the tropics flow the subtropical jet streams. They are strongest in the winter when the temperature difference between the tropical and temperate air zones is the greatest. Every once in a while, the polar front and the subtropical jet streams merge, and their combined power can generate severe storms below.

WEATHER RADAR

One of the most important meteorological tools to come out of World War II was radar. The Radiation Laboratory at MIT housed one of the nation's largest wartime projects and one of the most well-kept secrets of the war. Radar gave America a decisive edge because it was able to detect enemy ships and aircraft from great distances. One important bonus was radar's ability to track storms, and so warn ships and aircraft to stay clear.

Since the war, radar has been used to observe the location, size, movement, and intensity of thunderstorms. A network of radars throughout the United States monitors the formation and behavior of thunderstorms and other rain and snow storms. A conventional radar of the type used by the National Weather Service (FIG. 10-5) detects the presence of water drops and ice particles in the air. The greater the size and concentration of the precipitation particles, the more intense the radar echo. Thus, radar can be used to measure the intensity of rain and snow.

A special type of radar, called *Doppler radar*, has the ability to measure the speed, either toward or away from the radar station, of targets such as raindrops or other liquid or solid objects. Doppler radar operates similarly to the radar used in police speed traps.

Because one characteristic of tornadoes is their high wind speed, Doppler radar is well suited to detect them. In some cases, it is possible to detect evidence of tornado development as much as 20 minutes before the funnel reaches the ground. Tornadoes also produce a pronounced hook-shaped image on the radar screen, reflecting the tight spiral of the cloud formation of the storm. The hook echoes represent the heavy rain or hail that often occurs along the flanks of severe storms. Tornadoes typically emerge from the southwest regions of these storms. Unfortunately, not all tornado-breeding storms have this characteristic feature; however, the sight of such an echo in a thunderstorm usually leads to a tornado warning.

High-powered radars are used to track hurricanes and typhoons when they are within a couple hundred miles of land. The distinct spiral rainbands show up on the radar scope like the spiral arms of some distant galaxy. The heading and speed of the hurricane are calculated to determine where and

FIG. 10-5. Radar dome at the National Weather Service, North Little Rock, Arkansas.

when the storm will make its landfall and provide residents of affected areas plenty of time for evacuation to safer ground.

Specially equipped aircraft, called *hurricane hunters* (FIG. 10-6), are used to make measurements of the storm's position, as well as its pressure and wind patterns. Aircraft are also guided through storms and fog to a safe landing by radar.

WEATHER SATELLITES

In 1908, Robert Goddard had a dream. As with so many others like him, his dream was to explore

FIG. 10-6. (top) Navy weather reconnaissance aircraft. (bottom) Hurricane on weather radar.

space. In 1929, Goddard launched a rocket whose payload included a thermometer, a barometer, and a camera.

During World War II, the Germans vastly improved the rocket with the development of the V-2, which could deliver a 1-ton warhead 200 miles away. After the war, captured German V-2 rockets launched from the White Sands proving grounds in New Mexico carried a variety of payloads which led to the first pictures of clouds from high altitudes in the late 1940s. One V-2, used as a booster stage for a smaller rocket, set the world's altitude record of 244 miles on February 24, 1949.

In 1955, the Eisenhower administration announced plans to launch the first American satellite during the International Geophysical Year (IGY), 1957-58. Ironically, the Soviet Union, which felt challenged by America's boast, beat the United States by four months with the launching of Sputnik on October 4, 1957. Finally, Explorer I was blasted into orbit by an Army Redstone rocket on January 31, 1958, and the world entered the space age.

The first weather satellite, called TIROS for Television Infra-Red Observation Satellite (FIG. 10-7), was launched from Cape Canaveral on April 1, 1960. TIROS I, weighing 270 pounds, operated for 78 days, and in that time produced over 20,000 pictures of the earth.

Scientists wanted a satellite system able to view the global atmosphere on a regular basis both day and night. Therefore, one year after the launching of TIROS I, President Kennedy requested funds to develop the National Operational Meteorological Satellite System. TIROS I was an experimental craft, and the first in a series of polar-orbiting weather satellites.

The Earth rotates beneath the satellites as they circle the Earth in near polar, Sun-synchronous orbits at approximately 500 miles altitude. The satellites provide about 16,000 global atmospheric

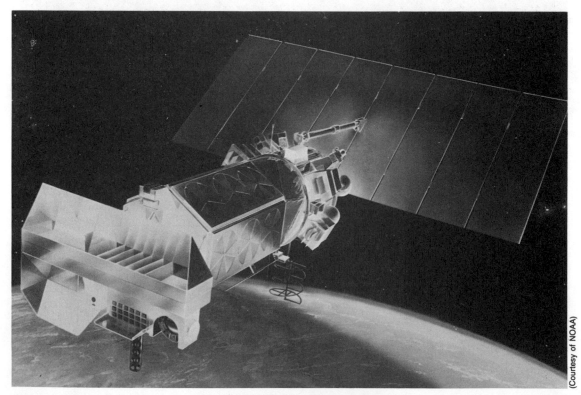

(Courtesy of NOAA)

FIG. 10-7. TIROS weather satellite.

soundings daily to the National Weather Service. The satellites also provide valuable information about weather conditions over ocean areas where conventional data are lacking.

A different type of satellite was required to meet the need for continuous surveillance of North American weather systems. The solution was to send a satellite into a circular orbit over the equator at an altitude of about 22,300 miles. This is called a *geostationary orbit*, in which the satellite orbits the Earth at the same rate the Earth rotates, or once every 24 hours. Two experimental geostationary satellites were launched in 1966 and 1967, providing the technological base for the Geostationary Operational Environmental Satellites, or GOES, (FIG. 10-8) operated by the National Oceanographic and Atmospheric Administration (NOAA). The first GOES prototype was launched on May 17, 1974, and a second on February 6, 1975.

GOES 5, positioned to cover the East Coast of the United States, and GOES 6, centered over the central Pacific, were launched in the early 1980s. Each satellite viewed almost one-third of the Earth's surface and provided images every 30 minutes, day or night. In 1984, GOES 5's weather-tracking camera failed after 3 years of service, requiring GOES 6 to do double duty, and it was moved to a more central position to cover the entire United States by itself. In May 1986, GOES 7 was launched by a Delta rocket, which malfunctioned shortly after liftoff and had to be destroyed together with the satellite. The eighth and final satellite in the GOES series was successfully launched by another Delta rocket on February 25, 1987.

The satellites are particularly important for early warning of tropical storms (FIG. 10-9) and cyclones. Almost every storm system that strikes the United States forms either off the southern coast of Alaska or the west coast of Africa. GOES satellite imagery was the only warning of Typhoon Iwa's approach to the Hawaiian Islands in November 1982. Iwa was monitored closely as it developed southwest of Ha-

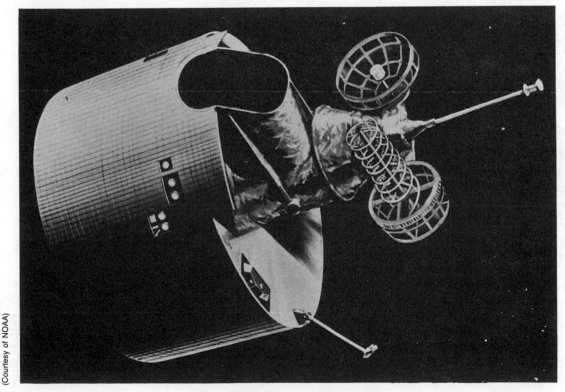

(Courtesy of NOAA)

FIG. 10-8. GEOS weather satellite.

Fig. 10-9. Typhoon Pat viewed from space.

(Courtesy of NASA)

waii. After moving northward for several days, it abruptly turned toward the islands, and within 24 hours, it struck Kauai and Oahu. Based on the satellite imagery, the National Weather Service was able to give timely typhoon warnings, and only one life was lost, even though property damage in heavily populated coastal areas totaled $200 million.

Satellites also provide near continuous coverage of the atmospheric conditions that produce tornadoes, squall lines, and other local, severe convective storms. Telltale signs of strong convection often can be detected in satellite imagery before severe storms develop. When they do, the satellites monitor their life cycles and track their movements. When necessary, the Weather Service gives warning of impending danger.

The satellite imagery is also used to estimate rainfall amounts for flash-flood warnings. In the winter, satellites monitor mountain snowpacks and river ice jams to warn of possible flooding. Satellite images are used to monitor the southward progress of freezing surface temperatures and provide warnings for citrus growers. The satellites are also sensitive to high heat sources and have been effective in pinpointing wild fires in remote areas. The smoke from forest fires as well as volcanic eruptions are also easily detected. The satellites monitor sea-surface temperature, which is not only of value to fishermen but can provide early warning of unusually strong El Nino currents.

NUMERICAL FORECASTING

The Norwegian meteorologist Vilhelm Bjerknes, who developed the polar front theory, proposed in 1904 that it should be possible to express the physical behavior of the atmosphere numerically and to stimulate its future behavior by a series of mathematical computations. The English meteorologist Lew Richardson took these ideas more seriously and tried to formulate laws that govern all atmospheric motions in precise mathematical equations. Unfortunately, the equations he used to describe the atmosphere took so long to solve by hand that, no matter how quickly he went, the weather always advanced much faster than his arithmetic.

In 1922, Richardson came up with the idea of a "forecast factory" where 64,000 mathematicians were equipped with mechanical desk calculators. Each individual would work on only one part of the atmospheric equation, which was combined with the work of all the others to create the whole weather picture for a timely forecast. Although Richardson's vision was impractical, it did show the need for the development of modern computers.

Shortly after World War II, the American mathematician John von Neumann and his colleagues at Princeton University fed the first peacetime meteorological data into ENIAC. Von Neumann managed to simplify Richardson's equations, and when they were fed into the primitive computer, the scientists could, for the first time, get ahead of the weather. In 1950, a model of large-scale atmospheric behavior was used to make the first successful numerical forecast, and by the mid 1950's, forecasts based on numerical methods were issued on a regular basis.

Today, high-speed computers (FIG. 10-10) are used to make long-range forecasts from 3 to 10 days in advance. They take information from a variety of sources, including satellites, radar, radiosondes, and a network of automated instrumented sites, along with sightings from sailors and aviators. This information is updated every few minutes. The data are manipulated by the computer and displayed on banks of video monitors, which enables the forecaster to select and combine certain features and observations. He might overlay a satellite image on a radar scan, or he might overlay a radar scan on

(Courtesy of NOAA)

FIG. 10-10. Weather computer system.

a display of temperature, pressure, dew point, and wind velocity. This ability becomes most important when he is attempting to forecast severe storms which might last for no more than 20 minutes. Each year severe storms cost an estimated $20 billion in economic losses, but even worse, they take an average of about 400 lives.

The computer could never fully replace the weatherman, however. In many cases, weather forecasting requires time-proven experience and an intuitive "sense" about the weather, which only the human operator can possess.

Supercomputers such as the National Meteorological Center's Cyber 205 in Camp Springs, Maryland, and the European Center's Cray X-MP in Reading, England, can produce a global atmospheric model, which is a computer simulation of the weather of the entire planet. It is a very refined mathematical model that includes cloud formation and dissipation, snow fall and melt, water evaporation and precipitation, and changes in sea-surface temperature. It also takes into account the effects of mountains and the geography of the whole world.

Intricate reactions in the troposphere affect the weather the world over, and large-scale weather phenomena are felt worldwide. These large events are a result of collisions between masses of moving air that can cover a whole hemisphere. In order to predict large-scale weather patterns, meteorologists must measure the constantly changing conditions in the atmosphere at various levels by radiosonde or satellite.

These global predictions have, in turn, improved local forecasts. Regional offices of the National Weather Service are connected to the main computer in Camp Springs, and forecasters can call up large-scale maps on their own screens, superimpose local observations, and zoom-in on up-to-date pictures of neighboring areas (FIG. 10-11).

LONG-RANGE PREDICTIONS

Since the early days of synoptic meteorology, it has been highly desirable to make weather forecasts on a monthly or even a seasonal basis. Failure of the monsoons in India led to a severe famine in 1877, which prompted attempts to forecast future monsoons.

Recognition of large-scale features of the general circulation system, such as semi-permanent areas of high and low pressure, was an important step forward in long-range predictions. The evolution of small-scale weather is closely related to correspondingly large-scale and slowly evolving systems in the upper atmosphere. In 1948, the U.S. Weather Bureau began issuing forecasts for the Northern Hemisphere, showing areas that were expected to be warmer or cooler, wetter or dryer than average during the forthcoming 30-day period.

It was also found that weather systems, such as lows and highs, travel in series often less than a week apart, and are steered along fairly definite paths by certain large-scale features of the general circulation. Computer projections can compare the month in question with those of previous years. When a close resemblance in weather patterns is found, a forecast is prepared based on developments that occurred in previous analogous situations. Boundary conditions, such as the interaction of oceans, snow, ice, and soil moisture with the atmosphere, also might aid as predictors of large-scale atmospheric phenomena in long time scales.

Computer simulation also can provide fairly reliable long-range forecasts. The computer is coming to the aid of the long-range forecasters in much the way it aided short-range forecasters 30 years ago. With no more knowledge than the weather around the globe on January 1, 1977, one of the coldest months on record, a computer model developed in 1983 successfully generated a reasonably good facsimile of the general weather pattern for the rest of that month. January's cold weather was a result of a strong ridge of high pressure over Alaska and Canada, which blocked the normal air flow and steered frigid air into eastern North America. All attempts at simulating this blocking pattern involved general circulation models that described the processes which cause the atmosphere to depart from an ideal gas such as precipitation, evaporation, and cloudiness.

This method paints a more realistic picture of the world, especially where the atmosphere inter-

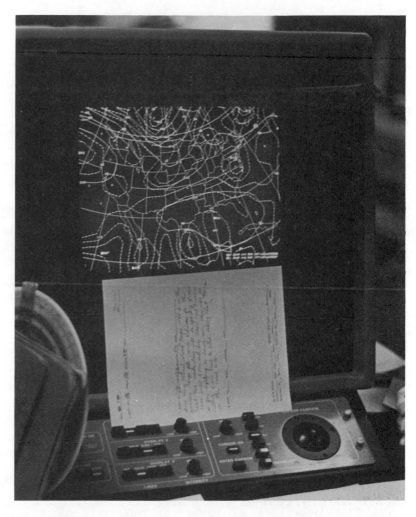

FIG. 10-11. Weather projected on a video monitor.

acts with land and water. No long-range forecasting method will, however, be able to describe the weather 30 days hence in the detail of a daily forecast, and can only give predictions of average conditions over large regions.

The stakes involved in reliable weather prediction are enormous. Every summer, severe thunderstorm warnings send people scrambling for the safety of their cellars; every winter, blizzards shut down traffic in the big cities. Foul weather closes airports, and sudden blasts of wind, called *microbursts*, can knock planes out of the sky. In 1983, hail, floods, freezes, lightning, tornadoes, and hurricanes in the United States destroyed $27 bil-

lion in property, crops, and livestock, killed 700 people, and 5000 more were injured. In the following two winters, cold snaps cost Florida growers more than $2 billion.

Millions of people depend on accurate forecasts for their livelihood. When meteorologists make mistakes, people's lives are at risk, and suits are brought against the government. Such legal battles might have a detrimental effect and cause weathermen to be too cautious and nonspecific about the weather. Forecasts might be veiled in vague language that only weathermen understand, and the people would be left out in the cold.

11

Man-made Weather

PERHAPS it is the ego in man that makes him believe he can control nature. Most of the time, nature humbles mankind with her enormous power. Hurricanes, tornadoes, floods, and droughts seem to come and go at her pleasure. She will dump several inches of rain in areas that are normally dry and leave other areas that are normally wet baked and parched.

It is these extremes of nature that people would like to modify. With a fine-tuning of nature, deserts might once again bloom, swamps might dry up, monsoons might become more regular, and hurricanes might be steered away from the coasts. Owners of ski resorts help nature along by seeding clouds over ski slopes to improve the snow base (FIG. 11-1). Cloud seeders claim success in reducing hail damage to crops, but it is not certain whether doing nothing at all would have brought about the same results. Farmers in drought-stricken areas would gladly pay the high price for a rainmaker in order to spare their crops. Unfortunately, flooding might result from their tampering with nature, and their crops could

still be lost. Also, stealing rain out of clouds could pose serious legal problems, and farmers downwind might not appreciate having their rain commandeered by someone else.

THE FORMATION OF CLOUDS

The first to develop theories about the clouds were the eighth century B.C. Ionian philosophers of Asia Minor. They believed that clouds were a thickened form of moist air, an idea that persisted until about the mid-seventeenth century when the French mathematician Rene Descartes declared that air and water vapor were two different things. Descartes' ideas were essentially ignored, however, until another century had passed.

In 1751, the French physician Charles Le Roy observed that sealing damp air in a glass container and allowing it to cool would produce dew on the inside of the glass at a certain temperature. When he heated the vessel above that temperature, the dew disappeared. Le Roy concluded that any parcel of air has a specific temperature, called the *dew*

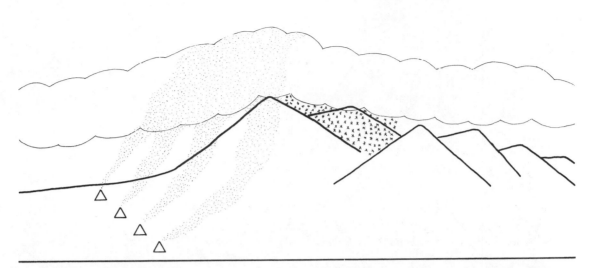

FIG. 11-1. Cloud seeding with ground-based silver iodide burners to augment snowfall at ski resorts.

point, at which the water vapor it contains will condense to a liquid. He also reasoned that warm air can hold more water vapor and feel less humid than cold air; therefore, the humidity is relative and depends on the temperature of the air.

Le Roy thought the water was dissolved in the air, like salt is dissolved in water. He thought it was then precipitated out as rain, dew, or snow, like salt is precipitated out of water when it evaporates. Although the term precipitation is chemically inaccurate in this case, it still remains in the meteorological vocabulary.

Another misconception which claimed adherents throughout the eighteenth century was that water vapor was like tiny bubbles of water whose low specific gravity allowed them to rise through the air until they reached a certain altitude, where the air was thin and equally light. In 1802, the English chemist John Dalton put forth the theory that water vapor was a gas that behaves in air much like any other gas. It mixes with the gases in the air, but does not combine chemically in solution. Molecules of water in the air exert a water vapor pressure that is independent of the other gases. When the water vapor pressure is high, the air becomes saturated with water vapor and any additional water evaporating into the air often results in precipitation. *Relative humidity*, therefore, is the ratio of the existing va-

por pressure to the maximum possible vapor pressure, and is usually expressed as a percentage.

Warm air has a greater capacity to hold water vapor than cold air; therefore, as moist, warm air ascends, it cools to the point where it becomes saturated with water vapor. Water vapor can condense to a liquid before the air reaches the saturation point. Conversely, when saturation is reached, condensation does not necessarily begin.

In 1875, the French scientist Paul Coulier discovered during his fog experiments that air meeting all the requirements of temperature, pressure, and relative humidity could not produce fog without dust particles. Atmospheric dust particles are produced by ash from volcanic eruptions, wind-blown clay particles, salt from the ocean spray, soot from forest fires, and more recently, pollution from man's activities. The dust forms the nuclei around which water vapor condenses. Without condensation nuclei, the air would become supersaturated with water vapor without forming clouds. Then suddenly, massive clouds would condense out of nowhere, and heavy downpours would lash the earth.

Clouds are formed when a moisture-laden parcel of air is heated and rises through the atmosphere. As the air slowly ascends, the atmospheric pressure gradually decreases, causing the air to expand. The energy needed for this expansion comes from within

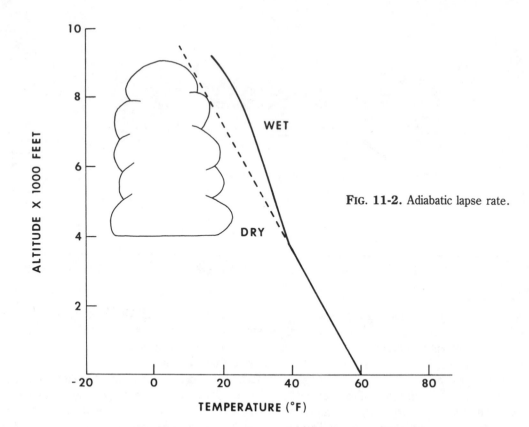

FIG. 11-2. Adiabatic lapse rate.

the parcel of air itself in the form of heat, resulting in a drop in temperature. The rate of loss of temperature is called the *adiabadic lapse rate* and is about 5 degrees Fahrenheit per 1000 feet or 1 degree Celsius per 100 meters (FIG. 11-2). If the parcel of moist air continues to rise, it eventually reaches its dew point, and water vapor condenses around minute dust particles. As the water vapor condenses, it releases *latent heat*, which is heat given off when water changes state from a gas to a liquid or a liquid to a solid (FIG. 11-3). The release of latent heat in turn slows the cooling of the air. The air maintains its buoyancy, which contributes to the upward growth of the cloud (FIG. 11-4). Moist air is more buoyant than dry air and once the saturation point is reached, the air becomes even more buoyant. It also explains why clouds are associated with the slowly ascending air in low-pressure systems.

Clouds are also produced orographically when moist air currents are forced upward by mountains

blocking their way. The results are clouds and heavy precipitation on the windward side of the mountain, while the lee side of the mountain is left high and dry, and deserts are often formed.

The first classification of clouds was made by the English pharmacist and meteorologist Luke Howard in 1803. Howard, who is considered Britain's father of meteorology, thought that clouds could be classified according to their appearance and behavior. Howard recognized three basic types of clouds and gave them Latin names. The high-level wispy clouds he named *cirrus*, meaning a lock of hair. The lumpy, individual clouds nearer the ground he called *cumulus*, which is Latin for heap. The horizontal blankets of clouds that extend over large areas he gave the name *stratus*, meaning layered.

Howard combined the names to describe various cloud combinations, such as cirrostratus to denote a high-altitude layered cloud. The Latin word *nimbus*, meaning shower, was tacked on a cloud name to denote that it was a cloud in the act of

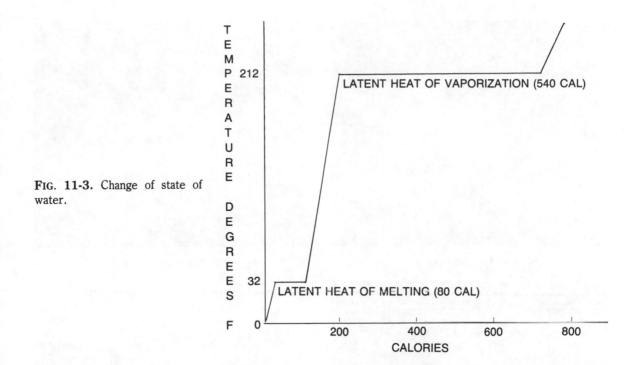

FIG. 11-3. Change of state of water.

precipitation, such as cumulonimbus. Later, meteorologists added several more cloud names and prefixes to depict certain clouds that do not exactly fit into Howard's simple classification scheme (FIG. 11-5).

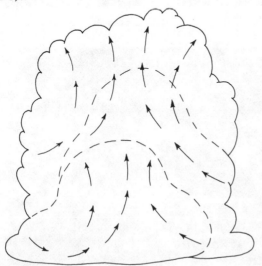

FIG. 11-4. The bubble theory of a thunderstorm. It visualizes a convective cloud not as a single column of rising air, but as a series of bubbles.

PRECIPITATION

Once the tiny cloud droplets are formed, any number of forces can come into play to cause precipitation. Ordinary raindrops are several million times larger than cloud droplets; therefore, they must grow by some sort of mechanism. In 1911, the German meteorologist Alfred Wegener, who is best known for his continental drift theory, suggested that almost all rain begins in the form of ice. Water droplets can be supercooled well below their freezing temperature without turning into ice because the microscopic water droplets are too small to freeze into a cohesive crystal structure. Ice also attracts water vapor because the vapor pressure near ice is lower than it is near water. This attraction causes water molecules to leave the cloud droplets and flow toward the ice, which then grows by accretion of water molecules. Clouds that rise to great heights often contain both ice crystals and supercooled water droplets. The ice crystals grow at the expense of the water droplets until the ice crystals are heavy enough to fall earthward. Upon reaching the warmer air below, the ice melts and forms rain. In the winter, the air nearer the ground might not be warm

Cumulonimbus ↑

Stratocumulus ↑

Nimbostratus ↑

Stratus ↑

Cirrus ↑

Cirrocumlus ↑

(Courtesy of NOAA)

FIG. 11-5. The classification of clouds, and cloud type and height.

Cumulus ↑

Cirrostratus ↑

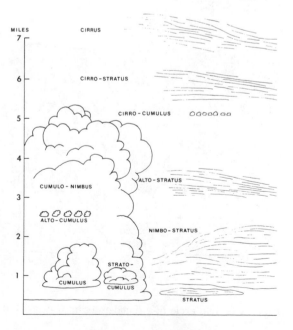

Altostratus ↑

Altocumulus ↑

enough to melt the ice crystals, and they fall as snow.

Clouds in the tropics are rarely cold enough to permit the formation of ice crystals; therefore, some other mechanism must be responsible for the merging of water droplets to form raindrops. Water droplets of uniform size rarely collide, and when they do, they simply bounce off each other. In order for raindrops to form, some of the water droplets must have started out larger than the others.

Larger droplets form by the condensation of water vapor around nuclei composed of large salt particles. The salt particles are produced by salt spray from ocean waves and the bursting of air bubbles on the surface of the sea. The salt particles are wafted aloft by tropical air currents and attract water vapor similar to the way salt in a salt shaker attracts moisture on a humid day and refuses to pour. The salt particles produce larger, heavier cloud droplets, and they are the first to overcome the lifting caused by rising warm air. On their way down, they collide and coalesce with smaller droplets and fall out of the cloud as rain. Static electricity in the cloud also might encourage the growth of raindrops because droplets of opposite charge would then attract one another.

Not all precipitation reaches the ground. The same warm updrafts that created the clouds in the first place might cause the evaporation of rain or snow soon after it leaves the cloud. Therefore, as long as there exists an upward movement of air, precipitation is inhibited. The release of latent heat of condensation keeps the rising air warmer than the surrounding air and maintains its upward movement. The air keeps rising until it enters a layer of warmer air, in which the rising parcel of air no longer has buoyancy. As long as the parcel of air can maintain buoyancy, the upward movement of air within a cloud retards the fall of precipitation until the raindrops or snow grow large and heavy enough to overcome the updraft (FIG. 11-6). This process produces a recurring precipitation-evaporation-condensation-precipitation cycle within the cloud. Eventually, a few large drops overcome this vicious circle and fall, splattering the ground in a random pattern. In a little while, the rain cools the surface, the updrafts cease, and the deluge begins.

An extreme example of the various combinations of precipitation and cloud turbulence is the formation of hail (FIG. 11-7). Generally, hailstones are about one-half inch in diameter, but they can grow to golfball size or larger. The largest known hailstone

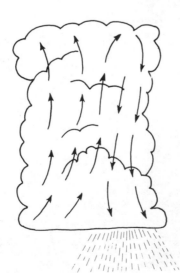

FIG. 11-6. Life cycle of a thunderstorm.

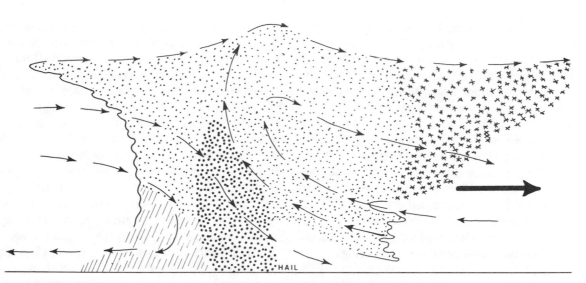

FIG. 11-7. Anatomy of a hailstorm.

was found at Coffeyville, Kansas, on September 3, 1970. It measured about one-half foot across and weighed over 1½ pounds.

Hailstones form when ice crystals remain airborne in a cloud of supercooled water droplets long enough to grow thousands of times larger than normal. This process requires turbulences generally found only in thunderheads, which form principally in the summer when the heat generates strong updrafts. The updrafts keep ice pellets suspended long enough to acquire several coatings of ice, giving the hailstone a layered structure, like an onion. The hail must fall rapidly through the air without melting and might even be helped along by strong downdrafts originating from the cloud. Often hail forewarns of the development of a tornado, which results from similar cloud turbulences.

EARLY CLOUD SEEDING

Many primitive cultures have held rain-making ceremonies, sometimes using animal or human sacrifices, either to cajole the gods into giving up some of their precious waters or to chase away evil demons who were holding back the rains. Even in modern societies, praying for rain is practiced.

There were a number of attempts to increase the rainfall by a variety of methods, from lighting large fires to the firing of cannon. The firing of guns and rockets into clouds and the ringing of church bells have long been practiced in Europe as a means of preventing the formation of damaging hailstorms. During World War I, it was noticed that there was a connection between cannon shots and the deluge of rain that fell almost constantly, turning the trenches into a quagmire. It was thought that either the smoke from the cannons or the loud noises they made might have caused the excessive rainfall.

During World War II, the American scientist Vincent Schaefer studied the various types of rime ice that formed on objects at the summit of Mount Washington in New Hampshire. He was particularly interested in the nature of the crystals that formed and the effect of certain types of surfaces that prevented ice from forming, even when the temperature was much less than the freezing point of water. These experiments were of crucial importance to the military, whose aircraft surfaces often became coated with ice when operating at high altitudes.

Schaefer's observations led to the discovery of clouds of supercooled water droplets. When Schaefer found a way of forming a supercooled water droplet cloud in his laboratory, he started an intensive search for substances that would cause such a cloud to condense into ice crystals. He tried a number of substances from minute clay particles to carbon smoke, to no avail. Then on July 13, 1946,

Schaefer used some dry ice (frozen carbon dioxide) to further cool his cold chamber. The instant the dry ice was placed inside the chamber, the supercooled fog practically exploded into a virtual snowstorm. He tried the experiment again, this time using only a small piece of dry ice, and again, tiny ice crystals immediately formed.

Four months later on November 13, 1946, Schaefer made the first field test of his new discovery. Flying over an altocumulus cloud whose temperature was well below zero, he seeded it by dropping 3 pounds of crushed dry ice along a line about 3 miles long. On the ground, snow was observed falling from the cloud for a distance of about 2000 feet before evaporating in the dry air.

A number of tests were conducted in the following months and gave similar results. Large areas of supercooled stratus clouds were converted into ice clouds, and on some occasions, snow fell from the seeded part of the cloud, leaving a clear lane in the sky behind. The effect of the dry ice is not to freeze the water droplets in the clouds, but rather, its intense cold produces a physical effect, called *homogeneous nucleation*. The dry ice cools some of the water vapor to below -40 degrees Fahrenheit, which initiates the formation of ice embryos. These ice embryos cause the supercooled water droplets in the cloud to evaporate into the embryos to form ice crystals.

Some clouds have a tendency to hold back water they might otherwise release as rain or snow. The unused water is in the form of water vapor or tiny cloud droplets. Despite the subzero temperatures, these cloud droplets do not freeze, and they are too small to fall through the cloud and collect other cloud droplets on their downward journey. Some of them can be started on their way to becoming precipitation by natural ice-forming nuclei, such as microscopic bits of clay, which mimic the ice crystal structure and can catalyze ice crystallization. A cloud droplet can turn to ice about the clay nucleant and grow at the expense of water vapor evaporated from surrounding cloud droplets until the new ice crystal is heavy enough to fall. The problem is that there are often not enough natural ice-forming nuclei to go around.

Any substance that mimics the crystal structure of ice can act as a seed crystal, similar to the way salt crystals form out of a supersaturated saltwater solution by dangling a seed crystal from a length of thread inside the container. Silver iodide and related compounds have become popular seeding agents because of the resemblance of their crystal structure to that of ice. They catalyze ice formation by providing an icelike template for the initiation of ice formation. The crystals grow, forming regular shapes to conserve energy because that is how to best minimize the free energy of the system. Layers upon layers of water molecules are added in such a way as to form sheets parallel to the crystal planes.

If there are too many new ice crystals and not enough water droplets around to feed them, the crystals will not grow large enough to fall. This was the experience of the Midwest in the late 1950s when rain-making experiments were conducted over south-central Missouri. The net effect of the seeding during five summers was a decrease in rainfall. Apparently, the Missouri clouds had all the natural ice-forming particles they needed to begin precipitation, and seeding only created an excess of very small ice particles that tended to remain in the cloud, rather than fall out as rain.

Israel has had a keen interest in rain-making because much of the country is desert wasteland. The first of two Israeli weather-modification experiments ran from 1961 to 1967 under the direction of the Hebrew University in Jerusalem. Researchers wanted to determine whether seeding wintertime clouds with fine particles of silver iodide would increase rainfall in northern Israel. In the beginning, the project was conducted in secrecy for fear that word of their work would leak out to their less friendly Arab neighbors downwind from the seeding targets. (The Arabs would not take it lightly if the Israelis stole their rain.) The first experiment appeared to be a success, and rainfall increased about 15 percent in the target areas after cloud seeding.

The second experiment, conducted between 1969 and 1975, was to determine if cloud seeding could enhance rainfall over an area that included the Golan Heights, captured during the 1967 war with Syria. This was a catchment for the Sea of Galilee, an important water resource. The experiment, helped along with some cooperative clouds, increased precipitation in the target area by 13 percent. No other weather-modification experiment enjoys as much acclaim as do those of the Israelis.

In the United States, the Climax experiments were conducted between 1960 and 1970 to enhance snowfall by cloud seeding in the Dillion and Leadville area of the Colorado Rockies. Some of the winter clouds encountering the high Rockies were not cold enough to produce many natural ice particles. It was thought that seeding the clouds with silver iodide could significantly increase the snowfall in the target area. When analyzing the impact of the seeding outside the target area, however, investigators found a serious problem. On days when clouds were seeded, more snow fell everywhere, not just in the target area, but also far beyond in all directions. Apparently, days randomly chosen for cloud-seeding also happened to be days that received more natural snowfall. When the numbers were adjusted for this natural variability of snowfall, the apparent snowfall enhancement was reduced from 18 to 9 percent. In another study, it was found that there was no significant seeding effect.

This is a basic problem of all cloud-seeding experiments; that is, knowing whether the observed changes were the result of natural variability or cloud seeding. In other words, it cannot be known with any certainty that the weather was actually modified, if it is not known what the weather would have been like if it were left alone in the first place.

MODERN WEATHER MODIFICATION

One of the boldest plans ever conceived was the seeding of hurricanes by aircraft in order to reduce their fury or even steer them away from populated sea coasts. This was an admirable endeavor, considering that the energy released by a full-blown hurricane is equivalent to a hydrogen bomb going off every minute it is alive. Clouds just outside the eye of a hurricane were seeded to invigorate their circulation. This process would widen the eye and snuff out the strongest winds of the storm on the edge of the eye (FIG. 11-8). The idea was to promote the freezing of liquid water droplets to ice. The latent heat released would then invigorate the growth of the seeded clouds.

Researchers seeded three hurricanes in the 1960s in a project known as Stormfury. The winds of Hurricane Debbie dropped as much as 30 percent, but then regained their strength after each of two seeding forays. In an earlier episode, disaster struck when a hurricane east of Jacksonville, Florida, was seeded, promptly changed its course, and smashed into Savannah, Georgia. Because there was so much uncertainty about the behavior of these dangerous storms, the federal government would not approve seeding operations unless the hurricane had a less than 10 percent chance of making landfall within 48 hours. This placed severe restrictions on the project, and when the Navy pulled out in 1972, it all but killed any further attempts at hurricane seeding in the Atlantic.

From there, the base of operations was shifted to the Pacific, where typhoons are more numerous, take many more lives, and destroy much more property. In 1973, a Typhoon Moderation Council was set up by the Marcos government in the Philippines. Of all the countries in the world, the Philippines is the most battered by tropical storms because it sprawls across the main thoroughfare of the Pacific typhoons. In an average year, nearly 20 typhoons hit the major islands that compose the nation (FIG. 11-9). For three months starting in September 1970,

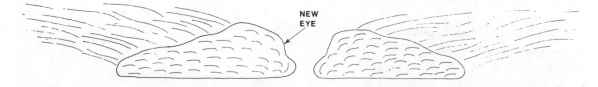

NEW EYE

FIG. 11-8. Seeding a hurricane.

FIG. 11-9. Floodwaters from the 1974 typhoon, Ivy, at Subic Bay, Philippines.

a succession of four typhoons struck the islands unusually hard, killing 1500 people.

Bays with shallow seabeds are the most vulnerable to the storm surge arising from a typhoon. More than 5000 Japanese lost their lives in Typhoon Vera which lifted the water of Ise Bay ashore in Nogoya, Japan in 1959. One of the worst disasters of the Pacific area was when a typhoon hit Hong Kong in 1937, killing 11,000 people. A similar storm in 1962 left 72,000 homeless, but the loss of life was not nearly as great. The saving of lives and property, therefore, becomes the greatest impetus for trying to tame these raging storms.

Opponents argue that hurricanes and typhoons are an important link in the worldwide heat transport system, and are important sources of rainfall. Attempts to smash Atlantic hurricanes, for example, might reduce the rainfall in Europe. There were also fears that tampering with the storms might even make them worse. If they are to be controlled at all, it might be better to steer them away from densely populated areas, rather than moderate their force. Also, funds might be better spent on more

efficient methods of early warning, evacuation, and rescue operations.

In the 1960s, scientists from the Soviet Union devised a method of firing rockets and antiaircraft shells into clouds suspected of harboring hail. Special hail-control stations were scattered throughout the countryside. The stations were equipped with radars and batteries of rocket launchers or antiaircraft guns, looking almost as though they were preparing for war. Star bursts from the exploding shells infiltrated the clouds with silver iodide, and rockets strewed the clouds with silver iodide smoke as they passed through. The purpose was to encourage the clouds to make many small particles of ice, instead of the fewer, larger hailstones that caused damage to crops.

The Soviets claimed 60 to 90 percent reductions in hail by these cloud-seeding methods, which impressed American researchers enough to visit the Soviets to learn more. In the United States, hail damage to crops (FIG. 11-10) amounts to more than $700 million yearly, so an effective hail-suppression technique would be most welcomed. Thus, began

FIG. 11-10. Damage to crops from hail.

a five-year National Hail Research Experiment in 1972 to verify the Soviet claims. After only 3 years, the tests were halted because the American scientists were unable to produce the claimed hail reductions. In some instances, seeded hailstorms actually produced more hail than those that were not seeded. Perhaps American clouds are different than Soviet clouds. To test this hypothesis, the Swiss exactly duplicated the Soviet methods and also failed to show any reduction in hail.

Farmers in the American Midwest are so confident that their cloud-seeding operations are effective during times of drought they are willing to pay a hefty price for it. Farmers in North Dakota targeted 6.6 million acres for the "store-bought" rain at a cost of 5 cents an acre. Their neighbors to the south actually enacted a state law for the control of the weather. Seeding aircraft fed smoke trails of silver iodide into the updrafts of clouds, and the planes were guided to their targets by ground-based radar.

Almost $1 million is spent annually for seeding clouds over half the state in order to give the farmers a few more inches of rain during the growing sea-

son (FIG. 11-11). In addition, the South Dakota Weather Control Commission offers to suppress hailstorms with fireworks shot from aircraft. Most farmers believe it all works and are willing to pay the 3 cents per acre for the service, but skeptics doubt that such seeding agents dispersed at or near the base of tall cumulus clouds could actually make their way up several tens of thousands of feet to the part of the cloud that contains moisture droplets, and thereby cause any more rain what would have occurred naturally.

Just about the only undisputed weather-modification scheme is the dispersal of fog, which can be considered as a low-lying cloud. The clearing of supercooled fogs over airports by means of ice-nuclei seeding is a proven technology used regularly in various countries (FIG. 11-12). Warmer fogs above the freezing point of water require the use of brute force for dispersal.

This method had its beginning in England during World War II and was used to make it possible for Royal Air Force planes to land after returning from combat missions. The system consisted of a

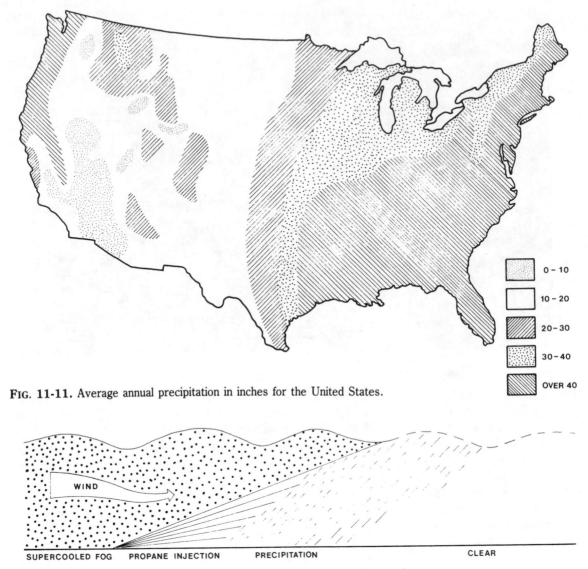

FIG. 11-11. Average annual precipitation in inches for the United States.

Legend:

	0 – 10
	10 – 20
	20 – 30
	30 – 40
	OVER 40

FIG. 11-12. Use of propane to disperse fog.

SUPERCOOLED FOG   PROPANE INJECTION   PRECIPITATION   CLEAR   WIND

perforated pipeline running along the sides of runways, in which aviation fuel was pumped and burned. In 1970, a more sophisticated thermal fog-dissipation system known as Turboclair was installed at Orly Airport in Paris, France. Twelve jet engines in specially designed pits along the edges of the runway generate streams of hot air that cause the fogs to evaporate. Many countries, including the United States, consider the system too costly for routine use by commercial aviation, and instead, more emphasis is placed on electronic landing systems.

WEATHER AS A WEAPON

Through the ages, battles have been won and lost because of the weather. Had Nelson kept his fleet in port, it might have been spared a furious storm which tore the sailing ships into tattered remnants—one of the worst disasters of the British Navy. If Napolean knew beforehand that he would be fighting winter as well as Russian soldiers, he might have stayed home and left Russia alone. Over 100 years later, Hitler made the same mistake, and one of the worst winters on record, among other things, cost him the war. In December 1944, just off the Philippine islands, a typhoon intervened in the Pacific war, catching a huge American fleet in the midst of refueling at sea. The raging water swept the flight decks of the carriers, made battleships heave to, and sank three destroyers with all hands. The weather did a more effective job of destroying the U.S. Navy than could the Japanese.

Since the American Civil War, weather has been used in battle operations. In offense and defense, military commanders made use of accurate weather predictions either to trap their opponents or stay out of harm's way. It is one thing to adjust military actions to the weather, though, and quite another to adjust the weather to suit military actions.

The tactical commander's bag of tricks might include the creation or dispersal of fog, depending on whether it is used to conceal his own or the enemy's movements. A barrage of storms could be called in to pin down the enemy, or at least make his travel difficult. Weather control at sea could hamper enemy ships with fog or rain, or it could disperse the weather to make the enemy's ships clear-weather targets. Civilians could be made targets as well, and a constant bombardment of poor weather—causing blizzards, floods, or droughts—could ruin morale.

In the cold war, one side could try to topple the other by severely damaging its economy and civil population by climate control. The Soviet Union in a guise of building peaceful water projects or weather modification to improve its own climate might bring about an unfavorable modification of the climate of North America. An example would be the building of a dam across the 32-mile Bering Strait between Siberia and Alaska. The idea was first proposed by the Soviets at the 1974 arms control meeting in Vladivostok. This dam would keep warm Pacific waters from being chilled by the cold Arctic Ocean, giving Siberia a warmer climate for agriculture and open up otherwise frozen seaports. However, the scheme could have been a disaster for North America because the icy polar waters might then drain across the top of the continent and down the east coast of Canada and chill it. Without firing a shot, the Soviet Union could bring America to her knees, and fear of this bleak prospect might have produced a fierce weather weapons race.

12

Severe Storms

HARDLY a day goes by that there is not a major storm which takes lives and destroys property in some part of the world. When statistics show that the death toll and property damage is on the increase, it does not necessarily mean that nature is becoming more violent, but that the world is becoming more crowded. Third-world nations, struggling to keep abreast of dwindling food supplies and natural resources, are particularly hard hit by the weather. Their cities are overcrowded, and dwellers are forced to live under squalid conditions. When a natural disaster strikes, people are practically trapped, and many are trampled underfoot when others try in vain to escape.

Even modern nations like Japan, which have high population densities, are frequently hit with dangerous storms, resulting in the loss of many lives and much property. In the United States, even with a well-equipped National Weather Service, storms cost hundreds of lives yearly and destroy several billion dollars in property and crops. However, modern nations still have a great advantage over poorer countries in that they have advanced warning of impending danger and can build structures that can resist the worst nature can dish out.

HURRICANES

Hurricanes, typhoons, and cyclones are all specific names of a general product called a *tropical cyclone*. They are nature's most spectacular and most destructive storms. Hurricanes make their home in the Atlantic, typhoons settle in the North Pacific, and cyclones find their niche in the Indian Ocean and around Australia.

Tropical cyclones are born as tropical depressions in the oceans, between latitudes 5 and 20 degrees north and south, where the surface temperature of the sea is 80 degrees Fahrenheit or more. They must be fairly close to the equator, but not too close, or the Coriolis effect will not provide the necessary spin to create vigorous vortexes in the air. This is why tropical cyclones are more common in summer and autumn, when the Sun can heat the sea well to the north or south of the equator.

Only one out of ten tropical depressions grow up to become full-blown tropical cyclones, whose lifetime averages about ten days. Once formed, the storms normally head in a westwardly direction, guided by the trade winds, as the Earth spins beneath them. Because they travel to the west, the countries in the western portions of the oceans are at the greatest risk (FIG. 12-1). Sometimes hurricanes will curve sharply away from the equator, enter colder water, and when deprived of their source of heat energy, die away to become ordinary tropical depressions again.

A typical hurricane is 300 to 400 miles in diameter, with its circulating winds spiraling in toward the center, or *eye*, at speeds of over 75 miles per hour. The winds in the eye, which ranges from about 5 to 25 miles in diameter, are calm and the skies are clear, or nearly so.

A hurricane formed off the west coast of Africa might trample the West Indies, take a swipe at Cuba or the Bahamas, and tear into the American mainland from the Gulf of Mexico or the southern East Coast. The hurricane is accompanied by a tremendous storm surge or tidal wave, which wrecks property and erodes beach fronts (FIG. 12-2). Winds of 100 miles per hour or more pile up water on the shore, while the very low pressure in the eye of the hurricane sucks the water up into a mound several feet high. Once on land, the hurricane is deprived of its primary source of energy and must depend on heavy rainfall, which releases large amounts of latent heat to keep the storm alive. Rainfall amounts between 3 to 6 inches are common, but upwards of several tens of inches is possible, causing severe flooding.

As the hurricane treks its way across land, the air flowing in at the base is no longer as moist as it was over the ocean, the tight vortex fills out, and the eye finally dissipates. The hurricane can only regain its strength if it returns to the sea. Otherwise, it ends its days as just another low-pressure system.

The erratic behavior of hurricanes is best described by Hurricane Elena (FIG. 12-3). Elena was born a tropical disturbance off the western coast of Africa on August 22, 1985. During the following week, it moved rapidly westward across the Atlantic, carried by the trade winds at 30 miles per hour with sustained circular winds of about 25 miles per hour. By the time the disturbance reached Cuba on August 27, it was classified as a tropical storm, with sustained circular winds of about 50 miles per hour. Two days later, with sustained circular winds of

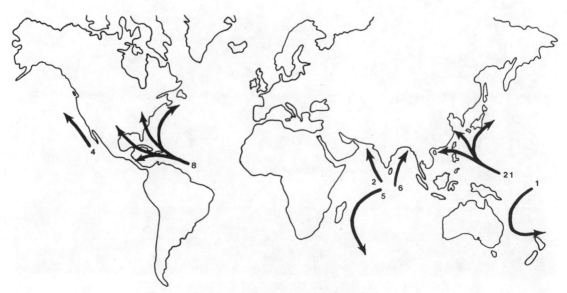

FIG. 12-1. The yearly occurrence of tropical storms.

FIG. 12-2. (top) The mechanics of a plunging breaker.
(bottom) Beach wave erosion from hurricanes near Grand Isle, Louisiana in 1985.

(Courtesy of U.S. Army Corps of Engineers)

FIG. 12-3. Hurricane Elena viewed from the space shuttle *Discovery*.

about 75 miles per hour, the storm was upgraded to hurricane status, and the list of hurricane names was consulted.

Hurricane Elena then moved through the open waters of the Gulf of Mexico toward New Orleans. Then suddenly, as though she were unable to make up her mind, she veered eastward, headed toward Florida, then stalled, retreated, changed course again, and made straight for the coast of Mississippi. Elena finally struck the Gulfport-Biloxi area on September 2, with 130-mile-per-hour winds. During her five-day rampage, nearly half of the Gulf coastline was put under hurricane warning at one time or another, requiring the evacuation of 1.5 million people. Elena was the forth costliest hurricane on record, running up a bill for more than $0.5 billion in property damages.

TORNADOES

Tornadoes (FIG. 12-4) have long been an enigma, striking sporadically and violently, generating the strongest of all surface winds, and causing

FIG. **12-4.** 1937 tornado in central Colorado.

:aths annually in the United States than any ntural phenomenon other than lightning. It nted that tornadoes can generate a maximum eed of 300 miles per hour, based on analy-notion pictures and damage to structures. nadoes are formed in the updrafts of a thun-n or are associated with hurricanes when ss over land. They are tightly wound vor-' air, rarely more than several hundred feet They rotate in a counterclockwise direction orthern Hemisphere and a clockwise direc-the Southern Hemisphere. Drawn by the reduced atmospheric pressure in the cen-, air streams into the base of the vortex from tions. The air then turns abruptly to spiral around the core, and finally merges with the n the parent cloud at the upper end of the . The pressure within the core might be as 10 percent lower than the surrounding at-re, which would be equivalent to a sudden pressure from that at sea level to an altitude feet.

: vortex frequently becomes visible as a nrk funnel cloud hanging partway or all the the ground. A funnel cloud can only form if sure drop in the core reaches a critical value, epends on the temperature and humidity of wing air. As air flows into the area of lower e, it expands and cools, causing water va-ondense and form water droplets.

Sometimes, no condensation cloud forms, and the only way a tornado can reveal itself is by the dust and debris it carries aloft over land or water spray over the ocean. In that case, it becomes a waterspout, which often frequent the Florida coast and the Bahamas (FIG. 12-5).

The funnel is usually cone shaped, but short, broad, cylindrical pillars up to a mile wide are formed by very strong tornadoes, and often, long, ropelike tubes dangle from the storm cloud. Over the tor-nado's brief lifetime, usually no more than a few hours, the size, shape, and color of the funnel might change markedly, depending on the intensity of the winds, the properties of the inflowing air, and the type of ground over which it hovers. The color varies from a dirty white to a blue gray when it consists mostly of water droplets, but if the core fills with dust, it takes on the color of the soil and other de-bris. Tornadoes are also noisy, often roaring, like a laboring freight train or a jet plane taking off. The sound results from the interaction of the concen-trated high winds with the ground.

The world's tornado hot spot, with about 700 tornadoes yearly, is the United States, particularly the central and southeastern portions of the coun-try, known as *tornado alley* (FIG. 12-6). The states most frequently visited by tornadoes are Texas, Ar-kansas, Oklahoma, Kansas, Nebraska, and Missouri, with a high occurrence of tornadoes continuing on up into Canada.

FIG. 12-5. Waterspouts near the Bahama Islands.

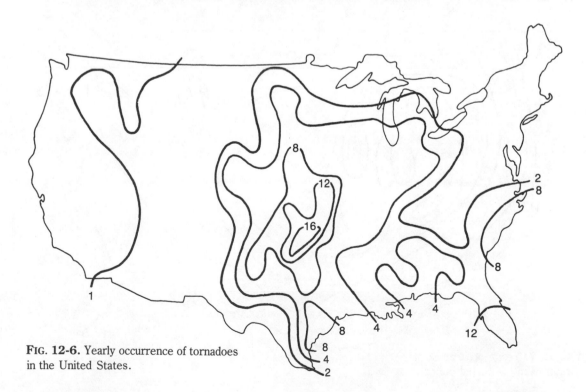

FIG. 12-6. Yearly occurrence of tornadoes
in the United States.

Tornadoes develop in the spring and to a lesser extent in the fall, when conditions are ripe for the formation of tornado-generating thunderstorms. These conditions include a highly unstable distribution of temperature and humidity in the atmosphere, strong cold fronts that provide the lift needed to start convection, and winds in the upper atmosphere favorable for the formation of strong updrafts.

For a tornado to form, the air in the updraft must begin to rotate. This is accomplished by a wind shear where the wind speed increases with height and veers from southeast to west. Once rotation begins, the tornado builds down toward the ground, although not all tornadoes actually reach the ground. When on the ground, the tornado funnel sucks up air at its lower end, like the hose of a vacuum cleaner.

Tornadoes are steered by the jet stream, and generally travel in a northeasterly direction for about 5 to 15 miles. Their forward groundspeed is normally slow enough (30 to 60 miles per hour) for them to be outrun by an automobile, although this is not always a recommended practice because of the unpredictable nature of tornadoes, which often hop about from place to place. Members of NOAA's National Severe Storms Laboratory at the University of Oklahoma actually chase tornadoes in vehicles carrying an instrument package known as TOTO which stands for Totable Tornado Observatory. This package is placed in the path of the tornado. TOTO is equipped to measure a tornado's behavior such as wind speed, wind direction, atmospheric temperature and pressure, and electric field strength. These measurements are used to acquire a better understanding of how tornadoes begin and how they do their damage.

Buildings are generally destroyed in the quarter-mile-wide path of a tornado by fierce winds blowing against the structure. The lifting power of tornadoes is impressive. They sometimes pick up heavy trucks and locomotives, and they often carry livestock and people away for long distances. Loose objects become deadly high-speed missiles, and straw has been known to be driven deep into wooden planks. This makes it vitally important for people caught in the path of a tornado to find shelter quickly, preferably in a storm shelter or a cellar.

FIG. 12-7. Yearly occurrence of hailstorms in the United States.

THUNDERSTORMS

Thunderstorms are widespread, commonplace, very dangerous, and costly. It is estimated that at any given moment, there are nearly 2000 thunderstorms in progress over the earth's surface, generating 100 lightning strikes per second. Every day there are about 45,000 thunderstorms, or about 16 million in a year. Of these, 100,000 hit the United States, with Florida ranking number one in frequency (FIG. 12-8). Their sheer quantity make them the primary balancers of the Earth's heat budget.

Thunderstorms are most common in spring and summer afternoon and evening hours. Although they can occur in winter, they are much less intense then. Thunderstorms are a welcome sight to farmers, particularly in the parched Midwest and the high plains, but their visitations might also bring damaging hail and flash floods. Because thunderstorm fatalities only come in ones or twos, they do not make the headlines, like hurricanes or floods. Yet, on the average, over 100 Americans are killed and about 250 are seriously injured each year, mostly by lightning. Property loss is estimated in the hundreds of millions of dollars annually.

Thunderstorms, generated by temperature imbalances in the atmosphere, are violent examples of the upward transfer of heat, called *convection*. Under certain atmospheric conditions, colder, denser layers of air are placed over warmer, lighter air layers. The resulting instability causes convective overturning, with the heavier, denser layers sinking to the bottom, while the lighter, warmer air rises rapidly to the top. Warm, buoyant air also might be forced upward by the wedgelike undercutting of a cold air mass or by a mountain slope.

Winds blowing into a strong low-pressure center force warm air near the center upward. These updrafts carry the warm air to a level where the air becomes saturated with moisture, resulting in condensation, where visible droplets appear and a cloud begins to form. Continued upward movement of air produces large, rising cumulus clouds. Strong winds above the developing clouds might further enhance the updraft. As the cloud continues to grow, water vapor changes to liquid or frozen particles,

resulting in a release of latent heat, which takes over as the principal energy source of the developing cloud. The cloud particles continue to grow by colliding and combining with each other until they are heavy enough to overcome the updraft and fall to earth as rain, snow, or hail.

Once reaching its final stage of growth, the cumulonimbus cloud might be several miles across at its flattened base and tower 40,000 feet or more. High-level winds shear off the cloud top, giving it an anvillike form (FIG. 12-9). These towering clouds are sometimes visible as lone giants. If several are moving abreast, they are known as a *squall line*. As the final stage approaches, the updraft that initiated the cloud's growth no longer prevails and is joined by a downdraft generated by the precipitation. This updraft-downdraft combination constitutes a single storm cell.

Most thunderstorms are composed of several cells whose life span is about 20 minutes. Old cells are replaced by new cells, making it possible for some storms to last for several hours. Strong gusts of cold wind from the downdraft often occur on the ground beneath and outward from the mature thunderstorm, and are a welcome relief to the long, hot days of summer. Eventually, the violent downdraft strangles the sustaining updraft, precipitation weakens, and the thunderstorm spreads and eventually dies.

One particularly dangerous aspect of the violent downdrafts associated with thunderstorms, especially to aviation, is a feature called a *microburst*, or downburst. This is a small, intense downdraft that is accompanied by what is called a *rain shaft*, which is a narrowly confined, heavy fall of rain. Sometimes the rainshaft evaporates before reaching the ground, rendering the microburst invisible. Upon hitting the ground the winds of the microburst spread out laterally, like the water flowing from a faucet spreads out at the bottom of a sink, creating horizontal winds of hurricane force with speeds upwards of 100 miles per hour and more. For a several-block area, it can blow down trees and power lines, break out windows, tear shingles off roofs, and cause structural damage to buildings (FIG. 12-10).

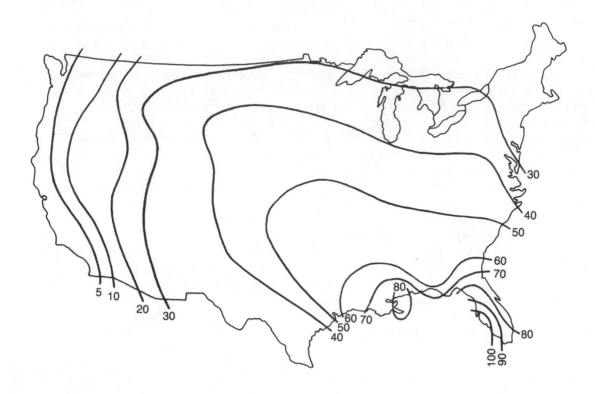

FIG. 12-8. (top) Yearly occurrence of thunderstorms in the United States. (bottom) A western-style thunderstorm.

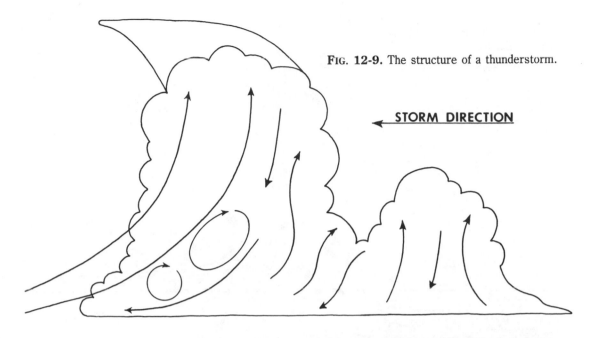

FIG. **12-9.** The structure of a thunderstorm.

◄— STORM DIRECTION

FIG. **12-10.** A house damaged by a microburst in Grand Junction, Colorado, July 16, 1986.

When an aircraft flies through a microburst on takeoff or landing, the encounter can be lethal (FIG. 12-11). Since 1964, 491 people have lost their lives and 206 have been injured in airline accidents involving microbursts. The plane first encounters a strong headwind from the microburst outflow, which increases lift. The plane then pitches up and the pilot compensates by leveling off. In only a matter of seconds, the plane encounters a decreasing headwind, then a downdraft, then a strong tail wind. By that time the plane has lost lift, is flying too low, and does not have sufficient air speed to avoid a crash.

Thunderstorms **153**

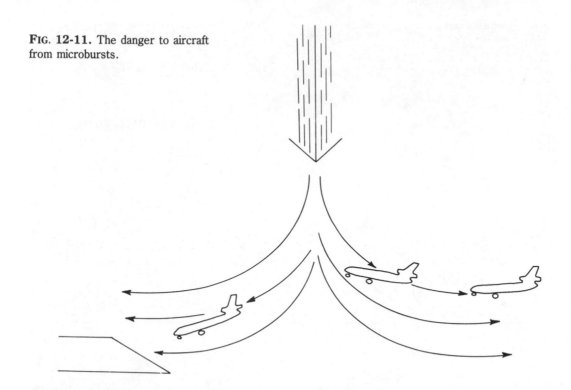

FIG. 12-11. The danger to aircraft from microbursts.

LIGHTNING

Of all of nature's violence, nothing compares with lightning for an instantaneous release of intense energy (FIG. 12-12). Lightning is very destructive to structures, causes most forest fires, and kills more people than any other weather phenomenon. Over the past 20 years, an average of 100 people per year have been killed by lightning in the United States, with 10 percent of those claimed by Florida alone. People are killed or injured while standing in the open or under a tree, taking a bath, talking on the telephone, or just watching television.

Lightning takes the path of least resistance, which is usually the shortest distance between the cloud and the ground. Any object taller than ground level, such as a building, a tree, or a person standing in the open or in a boat on a lake can attract lightning. Lightning finds its way into a house through power or telephone lines, outdoor antennas, or ventilation ducts. An automobile happens to be one of the safest places to be during a lightning storm, not because it is insulated from the ground by its rubber tires, but because the surrounding metal acts

like a Faraday shield, keeping the electricity on the outside of the vehicle. An airplane flying through a thunderstorm experiences this same effect when struck by lightning, and sometimes a ball of lightning is observed rolling from wingtip to wingtip.

Lightning is the atmosphere's way of balancing the electrical charges between the ionosphere and the Earth's surface with thunderstorms acting as mediators (FIG. 12-13). The Earth is normally negatively charged with respect to the atmosphere, but as the thunderstorm passes over the ground, the negative charge in the base of the cloud induces a positive charge on the ground below and for several miles around the storm. This charge enables lightning to strike an object or person even when the thundercloud is not directly over it.

The ground charge follows the storm, like an electrical shadow, growing stronger as the negative cloud charge increases. The electrical potential difference between the cloud and ground can be a few hundred million volts, but since air is a poor conductor of electricity and insulates the cloud from the ground, it prevents the flow of current. A discharge

FIG. 12-12. (top) Multiple Lightning flashes. (bottom) Lightning at sea.

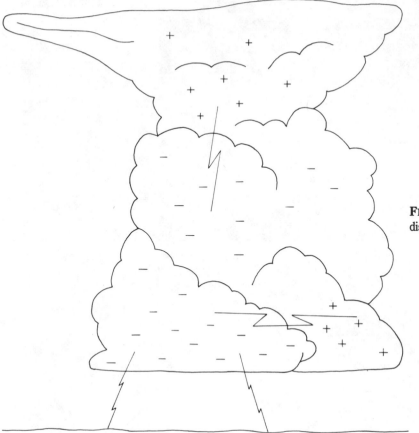

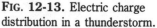

FIG. 12-13. Electric charge distribution in a thunderstorm.

can only occur after an ionized channel has been traced through the air by a preliminary discharge, called a *leader*, which zigzags its way toward the ground. Once the leader establishes contact with the ground, a conducting path between the cloud and the ground is completed, and a surge of current, called a *return stroke*, immediately follows. Commonly, a leader and stroke is repeated several times in the same channel, giving the characteristic multiple lightning strokes. Lightning strokes also proceed from cloud to cloud and from ground to cloud where high structures are involved.

Thunder is the result of sudden heating of the air in the path of a lightning flash. Because air has electrical resistance, it is heated by the passage of an electrical current, just as a wire connected to the poles of a battery is heated.

A common misconception is that a thunderclap is produced by the rapid expansion of the heated air, and a sudden collapse of air to fill the vacuum left behind. A better explanation suggests that each surge of current in the lightning flash creates a channel of gases at high temperatures and pressures. The gases expand into the surrounding air as a shock wave which, after traveling a short distance, decays into an acoustic wave. When lightning strikes close by, the thunder sounds like a sharp crack, while more distant strokes produce rumbling sounds.

Because the lightning flash is seen about 1 million times sooner than the thunder is heard, it is possible to estimate the distance in miles from the lightning. Simply count the number of seconds between the lightning and the thunder and divide by five.

FLOODS

Riverine floods are cause by large amounts of precipitation over large areas, by the melting of the winter's vast accumulation of snow, or both (FIG. 12-14). They are natural, recurring events, and they only become a hazard when people build on or farm in the floodplains.

The function of the floodplain is to carry excess water during a flood. Failure to recognize this function has led to rapid and haphazard development on the floodplains, with the subsequent result of unnecessary loss of life and property, thereby making floods a man-made disaster.

There are over 3 million miles of streams in the United States, and about 6 percent of the land area is prone to flooding. Many of the nation's cities were originally located near watercourses because they were the only means of transporting goods. However, it resulted in concentrating a substantial percentage of the nation's population and property in flood-prone areas. More than 20,000 communities have flood problems. Of these, 6000 have populations greater than 2500. The average annual flood loss in the United States is more than $3 billion. No price tag can be placed on the deaths, the hardships, and the suffering resulting from floods.

Flash floods are among the most severe floods. They occur when a violent thunderstorm or cloudburst pours a deluge of rain on a relatively small area over a very short time. They are particularly hazardous when the ground is already soaked with water from previous rains, or when streams are already at their capacity. Often, cities that have well-designed drainage systems that can handle normal high-water levels are simply swamped by a flash flood because the water level rises too rapidly for the drains to handle it. They become overloaded with water which overflows into the streets.

Runoff from intense rainfalls can result in high flood waves that destroy roads, bridges, homes, buildings, and other community developments. The discharges quickly reach a maximum and then diminish almost as rapidly. Flows often contain large quan-

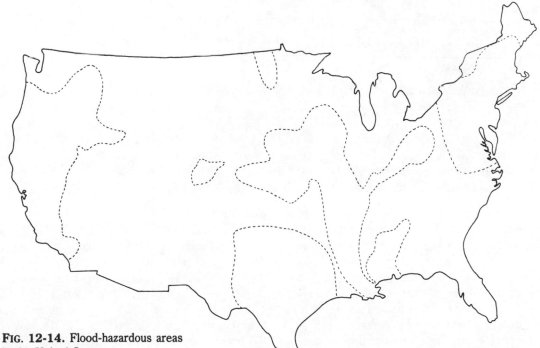

FIG. 12-14. Flood-hazardous areas in the United States.

(Photo by R. Dolan, courtesy of USGS)

FIG. 12-15. Storm surge near Cape Hatteras, North Carolina.

tities of sediments and debris collected as they scour the stream channels. These sediments and debris are deposited in annoying concentrations in streets, cellars, and the first stories of homes and buildings.

Flash floods are particularly common to mountainous areas and desert regions of the West. They are a potential source of destruction and a threat to public safety in areas where the terrain is steep, surface runoff rates are high, streams flow in narrow valleys and gullies, and severe thunderstorms are prominent.

Torrential downpours and tidal floods resulting from hurricanes cause more damage and take more lives than other forms of flooding (FIG. 12-15). By their very nature, hurricanes drop large amounts of rainfall over large areas, often within a day or so. The result is widespread flooding in natural drainage areas where streams are incapable of coping with the excess water caused by the onrush of heavy rains.

Tidal floods are overflows on coastal lands, such as bars spits and deltas, which are affected by the coastal current and occupy the same protective position relative to the sea that floodplains do to rivers. Most of the severe tidal floods are caused by tidal waves generated by high winds from a hurricane superimposed on the regular cycle of tides. Tidal floods might extend over great distances along a coastline.

The duration of tidal floods is usually short and is dependent upon the elevation of the tide, which generally rises and falls twice daily. The high velocities of hurricane winds often produce wave heights about 3 feet or more higher than the maximum level of the prevailing high tide.

Tidal floods can also be caused by the combination of flood runoff and waves generated by hurricane winds, resulting from the heavy rains that accompany hurricanes.

BLIZZARDS

A bad snow or ice storm (FIG. 12-16) can bring big-city traffic to a standstill, ground airlines, and generally make outdoor activities difficult. However, it is nothing compared to a blizzard, which is much more violent, combining strong winds, low temperatures, and enough snow in the air to reduce visibility to nearly zero. Technically, a blizzard exists when the temperature drops below 20 degrees Fahrenheit and there is a wind of 35 miles per hour or more, with blowing snow. The windchill temperature is then below −20 degrees Fahrenheit.

The snow literally blinds people and animals, and a condition known to many skiers as a *whiteout* makes the earth and sky indistinguishable. Only dark objects are discernible. Such conditions cause disorientation, which often leads to the skier getting lost or injured. A special form of whiteout is a ground

(Courtesy of NOAA)

FIG. 12-16. A severe ice storm.

blizzard, where restricted visibility is often less than 6 feet and can persist for many days.

During a blizzard, cattle unable to see, walk along with their backs to the wind until they are stopped by a fence or some other obstruction and can either starve or freeze to death in their tracks. People have been known to get lost in a blizzard trying to get from the house to the barn and freeze to death after walking around in circles. Some people who have been killed in blizzards died from suffocation; their lungs were choked with fine snow.

Blizzards are common in Canada and the northern United States east of the Rocky Mountains, especially around the Great Lakes region where they are called *lake-effect blizzards*. Arctic air moving southeastward over the Great Lakes lifts a considerable amount of available moisture to great heights, resulting in blowing and drifting snow downwind. In mountainous regions, blizzards can create conditions as severe as those found in the Arctic, where the temperatures are well below zero and winds blow upward of 100 miles per hour.

Snow falling in very cold weather (FIG. 12-17) is dry, more powdery, and less prone to sticking, thereby allowing it to be blown about easily. The blowing causes the snow crystals to fragment, yielding a finer, more compact mass. There might be a thin covering of snow in open fields where the wind is strong, while massive snow drifts pile up on the lee side of obstructions or in hollow places. Under some conditions, snow structures called a *sastrugi* form. They resemble sand dunes, but instead of sand, are composed of a compacted, rippled, icy substance. Like sand dunes, they are constantly on the move as long as the wind blows.

DUST STORMS

A dust storm is an awesome meteorological phenomenon, and dust storms play a crucial role in man's physical and economic well-being in many parts of the world. At times both people and animals have died of suffocation during a severe dust storm. A major dust storm in eastern Colorado (FIG. 12-18)

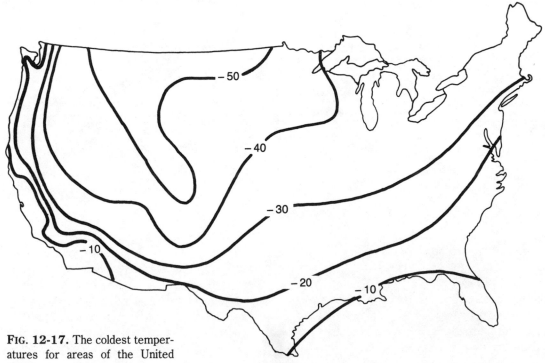

FIG. 12-17. The coldest temperatures for areas of the United States.

FIG. 12-18. Severe duststorm in eastern Colorado.

is reported to have caused the loss of 20 percent of the cattle in 1895.

A dust storm that forms over a desert during times of convective instability such as a thunderstorm is called a *haboob*, an Arabic term meaning "violent wind." They arise frequently in the Sudan where, around the capital city of Khartoum, they are experienced some 24 times a year. The haboobs are associated with the rainy season in the Sudan, and the amount of dust removed is remarkable. In 2 months, from 12 to 15 feet of sand can pile up against an obstruction that is exposed to the fury of these storms.

Quite a number of similar dust storms occur in the American Southwest. At Phoenix, Arizona, the frequency is about 12 per year. As in the Sudan, haboobs are most frequent during the rainy season, which is normally July and August. Surges of moist tropical air from the Pacific push up from the Gulf of California into Arizona and generate long, arch-ing squall lines with haboobs fanning out in front. These individual outflows often merge to form a solid wall of dust that stretches for hundreds of miles. The dust rises 8000 to 14,000 feet above the ground and travels at an average speed of 30 miles per hour, with gusts of 60 miles per hour possible.

Dust storms can give rise to small, short-lived, and intense whirlwinds, within the storms or out in front, that can damage buildings in their path. Visibility can drop to zero in such a storm, but average visibility is about one-quarter mile. After the storm, it takes about an hour or so for visibility to return to normal. If the parent thunderstorm arrives behind the dust storm, its precipitation will effectively clear the air, but as often happens, the trailing thunderstorm does not arrive or the precipitation evaporates before reaching the ground, and the dust can linger for several hours or even days.

Vast dust storms also can result from an enormous airstream that moves across the deserts of

Africa. Giant dust bands 1500 miles long and 400 miles wide often move across the area and are driven by strong cold fronts. Some large systems have even carried storms across the Atlantic to South America. The dust is raised to high altitudes, where westward-moving air currents transport it across the ocean.

Huge dust storms also arise in Arabia, central Asia, central China, and the deserts of Australia and South America, where the most obvious threat of dust storms is soil erosion. Each year the deserts claim more land. The tendency of the wind to erode the soil is often aggravated by improper agricultural practices. The primary method of controlling wind erosion is to maintain a surface cover of vegetation. Unfortunately, if rainfall is below normal, the surface cover might not be effective, and the fine topsoil is blown away.

LANDSLIDES

Landslides are violent shifts of the earth that are caused primarily by the weather. They are a mass movement of soil and rock material downslope under the influence of gravity. Landslides take place in virtually every state of the union and each year constitute a major threat to man and his works.

Although individual landslides generally are not as spectacular as other violent forms of nature, they are more widespread. Taken together they cause major economic losses and casualties. The direct costs resulting from damage to highways, buildings, and other facilities, and indirect costs resulting from loss of productivity amount to more than $1 billion annually in the United States. Single large landslides can run up damage bills in the tens of millions of dollars.

Landslides in the United States have not resulted in a major loss of life as they have in other parts of the world because most catastrophic slope failures have taken place in nonpopulated areas (FIG. 12-19). Nonetheless, the estimated total loss of life from landslides is more than 25 people per year.

Residents of California are all too familiar with landslides in their state (FIG. 12-20). Just within the last ten years, there have been 4000 landslides in the Los Angeles basin alone.

All slides involve the failure of earth materials under shear stress. The initiation of the process is a result of an increase in shear stress and a reduction of shear strength. The addition of water to a slope can contribute to both an increase in stress and a decrease in strength. Other factors involved include

(Courtesy of USGS)

FIG. 12-19. The 1959 Madison Canyon, Montana, slide.

FIG. 12-20. House damaged by a landslide in San Francisco on June 1, 1979.

the removal of lateral support by erosion from streams, glaciers, or waves, and along-shore or tidal currents. Man also can undercut support through his construction activities. Material can give way under excess loading by natural or human means, including the weight of rain, hail, or snow, which can also result in a special type of slide called an avalanche (FIG. 12-21). The weight of buildings and other man-made structures also can cause overloading of a slope.

The principal factors that contribute to low or reduced shear strength include the composition, texture, and structure of the soil, as well as the slope geometry. There might also be changes in water content and pore pressure, which acts like lubricant between rock layers. The principal triggering mechanisms include vibrations from earthquakes, blasting, machinery, traffic, and even thunder.

Other types of earth movements go under the general category of *mass wasting*; that is, the mass transfer of earth material which causes slipping, sliding, and creeping even down the gentlest of slopes.

Mass wasting is directly influenced by the amount of meteoric water in the soil. *Creep* is a slow down-slope movement of soil and is recognized by downhill-pointed poles, fence posts, and trees.

An increase in the amount of water in the soil increases weight and reduces stability by lowering the resistance to shear, resulting in an earthflow. An earthflow is a transition between the slow and rapid varieties of mass wasting and is a more visible form of movement. Earthflows usually have a spoon-shaped sliding surface, whereupon a tongue of soil breaks away and flows a short distance, leaving a large curved scarp at the breakaway point.

With increasing water content, an earthflow might grade into a *mudflow*, which is a highly viscous fluid that very often carries with it a tumbling mass of rocks and boulders, some the size of automobiles. Mudflows are the most impressive feature of many of the world's deserts. Heavy rainfall in bordering mountain regions causes sheets of water to rapidly run down steep mountain sides, picking up large amounts of material on their way and

Landslides 163

(Courtesy of USGS)

FIG. 12-21. A slab avalanche triggered by a skier.

producing a swift flood of muddy material, often with a steep wall-like front. Such a mudflow can cause much damage as it flows out of the mountains. Eventually, the mudflow loses its water through percolation into the dry desert floor, and sometimes a huge, strange-looking monolith is left out in the middle of nowhere as a monument attesting to the tremendous destructive power of water in motion.

13

Future Weather

IN order to project the weather into the distant future, it is necessary to understand the weather of the distant past. Throughout the ages, the climatological pendulum has swung from a tropical paradise to a full-blown ice age and back again many times during the Earth's long history. It is not really necessary to go back very far to find recurring patterns in the Earth's climate. The beginning of the Phanerozoic eon, about 600 million years ago, is far enough. This was a time when life began to flourish in the oceans on a grand scale and began to control its own destiny by exerting, to some extent, an influence on the climate.

According to the so-called Gaia hypothesis, proposed by the English chemist James Lovelock in 1979, the Earth is like a living organism that maintains the optimum conditions for life by regulating the climate, like the human body regulates its own temperature. However, there are times when Gaia seems to have lost control, such as during the great ice ages or during mass extinctions. Also, if industrialized nations think that Gaia will continue to clean

up after them, they might continue to pollute the planet with reckless abandon, forcing Gaia to forfeit control of the climate.

THE DISCOVERY OF ICE

Huge blocks of granite, called *erratic boulders*, lying on the slopes of the Jura Mountains and weighing up to 18,000 tons, were traced back to the Swiss Alps 50 miles away. Many thought they were swept there by Noah's Flood. Then in 1760, the Swiss geologist Horace de Saussure noticed that downstream from the foot of a glacier (FIG. 13-1) the surfaces of projecting rocks along the valley floor looked strikingly different from those up on the valley sides. The higher rocks were shattered by frost and were rough and jagged, while the lower rocks were rounded, smooth, and covered with scratches, aligned in a direction that pointed down the valley. Everywhere, rocks and boulders lay scattered about as though they were dumped there. From this, de Saussure concluded that the glaciers had once extended much

FIG. 13-1. Saskatchewan Glacier, Alberta, Canada.

farther down the valley, grinding the rocks on the valley floor as they advanced and receded.

In 1795, the Scottish geologist James Hutten described the Alps as once covered by a mass of ice with immense glaciers carrying blocks of granite for great distances. However, scientists would not believe that a floor of ice with rocks embedded in it could move along like a giant file and grind away the rocks beneath as it flowed over them. Nor were they likely to admit that the glaciers were much more widespread, dropping strange rocks in the most unlikely places.

The Swiss naturalist Louis Agassiz finally put the skeptics to rest. So convinced was he that glacial ice masses had once blanketed the Swiss mountains that he led an expedition, which included some of the most distinguished geologists in Europe, to the Jura Mountains in 1837. There on the valley floor were large areas of polished and deeply furrowed rocks miles from any existing glaciers. Heaped rocks, called *moraines*, marked the extent of former glaciers. The valley in which the scientists stood was

once buried in ice a mile thick, and the glaciers descended from the mountains and spread across most of Europe, killing everything in their path. Agassiz showed how glaciers formed by the slow accumulation of snow on the mountains. The snow crystals on the bottom were packed and compressed together into solid ice, and over the years, a thick, solid sea of ice formed. The ice was not stationary, but flowed outward or retreated, depending on the climate.

Agassiz discovered even more abundant evidence of glaciation in the British Isles, Scandinavia, and the north European Plain. In 1846, he immigrated to America and found that an even greater area, virtually all of the continent north of the Ohio and Missouri rivers, had been glaciated. Most geologists, however, could not imagine ice sheets of the magnitude that Agassiz described, and it took another 20 years before his views were accepted.

It did not take long after that for geologists to realize that there was not just a single episode of glaciation. Successive layers of glacial clay separated by soil or peat suggested a succession of ice ages. In 1909, the Swiss geologists Albrecht Penck and Edward Brukner confirmed that there were at least four ice ages. The ice ages in the Alps took their names from Bavarian streams that exposed traces of particular episodes of glaciation. In America, the names of states in the affected areas were given to corresponding episodes. From the youngest to oldest they were the Wisconsin, Illinoian, Kansan, and Nebraskan.

There were serious problems with this magic number of four ice ages, however, and although evidence showed the existence of several more, geologists, especially in America, simply chose to ignore it. Then in the mid-1950s, the Italian-born climatologist Cesare Emiliana, working at the University of Chicago, produced unrefutable evidence for rapid and rhythmic successions of ice ages. His proof came from analyzing fossil shells from ocean-bottom cores for their heavy oxygen content. Since the higher proportion of heavy oxygen meant a colder climate, Emiliana recognized seven distinct ice ages within the last 700,000 years.

ANCIENT ICE AGES

The first ice age ever recorded in geologic history took place around 2 billion years ago. At that time, the land mass was composed of small odds and ends of continents, called *cratons*, much like a giant jigsaw puzzle. This supercontinent was probably located near one of the poles where ice forms easily.

This was a period of transition when atmospheric carbon dioxide was being replaced by oxygen, generated by photosynthesis. The loss of this greenhouse gas caused the planet to cool considerably, placing the land mass in the grips of a great ice age.

This ice age was followed about 1 billion years later by a much more extensive period of glaciation (FIG. 13-2). It was perhaps the greatest ice age the Earth has ever experienced, ending about 700 million years ago. Evidence for this widespread glaciation is found in thick sequences of Precambrian *tillites*, which are cemented glacial till composed of an assortment of sediments from clay to boulders. These rocks have been found and dated on every continent except Antarctica.

Around 280 million years ago, near the end of the Paleozoic era, the land began to dry out and the temperature began to drop. The southern continent of Gondwanaland passed into the south polar regions where glacial centers expanded in all directions (FIG. 13-3). Ice sheets covered large portions of east cen-

FIG. 13-2. The extent of late Precambrian glaciation worldwide.

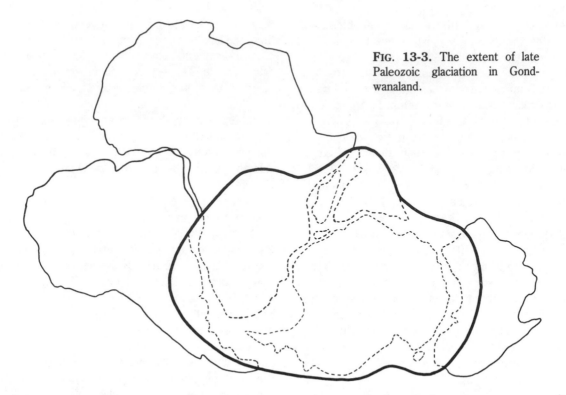

FIG. 13-3. The extent of late Paleozoic glaciation in Gondwanaland.

tral South America, Antarctica, South Africa, India, and Australia. In Australia, marine beds with fossils were found interbedded with glacial deposits. In South Africa, tillites several thousand feet thick covered many thousands of square miles.

Early in the ice age, the maximum glacial effects were in South America and South Africa. Later, the chief glacial centers moved to Australia and Antarctica. The late Paleozoic ice age is good evidence that the continents were at one time together in one large supercontinent. Instead of thick ice caps forming and spreading into tropical and semitropical lands, the continents existed near the South Pole and were later displaced to their present positions. Glacial evidence also supports the theory that the South Pole wandered across Africa into Antarctica and Australia.

THE PLEISTOCENE ICE AGE

The English geologist Charles Lyell originally coined the word *Pleistocene* in the 1830s, meaning a period of recent life based on fossil evidence. Because widespread glaciation also occurred in this time, however, the term became synonymous with the ice age. Lyell was also a strong supporter of the theory of uniformitarianism, which maintains that the slow geological processes were the same in the past as they are today. Yet the ice age was a catastrophic event. The Pleistocene epoch began about two million years ago, a time that also coincides with the appearance of Homo habilis, or man the toolmaker. The end of the Pleistocene is the end of the last ice age and gave way to the Holocene, or age of modern life, which began about 10,000 years ago.

The term *ice age* is currently taken to mean a time of maximum extent of the ice sheets during the Pleistocene. In the past million years, there have been about ten ice ages.

The most recent ice age peaked about 18,000 years ago when one-third of the land surface was covered with ice (FIG. 13-4). In North America, the ice was a mile or more thick in places and extended as far south as Oregon and New York. Ice buried the mountains of Wyoming, Colorado, and California, and rivers of solid ice linked them with mountains in Mexico. Throughout the world, alpine

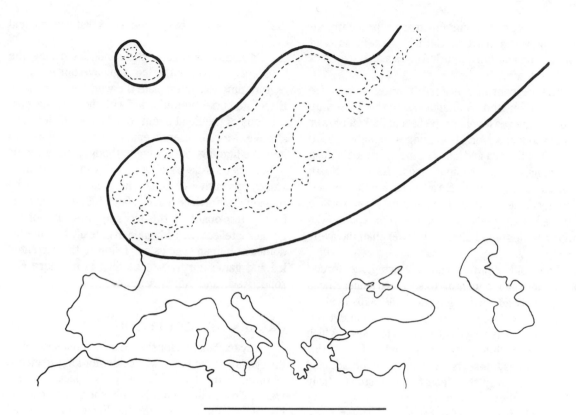

FIG. 13-4. The extent of Pleistocene glaciation in Europe (top) and
in North America (bottom).

glaciers existed on mountains that are presently ice free. Antarctica, part of Eurasia, Greenland, and western and southern South America also were covered with ice.

Five percent of the Earth's water was in the form of ice on land. So much water was locked up in ice that the sea level dropped about 300 feet lower than it is today. Several land bridges appeared above the level of the sea and allowed the migration of man and animals; for example, from Asia to North America via the Bering Strait. The Earth was significantly colder, and the temperature at the surface averaged over the entire globe year round was roughly 10 degrees Fahrenheit lower than the average is today.

The cold weather and advancing ice forced animals and man to migrate to southern lands. Ahead of the slowly advancing ice sheet, perhaps averaging only a few hundred feet per year, lush deciduous forests gave way to pine forests, which themselves gave way to barren tundra (FIG. 13-5). In other areas, deserts became widespread, and wind speeds over the deserts were substantially higher than they are today.

The deserts formed because with cooler global temperatures, less water was evaporated from the oceans, making less water available to the land. A reduction of precipitation seems to be a contradiction, though, because snowfall is needed to continue the growth of the glaciers. Only a few inches of snow would fall on the glaciers each year, but taken together over a period of several thousand years this became a phenomenal amount of precipitation. Also, cooler summers mean that less ice melted.

During the last ice age, a period anthropologists call the Upper Paleolithic period, between 35,000 and 10,000 years ago, saw the development of a species known as Cro-Magnon, or human beings as they are today. It was a time that witnessed an explosion of human progress and creativity and served as the cradle of human culture. Humans made more technological and artistic advancements in these 250 centuries than the entire 2 million years since stone tools were first used. In a quantum leap forward, humans invented language, art (which could be considered a form of writing), and music, and laid down the foundations of laws, trade, class distinctions, and even fashion.

Perhaps being cooped up indoors during the long, cold winters of the Ice Age gave our early ancestors time to contemplate the world around them. Elaborate burial sites adorned with the personal possessions of the dead seem to indicate a belief in an afterlife. More efficient weapons were developed to improve hunting. Surprisingly, though, there seems to have been little tribal warfare even against their stocky, primitive cousins, the Neanderthals, who roamed the Earth beginning about 100,000 years ago before the onset of the ice age. Because of his greater intellect, Cro-Magnon eventually became the dominant human species and followed the retreat of ice and game northward, settling in northern Europe, Asia, and North America.

CAUSES OF GLACIATION

Any explanation for the ice ages must show why the climate of the Earth was colder for long stretches of time. It must consider why the glacial periods were followed by such relatively short, warm interglacial periods, like the one the Earth is experiencing now. The theory also must take into account that once large ice sheets form, they cause still more cooling of the climate because the additional ice reflects more solar heat away from the Earth's surface in what is called the albedo (FIG. 13-6). With more heat lost, the climate becomes colder still, and the glaciers grow even more. It would seem that with such a feedback mechanism in place, glaciation would be difficult to stop. Yet, geologic history shows that something dramatic did happen to warm the climate and force the retreat of the ice sheets. The problem is finding a mechanism that regularly changed the climate over the past million years or so and turned the ice ages on, and then off again.

Several forces can be responsible for triggering an ice age, and they go under the general headings of extraterrestrial and terrestrial effects. An *extraterrestrial effect* is any process operating outside the Earth that reduces the amount of sunlight reaching the planet. It can be anything from the passage of the Solar System through a galactic dust

NORTH
POLE

FIG. 13-5. (top) The arctic tundra, southwestern Copper River Basin, Alaska. (bottom) The arctic tundra line, north of which the ground remains frozen year round.

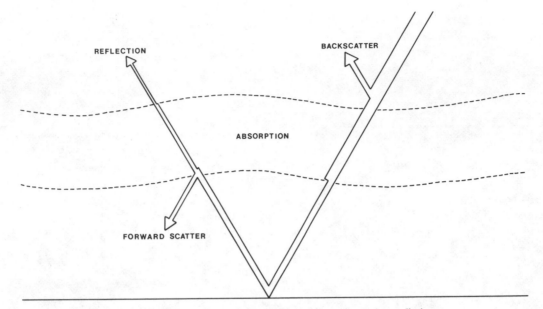

FIG. 13-6. The effect of the albedo on incoming solar radiation.

cloud to a collision with one of more meteors. One restraint must apply, however, and that is it must also be somewhat periodic since the ice ages themselves seem to follow a roughly regular pattern, recurring every 100,000 years.

The Sun might be the culprit with its rhythmic fluctuations of output from sunspot activity, which occurs in roughly 11-year cycles. The lack of sunspot activity during the 1600s might have been the cause of the "Little Ice Age," when creeping glaciers chased people out of the northlands of Europe.

There are cyclical changes in the Earth's orbital parameters that affect the amount of heat the Earth receives from the Sun, including the degree of tilt, the amount of precession of its orbital axis, and the eccentricity of its orbit around the Sun. The axial tilt and precession determines the distribution of solar radiation with respect to latitude and season, but do not affect the overall amount of heat the Earth receives during the year. The eccentricity is determined by the gravitational pull on the Earth by the other planets, causing its orbit to change from nearly circular to highly elliptical, which takes it much farther away from the Sun at aphelion and cools it.

Terrestrial effects are those that originate within the Earth itself, although they could be influenced by outside forces such as the gravitational pull of the Sun, Moon, and planets, which could make these events somewhat cyclical. They include any processes that affect the atmosphere, which can in turn block out the heat from the Sun.

Large volcanic eruptions, such as Tambora in 1815 and Krakatoa in 1883, have been known to cool the climate for several years. It might require several large eruptions over a long time to bring on an ice age, however, and evidence for unusually high amounts of volcanic activity has yet to be found in the geologic record.

Changes in the level of carbon dioxide along with water vapor and cloud cover affect the temperature of the Earth's surface. These changes generate a greenhouse effect, which keeps the Earth warm by allowing the Sun's heat to come in but not permitting all of it to escape. A loss of half the carbon dioxide would cause the planet to cool enough to bring on an ice age, but there is yet to be a good explanation how the gas could suddenly become unusually low. Perhaps an explosive growth of blue-green algae brought on by changing ocean conditions could deplete the carbon dioxide in the atmosphere.

The drifting of the continents near the polar

regions and the growth of mountain ranges could provide the right geological conditions for the growth of glaciers, but geological processes are extremely slow; therefore, they only provide the proper ground, not the cause for glaciation. There is an exception, and a theory that demonstrates how glaciers can suddenly gallop across huge land masses and just as suddenly retreat again must take into account the continent of ice.

THE ANTARCTIC ICE

When Antarctica (FIG. 13-7) broke away from Australia and later South America about 40 million years ago and moved into the South Polar region, it began to accumulate layer upon layer of ice, until today the average thickness is about 1.3 miles. Antarctica has an average area of 5.5 million square miles and is larger in winter than in the summer. The additional ice in winter makes Antarctica nearly twice the size of the continental United States.

The continent is divided by the Transantarctic Mountains into a large East Antarctic ice mass and a smaller West Antarctica lobe, which is as large as Greenland. Antarctica has land features like most other continents, with major mountain chains, deep canyons, plateaus, and plains, but they are buried under a thick sheet of ice. Large, flat areas are thought to be subglacial lakes, kept from freezing by the interior heat of the Earth. The temperature 6000 feet below the surface of an ice sheet can be 25 degrees warmer than at the top. Because of the high pressures that can exist at such depths, liquid water can exist several degrees colder than its normal freezing point.

Each year, Antarctica discharges over 1 trillion tons of ice into the seas that surround the continent. The ice flowing into the ocean breaks off to form icebergs (FIG. 13-8). The ice in East Antarctica is firmly anchored on land, but the ice in West Antarctica rests below water on an ocean shelf and is fringed by floating ice that is pinned in by small islands buried under the ice.

(Courtesy of U.S. Navy)

FIG. 13-7. McMurdo Sound, Antarctica.

(Courtesy of U.S. Navy)

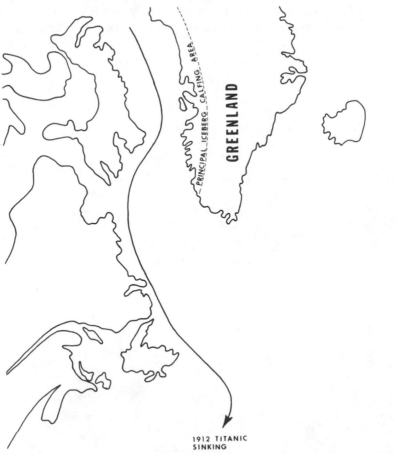

GREENLAND

PRINCIPAL ICEBERG CALFING AREA

1912 TITANIC SINKING

FIG. 13-8. (top) A huge iceberg off the Antarctic Peninsula. (bottom) The principal path of arctic icebergs.

Normally, the flow of ice into the oceans surrounding Antarctica compensates for the accumulation of snow, so the ice sheet is perfectly balanced and does not change its volume with time. This balance is achieved because a growing ice sheet tends to cool the surrounding atmosphere, thereby reducing the rate of snowfall, and because an increase of the load of ice depresses the continent, lowering the ice-sheet surface and raising its temperature. However, a concurrent development of ice sheets in the Northern Hemisphere would reduce the sea level, exposing submerged land over which the Antarctic ice could spread. As long as the equilibrium is maintained, the ice will continue to adjust itself to variable climatic influences.

West Antarctica is traversed by ice streams, which are rivers of solid ice several miles broad that flow down mountain valleys to the sea. The banks of the ice streams are marked by deep crevasses. At the bottom of the streams there might be muddy pools of melted water, which lubricate the ice streams and allow them to glide along smoothly.

Normally, because of its great weight, a glacier acts like a viscous solid and creeps over the landscape at a snail's pace, moving approximately one-half mile a year. In a warmer climate, however, friction at the base is lost because of huge subglacial lakes and streams, and this watery undercoat could act like a lubricant and send large parts of the ice sheet surging along the ice streams toward the sea at several times faster than normal speed. This rapid flow of ice into the sea, called a *glacial surge*, could raise the sea level 15 feet and inundate coastal areas worldwide, flooding over $1 trillion worth of real estate, and bringing on an ice age.

About 800 years ago, Hubbard Glacier charged toward the Gulf of Alaska, shrank back, then advanced again 500 years later. The last time the glacier began to advance was around 1900. At that time it was 30 stories tall. For 85 years Hubbard flowed toward the gulf at a steady rate of a couple of hundred feet per year. Then in June 1986, the 80-mile-long river of ice was on a veritable sprint, surging ahead as much as 46 feet a day. It and its tributary, Valerie Glacier, blocked off the mouth of Russell

Fjord, turning it into a lake, and the rising waters threatened the town of Yakutat.

There are 20 such glaciers around the Gulf of Alaska that are in high gear. If enough of them reach the ocean and raise the sea level high enough, West Antarctic ice shelves (FIG. 13-9) now pinned to underwater islands would rise too, and could be ripped from their moorings with catastrophic results.

MASS EXTINCTIONS

The geologic time scale is divided into four major eras: the Precambrian, the age of prelife; the Paleozoic, the age of ancient life; the Mesozoic, the age of middle life; and the Cenozoic, the age of recent life. Except for the Precambrian era, the eras are further subdivided into periods, which are themselves divided into epochs. Each chunk of time is distinguishable from the next by the type of life forms that existed, and the boundaries between the time frames represent mass extinctions or rapid expansion of species. Such catastrophes seem to be in direct conflict with uniformitarian concepts, which assert that Earth processes are slow and steady.

During the Phanerozoic eon, the past 600 million years, there have been five notable mass extinctions. The largest was the Permian extinction, 240 million years ago, in which upwards of 95 percent of all marine species disappeared. This followed a time when much of the Earth was blanketed in a sheet of ice from one of the greatest ice ages in geologic history.

Since then, there have been five additional lesser extinctions. A classic example is the extinction of the dinosaurs, along with 70 percent of all other known species 65 million years ago. Taking the lesser extinctions into account, there seems to be a periodic occurrence of roughly 26 million years since the great Permian die out. This would imply a common cause for such events, which could be either earthbound or extraterrestrial.

The reason species die out on such a grand scale probably has to do with some drastic change in the climate. Plate tectonics, which began to push the continents around roughly 200 million years ago,

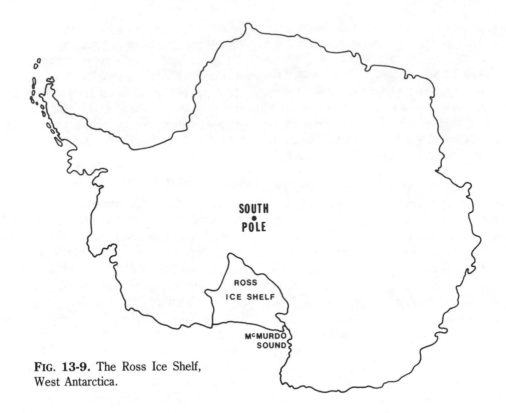

FIG. 13-9. The Ross Ice Shelf,
West Antarctica.

could cause shifts in atmospheric and oceanic circulation. This shift might inflict mass extinction on a global scale, but operates only over a very long period.

The collision with a extraterrestrial body such as a large asteroid could cause extinctions almost instantaneously. Meteor Crater in Arizona (FIG. 13-10) 1 mile across and nearly 600 feet deep, is comparatively small as meteor craters go, and is relatively young at only 25,000 years old. Because it exists in the desert, it has escaped erosion, which has erased all but faint signs of the larger craters. The Earth can expect to incur a significant asteroid impact on the average roughly every 50 million years, which is about twice the extinction cycle. Such an impact would gouge a rather large hole in the ground and inject huge quantities of dust into the atmosphere. The heavy dust cloud would encircle the globe and linger for weeks or months. This cloud could cool the climate and cause a massive killing of species, especially in the tropics where species

are particularly sensitive to a change to a colder climate.

The most recent massive extinction occurred at the end of the last glacial period about 10,000 years ago. It was modest compared with most of its forerunners, and unusual in that it affected a large proportion of big land mammal species, especially in the Americas. Fifty-seven species of large mammals became extinct in the late Pleistocene period, compared with 54 in the previous 3 million years. They include the giant ground sloth, the mastodon, the mammoth, and the saber-toothed tiger.

As the glaciers retreated, there was a global environmental readjustment, and the cool but equable climes of the Ice Age gave way to the warmer but more seasonal climate of today. The rapid environmental switch from glacial to postglacial times caused a shrinking of the forests and expansion of the grasslands. This disrupted the food chain of the large animals. Deprived of their food resources, they became extinct.

FIG. 13-10. Meteor Crater, Arizona.

The death blow could also have been delivered by human hand. By this time, humans were efficient hunters and roamed far north in response to the retreating glaciers. A killing frenzy might have caused the demise of the big animals, just as it did for the buffalo of the American West.

THE CARBON DIOXIDE PUZZLE

The Earth of the Cretaceous period 100 million years ago was unaccountably warm, and it had been so since the end of the last great ice age 180 million years earlier. There is no evidence of any permanent ice caps, which today bury Antarctica and Greenland under a thick sheet of ice. Deep ocean water, which is now near freezing, was 25 degrees warmer. The average global temperature at the surface, which today is 60 degrees, was 20 degrees warmer. It was particularly warmer in the polar regions. The difference between the temperatures at the poles and the equator, which is now 75 degrees, was only 40 degrees.

The drifting of the continents into warmer equatorial waters could account for some of the mild climate. As the continents drifted poleward during the past 100 million years, the land accumulated snow and ice and reflected more heat back into space, which had a cooling effect on the climate. Although the geography was important, it could only supply a portion of the warming. The movement of the continents was faster than it is today, with more highly active plate tectonics. The greater activity in the plates produced higher volcanic activity, which in turn increased the carbon dioxide in the atmosphere with a consequential increase in the greenhouse effect.

During the coldest part of the last glacial period, 18,000 years ago, the concentration of carbon dioxide in the atmosphere was about half of that of the preindustrial period and about a quarter of what it is today. As the ice sheets began to melt, about 15,000 years ago, carbon dioxide began a rapid increase, stopping about 10,000 years ago. The carbon dioxide was taken up by the ocean, where microscopic organisms converted it into carbonates.

In effect, life in the ocean acts to pump carbon from the surface and atmosphere into the deep sea. The faster this biological pump works, the less carbon dioxide remains in the atmosphere. The speed of the pump is determined by the amount of nutrients in the ocean, which respond to changes in ice volume. The melting of glacial ice at the end of the last ice age flooded continental shelves, which depleted the sea of organic carbon and nutrients. With reduced nutrients, the pump slowed and deep-sea carbon returned to the surface through upwelling of water. It reentered the atmosphere as carbon dioxide, which enhanced the greenhouse effect.

Since the industrial revolution, the amount of atmospheric carbon dioxide and other trace gases has again been rapidly increasing from the burning of fossil fuels and forests. By the end of this century, these greenhouse gases might cause an appreciable warming of the Earth. With an additional warming of the polar regions, the Antarctic ice sheet might become extremely unstable, causing it to surge into the Antarctic Ocean. This would form an overlarge ice shelf that would increase the Earth's albedo, and the transfer of cooling to the Northern Hemisphere could lead to glaciation.

14

Climate and Hunger

TWO million years ago, an early food-gathering people of Africa, called Homo habilis, numbered around 100,000. By 10,000 B.C., about the time agriculture was invented, there were 5 to 10 million people in the world. By 3000 B.C., the time of the first dynasty in Egypt, the population had risen to 100 million. At the beginning of the first century A.D., the world's population was about 250 million, or nearly the present population of the United States. For eighteen centuries, the world's population steadily grew, tripling by the time of the Industrial Revolution in 1750. The population reached its first billion mark, after 2 million years of growth, around 1800. Only 130 years later, the figure doubled to 2 billion. Thirty years later in 1960, the world reached its third billion, and in less than 15 years after that came the fourth billion. The fifth billion was added in 1986 after only a dozen years had passed, and another billion is expected by the middle 1990s.

The 5 billion mark in human population was reached on July 7, 1986. In order to grasp the significance of this number, think of people marching in a column 100 abreast stretching clear around the world. If all the people in the world were stacked one upon the other, the pile of bodies would reach 1 million miles into space, or twice the distance to the moon and back. The total human mass is equal to a block of clay, roughly 1 mile on each side. Many demographers believe that the world is already at its carrying capacity, and it will be difficult to feed, clothe, shelter, and employ many more people at more than a subsistence level of life.

Rapid population growth has stretched the resources of the world, and the prospect of future increases raises serious questions of how to cope with people's growing needs. Meanwhile, the population growth of the developed nations has stabilized such that governments are calling for a higher birth rate in order to keep their economies growing in the future.

If the population continues to grow at this astounding rate, it will double by the year 2020, with 80 percent of the increase in underdeveloped countries. By the year 2000, half the people in these countries will be under the age of 15. Some 600 million new jobs will be required as these people reach maturity and begin to raise families of their own. Many Third-World cities will become sprawling slums with few services and much disease, pollution, crime, unemployment, and political unrest. Mexico City, the largest of them all, will double its population by the year 2000 to 31 million. Bangladesh, which is about the size of Wisconsin, will have 160 million people, a 60 percent increase. In Kenya, which has the world's highest birth rate, the average woman once had eight babies and four living children. Now, with improved health care she has eight living children.

THE BIRTH OF AGRICULTURE

When the continental glaciers of the last ice age began to retreat about 15,000 years ago, the eastern shores of the Mediterranean witnessed one of the most momentous events in man's long climb up the ladder of progress. While hunting deer and wildebeest and gathering food along the North African coast, primitive people stumbled across the fertile Levant region, which includes the countries bordering on the eastern Mediterranean. They also discovered an area known as the Fertile Crescent, stretching from the southeast coast of the Mediterranean to the Persian Gulf.

In these regions, stands of wild wheat and barley grew thickly in the uplands. The people gathered the wild plants and used primitive stone grinders to process the cereals. The stability of this food supply encouraged the people to build permanent settlements and devise a number of tools to harvest the crop and invent pottery in which to cook it. They might have herded gazelle instead of just hunting them, beginning a new system of animal husbandry.

When the glaciers were gone, about 10,000 years ago, the Neolithic era and the food-producing revolution began. Man slowly learned the best combinations of resources at his disposal. Instead of merely gathering wild foods, he collected plants and tried to control and nurture them. Sheep, goats, pigs, and cattle were domesticated, thus providing a ready supply of wool, milk, and meat, and an alternative source of food should the harvest fail. Even

at this early stage, farming was so productive that it could support ten times as many people in a given area of land as could the foraging way of life.

It is not surprising that agriculture not only supported, but encouraged the growth of population. Since farming was labor intensive, large families were needed to till and harvest the land. Villages sprang up everywhere with houses that were built to last. The ownership of land made man territorial. It had to be guarded and tended with care by the whole village so that it could be passed on to succeeding generations.

Increasing populations required innovations to increase food production by improving farming techniques, which led to irrigation and the invention of the plow. Even this was not enough, and some people were forced to migrate northward.

Farmers roamed across Europe following the tracks of the hunter-gatherers. Starting about 6000 B.C., agriculture spread from Greece through the Balkans. It eventually reached Great Britain and northern Europe by about 3000 B.C. Europe was largely forested (FIG. 14-1) and the land had to be cleared for planting and cattle grazing. The climate was colder and wetter and houses had to be specially constructed. The expansion of farming into limited areas with the most easily cultivable soils brought on overpopulation, forcing people to move to less desirable locations.

In contrast, on the plains of Mesopotamia, the problem was not the lack of fertile soil but water. Large irrigation projects required the hard labor of hundreds of thousands of men and a system of centralized authority to rule over them. What was once a loose-knit egalitarian society was, in a mere thousand years (by 3000 B.C.), transformed through agriculture into an authoritarian society, equipped with kings, captains, and slaves. Huge armies of highly organized states fought each other over the control of people and their land. It was the dawn of civilization.

FOOD AND POPULATION

With the exception of the developed countries, most of the world is preoccupied with obtaining enough food in order to survive. The underdevel-

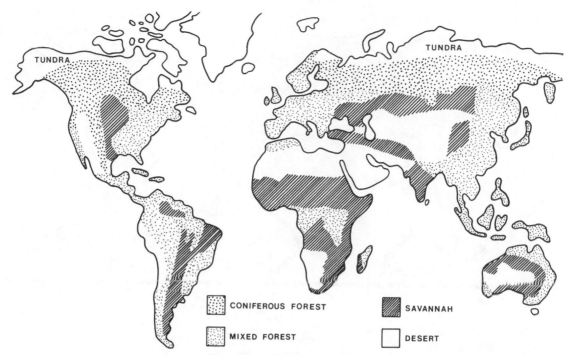

FIG. 14-1. World environments.

CONIFEROUS FOREST   SAVANNAH

MIXED FOREST   DESERT

oped countries in Asia, Africa, and South America are in a desperate race to keep food supplies growing at the same pace as population. Where agriculture is hard-pressed to support a population, that population is in danger because favorable climates aid agriculture and allow populations to grow beyond the limits of less advantageous climates. The human race might be coming closer to a precipice where mass starvation could occur whenever a drought or plant diseases result in below-average crop production (FIG. 14-2).

The total quantity of food directly and indirectly consumed by the human population is staggering and amounts to about a ton per person per year, or roughly 5 billion tons. This is equal to the tonnage of all the fossil fuels consumed annually and could fill 50,000 supertankers which, if tied end to end, would stretch halfway around the world. Nearly half of the total tonnage of crops and three-quarters of the energy and protein content is in wheat, rice, maize (corn), and other cereal grains. However, a large fraction of these grains is eaten by domestic animals including pets. Countries like India have a large population of cattle that freely roam the streets, consume large quantities of food, and spread disease. Because they are considered sacred, they cannot be eaten.

The average individual food intake is 1800 kilocalories per day for underdeveloped countries and 2700 kilocalories per day for developed countries. Furthermore, the diet of the poorer countries is not nearly as nutritious as those of the richer nations. The poor are condemned to a monotonous, low-quality diet, consisting of cereal grains or tubers and other starchy roots. For the poorest 20 percent of the population, the diet falls below the body's requirement for a normally active, healthy person.

The underdeveloped countries no longer are able to produce much, if any, surplus food in good years, which could be used as a reserve for lean years. As a result, they are extremely vulnerable to fluctuations in weather conditions. Before World War II, the underdeveloped countries as a whole were exporters of cereals. Since then they have become importers, with much of the tonnage obtained under food aid programs. Also, when food prices rise

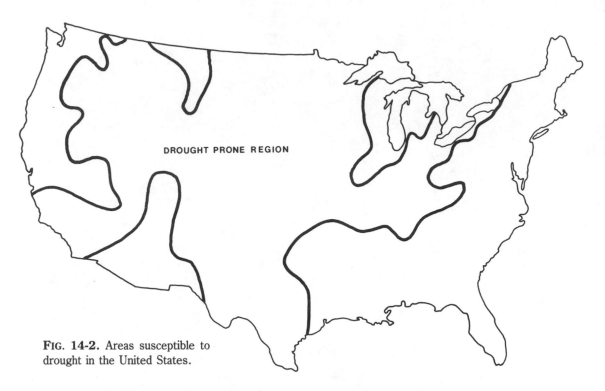

FIG. 14-2. Areas susceptible to drought in the United States.

because of a bad harvest, poor families must forego other wants, further lowering their standard of living, in order to obtain food. If supplies are already low, obtaining even food might prove to be difficult.

This situation prompted the suggestion in the early 1970s of an internationally managed world food bank, which could augment supplies of food during years of drought, pestilence, or disease. Unfortunately, the 1973 Arab oil embargo undermined these efforts by raising the cost of pumping groundwater for irrigation (FIG. 14-3) and by increasing the price for fertilizer, which was already in short supply. The developed nations with highly mechanized farming were particularly hard hit with the inflated oil prices, which resulted in higher food prices.

FAMINE IN AFRICA

Nearly 30 African countries are listed as hungry. When the rains fail, people by the hundreds of thousands die of starvation. In 1984, the worst famine in African history killed 200,000 people in Mozambique and 300,000 in Ethiopia.

FIG. 14-3. Irrigation is used extensively in the dry regions of the midwest and west United States. Unfortunately, aquifers are rapidly being depleted, requiring the drilling of deeper wells.

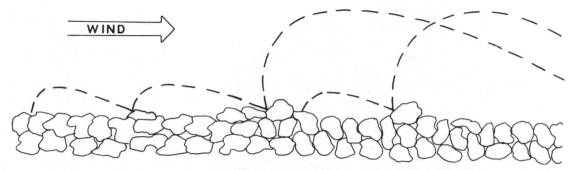

WIND

FIG. 14-4. Sand grains march across the desert floor through saltation.

In 20 years, Mozambique has lost more than three-quarters of its grazing land to the encroaching sands of the Sahara desert (FIG. 14-4). A vast belt of drought spreads across the continent, parching the land and starving its inhabitants (FIG. 14-5). The last big African famine occurred only ten years earlier in 1974, killing about 300,000 Africans, and relief agencies vowed it would never happen again. Experts insisted that famines were predictable. Yet warnings issued 2 years prior to the 1984 disaster were largely ignored by African and Western governments until it was too late. When the world was finally awakened to the tragedy, the drought was well underway in Ethiopia and other Black African countries.

Droughts are normal occurrences in Africa. The effects, however, are steadily getting worse because

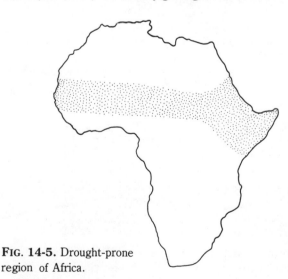

FIG. 14-5. Drought-prone region of Africa.

of Africa's deepening poverty, increasing population, and, worst of all, abuse of land. Much of the damage is done by mismanagement, corruption, and civil war, which only aggravate the natural disasters that have always beset the region. In the last drought, not only people, but hundreds of thousands of cattle, sheep, and goats, died, further reducing a country's food potential for the future. Refugees considered themselves fortunate if they received a meal from a relief organization once in every three or four days.

Africa's dependence on relief will most likely continue to grow in the years ahead. It seems that natural disasters are killing more people every year. Yet, there is no clear-cut evidence that the climatological mechanisms associated with droughts, floods, and cyclones are changing. Instead, the effects of natural disasters are worsened by poverty, environmental damage, and rapid population growth. Black Africa is the world's poorest area, and it is the only region where the population, which is experiencing the fastest growth of any continent in human history, is outpacing the food supply.

Agriculture never fully recovered from the devastating drought of 1974, mainly because previously arable land was wasted. Another problem is that, on the average, African governments spend four times as much on armaments as they do on agriculture.

Primitive farming techniques have devastated the land, causing a decline in African agriculture of about 25 percent since 1960. Under increasing pressure for food production, normally fallow fields have been placed under the plow, wearing out the soil.

Famine in Africa **183**

Most farmers have no chemical fertilizers, and the animal dung that they once used to enrich the soil must now be burned for fuel because the trees have been cut down. With deforestation, the soil loses much of its capacity to retain moisture, and consequently it loses its productivity and resistance to drought. Therefore, famine in Africa is as much a man-made disaster as it is a natural one.

CAUSES OF DROUGHT

Droughts occur when there is a shifting of precipitation activity around the world (FIG. 14-6). Since the total heat budget of the Earth does not change significantly from one year to the next, areas that become unusually dry are matched by other areas that become unusually wet. In other words, droughts in one region give rise to floods in another. For example, in 1983 and again in 1988, the United States had two of its worst droughts since the Dust Bowl years of the 1930s (FIG. 14-7) with crop losses approaching $10 billion. Australia had its most severe drought in over 100 years. An equally intense drought caused food shortages in southern Africa and affected West Africa and the Sahel region, a 250-mile-wide strip of land south of the Sahara desert from the west coast to Chad. Meanwhile, the worst flooding of the century struck Ecuador, northern Peru, and large areas of Brazil, Paraguay, and Argentina.

The droughts might be triggered by an unusually warm tropical Pacific caused by an El Niño current and its accompanying atmospheric changes. Of the most recent 28 El Niños, 22 have been associated with below normal rainfall in southeast Africa, whereas a colder than normal tropical Pacific probably leads to higher than normal rainfall.

El Niños apparently can bring drought to Australia and India as well, but droughts in the Sahel region seem to be associated with the appearance of warmer than normal water in the Atlantic off West Africa and south of latitude 10 degrees north. Colder than normal water appears at the same time across the Atlantic as far north as the Caribbean, where it also seems to influence precipitation. Changes in ocean currents, induced by atmospheric circulation, redistribute heat in the Atlantic to create the abnormal sea-surface temperature pattern. The drought-related sea-surface pattern develops in the months

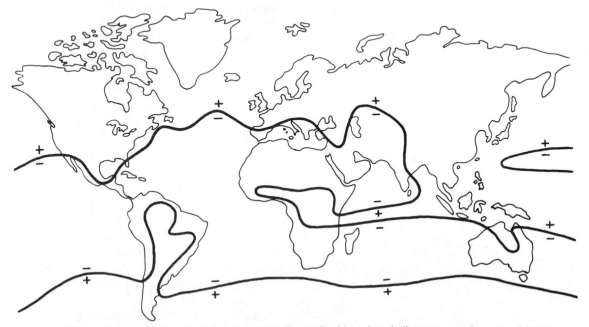

FIG. 14-6. The precipitation-evaporation balance of the Earth. Positive signs indicate areas where precipitation exceeds evaporation. Negative signs indicate areas where evaporation exceeds precipitation.

(Courtesy of USDA)

FIG. 14-7. Buried farm machinery in Gregory County, South Dakota, in 1936 as the result of the 1930s dust bowl.

before the crucial summer rainy season. The precipitation activity is then shifted hundreds of miles to the south, reducing the moisture-laden winds reaching into West Africa and the Sahel region.

These seasonal winds are called *monsoons* (FIG. 14-8) and they bring water to half the people of the world. The monsoon of southern Asia is possibly the most impressive seasonal phenomenon of the

FIG. 14-8. The summer monsoons.

tropics. The term *monsoon* is from the Arabic word *mausim*, meaning "season," and applies to the wind system of the Arabian Sea that blows from the southwest during half of the year and from the northeast during the other half. Generally, the term has come to signify any annual climatic cycle with seasonal wind reversals that cause wet summers and dry winters.

The largest and most vigorous monsoons are found on the continents of Asia, Africa, and Australia and their adjacent seas. During the active phase of the monsoon, the weather is unstable, with frequent storms that carry abundant rainfall, upwards of 200 inches per year and more. During the dormant phase, the weather is absent of tropical storms and is dry, hot, and stable. Variations in annual precipitation can lead to years of drought or flood, which can be expected about 30 times per century.

The monsoons fail to arrive in Africa because the deflection of the westerlies southward over Africa results in a displacement of a high-pressure system hovering over the Sahara desert. Normally, when the monsoon encounters the southern edge of the high, moisture condenses and rain falls over

the Sahel. When the high is displaced to the south, however, the monsoon drops its moisture before it reaches the Sahel.

The Ghat mountain chain in southwest India plays an important part in forcing moisture-laden air from the Arabian Sea upward, where it cools and releases its rain. The monsoon sweeps northward across India, drenching fields and flooding villages. Droughts occur when a blocking high exists south of the Himalayan Mountains, keeping the monsoons away from the Indian subcontinent. Sometimes the monsoons are delayed for several weeks because the lower temperature of the ocean upwind from the land limits the amount of moisture in the air above the water. When the ocean warms, the monsoons return.

DEGRADATION OF THE ENVIRONMENT

Perhaps the greatest limiting factor to man's continuing population growth is soil erosion (FIG. 14-9). Before the advent of agriculture, natural soil erosion was probably no more than 10 billion tons

(Photo by K.N. Phillips, courtesy of USGS)

FIG. 14-9. Severe cropland erosion.

per year: slow enough to be replaced by the generation of new soil. Estimates of present soil erosion rates are as much as three times greater. In other words, we are losing the very ground beneath our feet much faster than nature is putting it back.

Soil erodes when it loses its natural or man-made covering of vegetation whose root system holds the soil in place against the effects of wind and rain. Anytime the land is denuded of vegetation, the soil is exposed to the elements and, carried by streams and rivers, makes its way to the bottom of the ocean. In order to replace the soil, rock must be weathered into fine grains (FIG. 14-10), a process that takes lots of time.

Because of increasing world food demand, farmers are forced to adopt agricultural practices that have been proven in the past to lead to excessive soil erosion. Perhaps as much as one-third of the global cropland is losing soil at a rate that is undermining any long-term productivity. World food production per person will eventually begin to fall off if the loss of topsoil continues at present alarming rates.

CAUSES OF CHANGES IN CLIMATE

There is good reason to believe that increasing human populations cause changes in the climate. The famine that ravages Africa is frequently attributed to drought, but drought might only be a triggering mechanism. The root cause of Africa's crisis is growing population, soil erosion, and desertification. The sands of the Sahara desert are advancing inexorably, engulfing everything in their path as do other deserts of the world.

Desertification is a process of degradation of the environment, and is a product of climate and human activity. In the Sahel, it has been accelerating alarmingly. The process began over a millennium ago when nomads of the Sahel lived by herding and hunting. They cut trees and set fires to improve grazing and to aid in hunting, turning the tropical forests into grassland. The colonial era brought the nomadic life to a halt, and people of the Sahel were forced to live a more settled life as farmers and herdsmen. Over-

grazing by cattle further destroyed the already weakened soil, and desertification was accelerated. The more the land was denuded, the greater was the surface reflectance of solar radiation, which contributed to lesser rainfall and denuded more land.

This same process is happening all over the world, but particularly across the Atlantic in the Amazon jungle of Brazil. Here, tropical rain forests are cleared away on an unprecedented scale to make way for pastureland for grazing cattle. The trees are cut down and burned in a process called *slash-and-burn* agriculture so their ashes can fertilize the thin soil. After a year or two, the soil is robbed of its nutrients by improper farming techniques, the land is abandoned, and the farmers press farther into the forest. Meanwhile, heavy rains wash away the denuded topsoil, and without the soil, the rain forest has no chance of recovery and is lost for all time.

As a large part of the rain forest is being destroyed, precipitation patterns are changing, which can possibly turn the area into a man-made desert. Throughout the world, rain forests are disappearing at an alarming rate of about 27 million acres per year, which is an area about the size of Ohio. At this rate of forest destruction, all accessible tropical forests will be gone by the end of this century.

Along with the destruction of the tropical forests is the destruction of wildlife habitat. Presently, there are about 10 million species, but they are continuously being crowded out by human beings who destroy their ecological niches and pollute their environments with herbicides, insecticides, and industrial poisons. The human race is growing so explosively and so extensively that as a result, other species are perishing in tragically large numbers. Tropical rain forests cover only about 6 percent of the earth's land surface, but they contain two-thirds or more of the existing species.

Sometime during the next century, the rate of extinctions could surpass in scale the mass extinctions at the end of the Cretaceous period, some 65 million years ago which killed off the dinosaurs and 70 percent of all other species. So, not only will humans become the dominant species on Earth if they continue their rapid growth, but they might also find

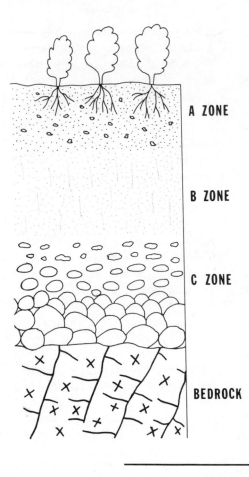

A ZONE

B ZONE

C ZONE

BEDROCK

FIG. 14-10. (top) The soil profile. Zone A indicates sand, silt, clay, and organic-rich soil. Zone B indicates sand, silt, clay, and organic-poor soil. Zone C indicates pieces of parent rock plus material leached from above. (bottom) Areas of wind-blown soil deposits in the United States.

Table 14-1. Major Deserts of the World.

DESERT	LOCATION	TYPE	AREA SQUARE MILES × 1000
Sahara	North Africa	Tropical	3500
Australian	Western/interior	Tropical	1300
Arabian	Arabian Peninsula	Tropical	1000
Turkestan	S. Central U.S.S.R.	Continental	750
North America	S.W. U.S./N. Mexico	Continental	500
Patagonian	Argentina	Continental	260
Thar	India/Pakistan	Tropical	230
Kalahari	S.W. Africa	Littoral	220
Gobi	Mongolia/China	Continental	200
Takla Makan	Sinkiang, China	Continental	200
Iranian	Iran/Afghanistan	Tropical	150
Atacama	Peru/Chile	Littoral	140

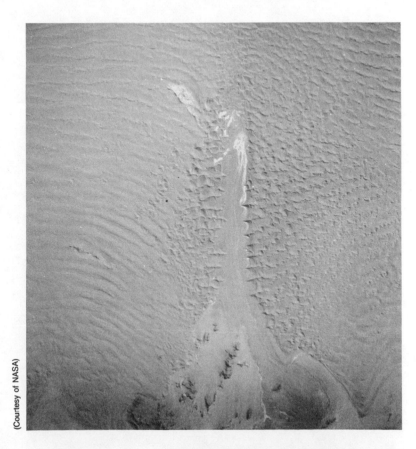

FIG. 14-11. The Namib desert in Namibia viewed from space. Note the large sand dunes, whose axes parallel the coast and are breached by a flash flood.

(Courtesy of NASA)

themselves living in a world devoid of all the beauty and diversity of life.

PREVENTING HUNGER

For the most part, people only react to disasters, rather than act to prevent them. Providing food aid to Africans to prevent a short-term famine does not prevent future famines from occurring. The most important way to prevent hunger is to improve methods of forecasting famine by improving climate forecasting. The 1984 African drought was predicted 2 years before the event, but unfortunately, those in responsible positions chose to ignore the warnings, resulting in more than a million people dead or dying of starvation.

To prevent the recurrence of such a tragedy, researchers are using satellites to map vegetation across an entire continent. On the edges of deserts, satellite images can chronicle just where the grassland is vanishing (FIG. 14-11). Color infrared photography from Landsat satellites can determine the amount of stress vegetation is experiencing during a drought. They can depict how much vegetative cover is lost from one year to the next. Satellites might ultimately help answer the larger ecological questions about vanishing tropical forests and burgeoning populations.

15

Nuclear Winter

SCIENTISTS have been plagued with a problem of proving "nuclear winter" without actually having a full-scale nuclear exchange between the two superpowers. However, the past might hold some clues as to what happens when the sky becomes clogged with dust and soot, as it would be in a nuclear war. The clues might be hidden in 65-million-year-old sediments that were laid down at the end of the Cretaceous period when the dinosaurs and nearly three-quarters of all other species mysteriously vanished. Something akin to nuclear war must have destroyed life on such a large scale.

The top of the Cretaceous sediments holds a thin layer of mud that has a high concentration of iridium, an isotope of platinum, which is very rare on Earth but is abundant in meteorites. The mud also shows a thin layer of common soot. A massive shower of meteors might have rained down on the Earth and set global forest fires. The soot would have blocked out the Sun, causing the Earth to cool and freeze its inhabitants.

In 1908, several hundred square miles of forest was leveled and burned in northern Siberia by what is suspected to be the fireball from an exploding meteor. More recently, in the spring of 1984, a mushroom cloud was spotted by airline pilots about 250 miles east of Japan, and was believed to have been the plume from a meteor explosion. If what happened to the dinosaurs is any indication of what could possibly result from nuclear war, then the human species could well find itself on a similar road to extinction.

THE PHYSICAL EFFECTS

The basic principle behind nuclear weapons is really quite simple—so much so that any university physics student can design a workable atomic bomb. Even Third-World nations are thought to have the technology to build them. The only drawback is obtaining enough plutonium or uranium. Although nuclear power plants around the world have safeguards to prevent the theft of plutonium, it can still be siphoned off to make atomic bombs. Any country that has a uranium mine can extract high-grade uranium by modern techniques and build a Hiroshima-type atomic bomb (FIG. 15-1). All that is needed is a crude cannon to blast one-half of the nuclear material into the other half. The combined mass, called the *critical mass*, produces a highly explosive fast chain reaction.

Modern nuclear weapons (FIG. 15-2) are more sophisticated and more efficient. The high temperatures from a small atomic bomb fuse hydrogen nuclei into helium: the same reaction that takes place in the Sun. The high-density neutrons produced by this reaction split uranium atoms, releasing tremendous power in a split second.

When a nuclear weapon is detonated, a fireball rapidly expands, creating a shock front that is literally a wall of compressed air traveling at supersonic speeds. As it passes, there is a nearly instantaneous rise in atmospheric pressure, crushing structures and people in its path. Following the shock wave are hurricane-force winds that could blow down anything that remains standing. People are at risk from being inside or near collapsing buildings, from being hit by flying debris, or from being hurled into a solid object.

The fireball also radiates thermal energy, which can cause severe burns and start fires well beyond the limits of blast damage. Clouds overhead would return any thermal energy that would otherwise escape into space. Under certain weather conditions, a 1-megaton burst, which would be about the average size used, could ignite fires as far as 10 miles away. Many fires might consolidate into a massive firestorm, which would be driven by a vigorous updraft and fanned by strong inflowing winds (FIG. 15-3). About one-half of the bomb's energy is in the blast wave, about one-third is released as thermal radiation, and the rest of the energy is nuclear radiation.

If a 1-megaton nuclear warhead were detonated at a height of about 1 mile above the heart of New York City, the fireball would not actually touch the ground, but it would emit intense thermal radiation

FIG. 15-1. Atomic bomb damage to Hiroshima, Japan, during World War II.

FIG. 15-2. Detonation of America's first hydrogen bomb.

FIG. 15-3. Firestorm created by a nuclear detonation on a city.

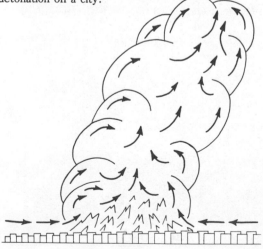

capable of severely burning anyone out in the open and would start fires a considerable distance away. Anyone up to several tens of miles away looking at the fireball would be permanently blinded. Prompt nuclear radiation would kill anyone not protected by a fallout shelter who is directly beneath or a short distance away from the fireball.

When the blast wave reached the ground, it would totally destroy the interior of the city and heavily damage buildings within a 5-mile radius. The velocity of the wind behind the shock wave would be upwards of 200 miles per hour. Forty seconds after the explosion, the shock wave would be 10 miles from ground zero, and the wind velocity would die down to 40 miles per hour. Buildings from this distance would suffer only moderate damage, but broken window panes and other objects flying through the air could still become deadly missiles.

The Physical Effects   193

Meanwhile, the fireball would be climbing at a rate of 300 miles per hour. This would set up a strong updraft, and inflowing winds would coalesce any fires started by the thermal radiation into a raging firestorm. Eventually, the fireball would cool and condense into a radioactive mushroom cloud that could reach 15 miles altitude ten minutes after the explosion (FIG. 15-4). In all likelihood, New York City, as well as other major cities, would be targeted with as many as eight such weapons.

Nuclear weapons produce about 300 radioactive isotopes, which are deposited mostly by fallout. The most short-lived radioactive isotopes have the highest radiation intensities; therefore, much of the radioactivity falls off fairly rapidly. As a rule, for every sevenfold increase in time, the radiation is reduced by a factor of 10. For example, a dose rate of 1000 *rads* (a unit of radiation exposure equal to 100 ergs of ionizing energy per gram of tissue) would be reduced to 100 rads in seven hours and 10 rads in 49 hours—a 99 percent reduction in two days.

Radiation is also cumulative, meaning that the longer the victim is exposed to radiation, the worse are his chances for survival. For example, exposure to 10 rads every hour would accumulate to a lethal dose in only two days. Such an exposure would be typical even in rural areas far from the target zones, which is why fallout shelters are so important. Most fallout shelters have a protection factor of at least 100, so an outside dose rate of 100 rads is reduced to 1 rad inside the shelter. Usually, a two-week stay in a fallout shelter would be sufficient in most circumstances.

THE BIOLOGICAL IMPACT

The immediate casualties of a full-scale nuclear war would be upwards of one-half the world's human population, mostly those living in the Northern Hemisphere. A large number of deaths would be directly attributed to blast effects, thermal radiation, and prompt nuclear radiation near the point of detonation. Many more deaths would result from fires set by the explosion, which would quickly spread out of control. Fallout shelters below the fires would become death traps where people would be baked in underground ovens.

Deaths also would occur downwind from the target area from local radioactive fallout deposited during the first 24 hours. The fallout would be composed

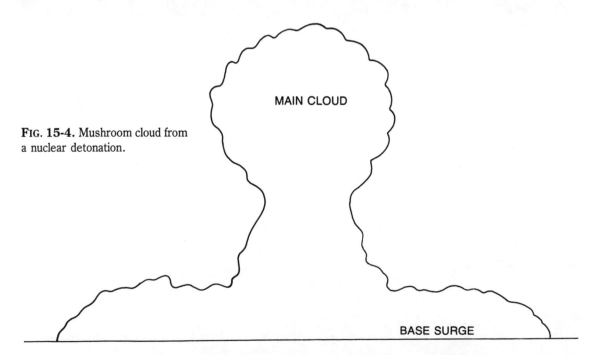

FIG. 15-4. Mushroom cloud from a nuclear detonation.

MAIN CLOUD

BASE SURGE

of dirt and crushed building material which would be carried aloft within the rising fireball. Radioactive byproducts from the nuclear explosion would be fused onto the material by the intense heat of the fireball. The heavier dirt-size particles would be the first to fall out and could cover a large area up to several inches thick with highly radioactive material.

World-wide radioactive fallout is dust-size material suspended in the air for long periods, and, riding on the wind, it travels for long distances. Kiloton-size nuclear weapons produce a mushroom cloud that can reach the top of the troposphere (FIG. 15-5). Within this weather zone, radioactive particles are rained out, producing "hot showers" of radioactive rain hundreds or thousands of miles away from the target areas. This fact means noncombatants would be casualties of a nuclear war as well, and is why a neutral country like Sweden has the best fallout shelters in the world.

Megaton-size nuclear weapons can push the mushroom cloud clear into the stratosphere, where radioactive particles are not rained out and therefore encircle the entire world. The mushroom cloud also contains large quantities of nitrous oxide, generated by the fireball, that could destroy the ozone layer. Possibly after a year or more, most of the particles fall through the troposphere and are eventually rained out. This type of fallout discredits the notion that the Southern Hemisphere is relatively safe from a nuclear war that takes place mostly in the Northern Hemisphere.

Nuclear radiation consists of alpha particles, which are helium nuclei; beta particles, which are free electrons; gamma rays, which are similar to X-rays; and neutrons. A dose of radiation measuring between 400 and 500 rads delivered over a period of several days would kill half the people exposed. About one-third of the mid-latitude land area of the Northern Hemisphere would receive such a dose in a full-scale nuclear war. Virtually all people would die from a radiation exposure of 600 rads or more without extensive medical treatment. Unfortunately, most medical facilities and personnel would be destroyed, so there would be very little medical aid.

A dose between 200 and 300 rads would kill less than 20 percent of the population, but would leave most victims debilitated with such maladies as vomiting, diarrhea, skin sores, fever, weakness, and fatigue. Radiation can also cause sterility in both sexes, cataracts, and rapid aging, which would cause people to die much earlier than they would had there been no war.

Radioactivity damages the body by interfering with the molecular structure of the cells. The cells might be able to repair themselves, but if genetic damage occurs, they might replicate in a mutated

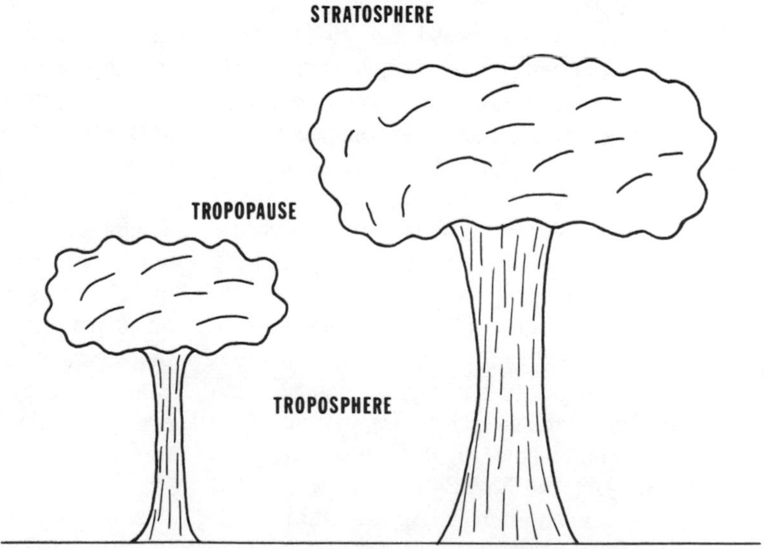

FIG. 15-5. Comparison between the effect of a detonation of a kiloton (left) and megaton (right) nuclear weapon.

STRATOSPHERE

TROPOPAUSE

TROPOSPHERE

form, causing cancer, birth defects, and other genetic diseases. The cells most affected are those that multiply rapidly, such as blood cells, which could lead to leukemia, and cells of the digestive system. In the latter case, if too many cells are denuded, a person could die of starvation or thirst no matter how much food or drink he ingests.

Those people who were already in poor health or severely injured in the explosion could find the added burden of radiation to be too much. Radiation adversely affects people at both age extremes: old people because they are generally weak and frail, and young children because of their rapid body growth. Pregnant women are particularly susceptible because radiation might induce abortion of the fetus or cause severe birth defects.

Most victims who have received an overdose of radiation would be in great agony. Vital functions could shut down or the circulatory system could become clogged with wastes, and death would probably follow within 2 weeks or less. Those who survive this period would suffer effects similar to radiation cancer treatment, with loss of hair, tendency to bleed easily, and damage to the immune system, making them highly susceptible to disease, which by then would be running rampant.

THE ECOLOGICAL CONSEQUENCES

Not only would people die in large numbers in a full-scale nuclear war, but so would plants and animals. Disease would spread like wildfire from decomposed, unburied corpses, both human and animal. Certain plants, like cereals and fruit trees, have a low tolerance for radiation. Many animals have a much lower tolerance for radiation than humans, while some pests, like insects and rats, have a considerably higher tolerance. Without natural predators like birds, they would multiply rapidly, spreading disease in epidemic proportions.

Radioactive fallout would contaminate the soil and water, possibly killing off microorganisms that are beneficial to plants and aquatic animals, and thereby disrupting the food chain. Destruction of the ozone layer would allow a high dose of ultraviolet radiation to reach the Earth's surface, where it is deadly to plants and animals. Agricultural production desperately needed for recovery would fall off sharply. Food grown in fallout-contaminated soil would concentrate radioactive substances in plant tissues, making it unfit to eat.

The burning of cities and factories would release huge quantities of toxic chemicals into the air and water, turning the Earth into a vast chemical waste dump. People might survive the initial effects of the explosion, only to be poisoned to death by toxic gases from the fires. Sulfur compounds in the air would mix with water vapor and fall to Earth as acid rain. If nuclear reactors were destroyed, large quantities of highly radioactive nuclear fuel and wastes would further contaminate the environment with high-intensity radioactivity that could last for thousands of years.

Roughly one-third of the land area in the northern temperate zone is covered by forest, and an equal area is covered by brush and grassland. Violent wildfires have been known to spread over millions of acres and occur about once every decade. Forests near targeted areas could catch fire from thermal radiation and burn out of control, destroying hundreds of thousands of square miles in a matter of days. These would be mass fires that burn bodily, and not the sort produced naturally, which are composed of moving fronts.

The forest fires, along with adjacent grassland fires, would inject huge quantities of soot into the air. The total smoke emission from a full-scale nuclear war could be as much as 300 million tons. If spread evenly around the world, the smoke could reduce the intensity of sunlight reaching the ground as much as 95 percent (FIG. 15-6). Typically, heavier smoke cover would exist in the target zones where noon would be as dim as a moonlit night.

The fires would generate large amounts of carbon monoxide and also increase the level of atmospheric carbon dioxide. Loss of wildlife habitat on such a grand scale would mean the extinction of thousands of species. The loss of vegetative cover would increase runoff and allow the soil to be easily eroded, causing massive mudflows, which would further devastate the landscape.

The consequences of having large quantities of dust and smoke in the atmosphere is that sunlight

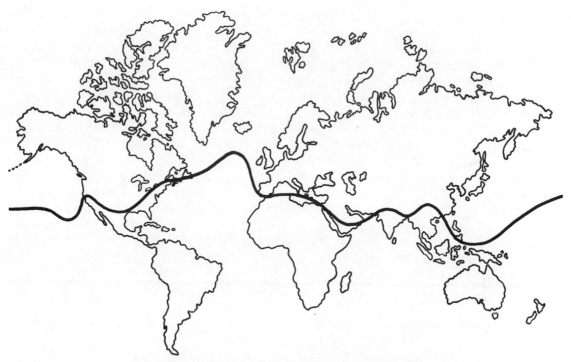

FIG. 15-6. July smoke line, above which sunlight is twilight or darker during daytime for three weeks following a general nuclear war.

is blocked from reaching the surface of the Earth. Instead, the radiant energy from the Sun goes to heat the upper atmosphere. This blockage of sunlight reduces condensation and precipitation, thus reducing the cleansing effect of rain and allowing the smoke to linger for a long time. The reduction of solar energy on the surface of the ocean would also reduce the amount of water vapor evaporated into the atmosphere.

The effect of lowered amounts of sunlight is that plants, which need it for photosynthesis, would wither and die. Plants would also suffer from a reduction of rainfall, and drought conditions would prevail over large areas of the Northern Hemisphere. Because the smoke could also extend into the midlatitudes of the Southern Hemisphere, this region could be affected as well, causing a serious problem for agriculture the world over.

The lack of sunlight would also make the surface colder (FIG. 15-7), and if temperatures fall below a certain level, plants cease to grow. If the war took place in the summer, killing frosts would claim much of the harvest, leaving survivors with little food to tide them over the winter, which would be considerably colder than normal.

THE CLIMATOLOGICAL CHANGES

When the Mariner 9 space probe made its rendezvous with Mars in 1971, it encountered a globalwide dust storm, which blocked its cameras from seeing the ground. The dust storm went on for months before it finally cleared enough for the spacecraft to see through the dust cloud.

The Martian dust storm prompted scientists to speculate what would happen on Earth should such an event take place. Dust storms on Earth do not reach such proportions, but large volcanoes such as the 1815 eruption of Tambora do loft huge amounts of dust into the atmosphere, bringing worldwide climatic effects, such as those which occurred during the "year without summer." The bombardment of

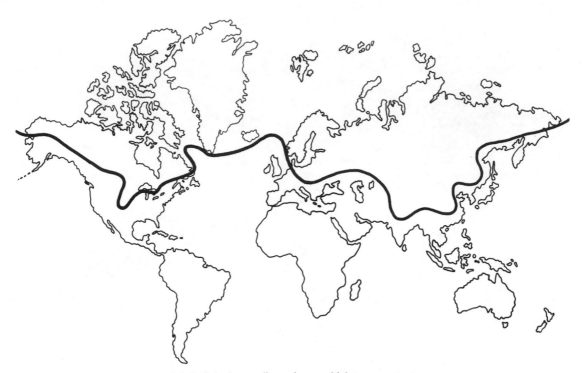

FIG. 15-7. July freeze line, above which temperatures are
freezing or below for three weeks following a general nuclear war.

one or more large meteors could also inject large quantities of dust into the air, and this is one theory for the extinction of the dinosaurs.

The detonation of large numbers of nuclear weapons near the ground would pump several hundred million tons of soil and dust-size particles into the atmosphere, along with soot from burning cities and forests. Global mixing would cause the dust cloud to encircle the entire planet, making it look much like Mars did during the Mariner 9 mission.

Since the beginning of the nuclear arms race four decades ago, scenarios for nuclear war assumed that the most devastating consequences would be large numbers of human casualties on both sides. The social and economic structure of the combatant nations would presumably collapse into total chaos, and for all practical purposes, people would be reduced to a primitive existence. Since the principal target zones would be in the Northern Hemisphere, it was thought that noncombatant nations and most of the Southern Hemisphere would be spared from the ef-

fects of nuclear war. Even the role of radioactive fallout was played down and was thought to be of only minor significance.

The concept of mutual assured destruction, with the ominous initials MAD, which is supposed to keep nuclear war at bay does not embody long-term effects of nuclear war because the short-term consequences were thought to be horrible enough. Now, it appears that the war itself would only be a triggering mechanism for dramatic environmental changes that could disrupt all life on Earth.

The long-term climatic effects of a nuclear war are likely to be much more severe and far-reaching than it has been imagined. Vast areas of the Earth would be subjected to prolonged darkness, cold temperatures, violent dust storms, toxic smog, and persistent radioactive fallout.

Following a massive nuclear exchange, convection currents over the land would be brought to a standstill as a result of excessive heating of the upper atmosphere by smoke and dust clouds, causing an intense temperature inversion. In effect, the stratosphere would descend to the level of the surface, creating a totally alien atmosphere. On the coasts, warm currents of air over the ocean would sweep onto the continents at ground level, producing thick stratus clouds and continuous precipitation. In some regions, cold offshore winds would interact with the ocean air currents to produce intense storms and heavy precipitation. In other areas, cold air flowing off the continents might warm over the ocean, rise, return to the continent, and subside over the land, causing large areas to be covered with a persistent radiation fog.

One result of the temperature inversion is that convective penetration of moist air from below would

would be all major cities, cities located near military targets, major industrial centers, and any town with a significant population. These could be hit with one or more megaton-size nuclear warheads, detonated both near the ground and in the air to inflict maximum damage with maximum fallout. Military targets located in remote areas, including missile silos, underground command centers, and air bases, would be hit with multimegaton ground bursts, producing mile-wide craters hundreds of feet deep and sending tremendous amounts of fallout downwind (FIG. 15-8).

People under heavy patches of dust and smoke would barely be able to distinguish day from night. The temperature would drop between 40 and 70

t, bringing freezing conditions
r. In addition to the cold and the
e a deathly silence, for all animals
d be dead. There would be no
no more croaking frogs, no more
eerie still, there would be mul-
various stages of disfigurement
ch would be awful, and with that
of burning rubble and an assort-
c fumes. The ground would be
e fog, and the air would be heavy
th. Insects and rats, which are
to radiation, would overrun the
ould be plenty for them to feed
redators to kill them off. The
infectious diseases, for which
nedicines or hospitals with doc-
them.
:cupation of everyone would be
for enough food and water just
d goods found in gutted out gro-
the primary source of food, but
last for long. There might be
ed in grain elevators out in the
vould be no means of transport-
ince all forms of transportation
a halt due to lack of fuel. Eat-
d animals would be out of the
l be spoiled and heavily contami-
l be no point in trying to grow
d be too dark, too cold, and the

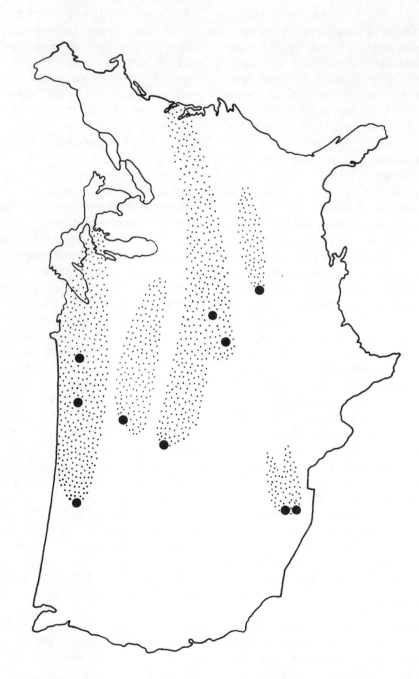

FIG. 15-8. Heavy fallout patterns from Soviet counterforce attack on American missile bases.

soil too contaminated with radioactive and chemical substances.

Since people can live about ten times longer without food than they can without water, obtaining a safe water supply would be of vital importance. The water mains most likely would be destroyed, and even if they were not, there would be no electricity to drive the pumps. Since it would not rain, water catchments would be of no use. The only safe source of water would be bottled water or canned drinks. Creek or river water, if it were available, would have to be decontaminated with special water tablets. Drinking contaminated water would cause serious sickness or disease, for which there would be no available curatives.

In a year of so, when clear skies and normal convection finally returned, the food stored in grain silos would start to run out. With the destruction of the ozone layer, people would be required to stay out of direct sunlight or take a chance of getting skin cancer or going blind from the exposure of ultraviolet rays. It is a distinct possibility that all sighted animals would go blind, and would be incapable of fending for themselves.

Farming would have to be done on a very rudimentary level since there would be no gasoline for farm machinery because the fuel stocks would have all gone up in smoke. There would also be no fertilizers to enrich the soil. Furthermore, it is doubtful whether anything grown could survive the barrage of ultraviolet rays without some form of protection.

There would be little or no cooperation toward reconstruction because people's main concern from one day to the next would be finding or growing enough food. There could even be armed conflicts as one group of starving people would attack another for their food. Weakened by hunger, disease, and radiation, resulting in high death tolls and large numbers of still births or birth defects and the lack of a social structure to organize labor and maintain order, the population of the survivors would rapidly dwindle, and eventually all would die.

APPENDIX

Forecasting the Weather

THE modern-day meteorologist has at his disposal a network of computer projections, radar and satellite images, and up-to-the-minute reports from points around the country. Forecasting has improved dramatically over the past three decades, and bears no resemblance to the archaic methods of the last century. Despite the miracles of our technological age, however, weathermen, much to their chagrin, still make mistakes. Instead of stating with confidence that it will rain tomorrow like they used to, weathermen give odds for the occurrence of such an event. It seems that a 20 percent chance of rain is a good enough reason to take along an umbrella. Then again, it might not rain at all, given even a 70 percent chance.

Generally though, the forecasters' track record is pretty good, running at better than 90 percent accuracy for 24-hour predictions. With each added day into the future, the accuracy drops another 10 to 15 percent, until on the fourth or fifth day, the forecast becomes nothing more than an educated guess.

Nevertheless, today's 5-day forecasts have the same accuracy of 2-day predictions 15 years ago.

The primary responsibility of the meteorologist is giving notice of life-threatening weather phenomena, such as hurricanes, tornadoes, thunderstorms, blizzards, and floods. He must know in what area a hurricane is likely to make landfall so that people can be evacuated to safety. He must keep a wary eye out for an unusual squall line development, which might have the potential for tornadoes. Even then, the best he can hope for is 20 minutes warning before a tornado touches down. Blizzards have the potential of shutting down an entire city or stranding a rancher's herd. With enough warning, people can take the needed precautions, which might spell the difference between life or death. A variety of meteorological and hydrological conditions can be responsible for floods. In the spring, rains might contribute to meltwater from heavy accumulations of snow, causing rivers to overflow their banks. The meteorologist must know how much moisture is already in the ground and how much will end up as runoff, which already swollen rivers are incapable of handling.

THE FORECAST SYSTEM

There are over 320 National Weather Service (NWS) facilities operated by the National Oceanic and Atmospheric Administration (NOAA) in the 50 states and elsewhere, employing some 5000 workers. Practically every state capital or major city has a forecast office. Large states like Texas, California, and Alaska might have two or three, while some smaller states might come under the jurisdiction of a single office. Domestic and overseas operating locations are linked by an extensive international communications system.

In a single year, over 20 million weather observations are processed by the NWS from all over the world, and approximately 2 million forecasts and warnings are issued. The forecasts include zone (several counties), local, agricultural, forest-fire weather, and marine. Also, a sizable effort of the NWS goes toward support of the aviation industry. In addition, the NWS operates River Forecast Centers to provide flood warnings and special flow forecasts, which are used by irrigation, navigation, recreation, and hydroelectric generation interests.

Meteorological data are collected from on the land, on the sea, and in the upper atmosphere by people from many countries. In the course of a typical day, the National Meteorological Center (NMC), the nerve center of the NWS located in Camp Springs, Maryland, receives approximately 50,000 surface reports from land, 3000 reports from ships, 4000 upper air observations, and 3000-4000 reports from aircraft. Additionally, satellite information— including cloud photographs, atmospheric temperature soundings, and sea-surface temperatures—is sent to many receiving stations on the ground. Ocean buoys provide additional information on sea temperatures, ocean currents, and air-sea interactions.

The collected data are sent by various communications methods to various NWS offices, where the data are used to prepare meteorological prod-

FIG. A-1. The National Weather Service provides "weather radar" services to local television stations.

ucts for the public and other users. The NOAA weather wire service and other localized circuits provide direct service to many radio and television stations, which provide a direct role of linking the NWS to the public (FIG. A-1). NOAA weather radio, AT&T weather-by-phone, and cable television weather channels also help provide weather information to a large number of people.

NATIONAL METEOROLOGICAL CENTER

The National Meteorological Center provides weather analysis and forecast guidance for use by field offices. It also provides a number of meteorological products, such as wind forecasts for domestic and international aviation, precipitation forecasts for hydrologic and public services, and ocean analysis and forecasts for mariners. These products cover the entire globe, but most cover the Northern Hemisphere.

The World Meteorological Organization (WMO) has designated the National Meteorological Center as the analysis and forecast arm of the World Meteorological Center, with offices located in Washington, Moscow, and Melbourne. The National Meteorological Center is also a World Area Forecast Center under the International Civil Aviation Organization (ICAO), along with Bracknell, England. The global responsibilities span meteorologic, oceanographic, and hydrologic activities, as well as international aviation in a cooperative effort known as the World Weather Watch.

In order to carry out these added responsibilities, all of the National Meteorological Center's divisions have expanded their services and products to cover the entire globe. The five divisions are as follows: The Meteorological Operations Division is primarily responsible for the preparation of forecast guidance products that are based on the interpretation of numerical weather forecasts. The guidance includes forecasts in the short range (12-72 hours) and medium range (3-10 days), temperature and precipitation forecasts in the 3- to 5-day range, and predicted anomalies of temperature and precipitation in the 6- to 10-day range. This division also serves as a Regional Area Forecast Center for commercial aviation over portions of the North Atlantic and Pacific oceans and much of the Southern Hemisphere. In addition, the Division provides detailed quantitative precipitation forecasts to the field offices in support of their heavy snow and flash-flood watch/warning responsibilities.

The Automation Division operates the communications computers and their interface with equipment operated by the NWS Communications Division. The Division manages the operational data, including that produced by the National Meteorological Center's atmospheric models. Graphical and alphanumerical analysis and forecast products are created from the models and distributed to users around the world. The division also investigates various computer programs and tests various techniques for automating the center's operations, including the development of automated graphics. These programs and techniques might or might not be initiated by the Automation Division; in any event, they receive final, preimplementation testing there. New operational computer programs and techniques also are implemented by this division.

The Development Division conducts research and development (R&D) in the techniques of numerical weather prediction. This R&D includes the initiation of atmospheric models, analysis and prediction by numerical methods, and four-dimensional data assimilation. The division adapts the results of its R&D in numerical weather prediction to the products of the National Meteorological Center. In addition, the division conducts a program of R&D in numerical oceanography and the development of various operational marine products.

The Climate Analysis Center prepares monthly and seasonal (90-day) outlooks, collects and analyzes data to depict current anomalies of climate, researches and develops predictive techniques to improve and extend the present outlooks, performs diagnostic studies of large-scale climate anomalies, and conducts a program of stratospheric research.

The Computer Operations Division operates the National Meteorological Center's large-scale computers. The division executes subroutines that analyze the data, runs the climate models, and produces the end products. Also, this division provides centralized computer support to other components of the NWS and to the National Ocean Service (NOS) and the National Environmental Satellite, Data, and Information Service (NESDIS), located in Boulder, Colorado.

The center's centralized preparation of data analysis, forecasts, and outlooks is designed to eliminate meteorological analysis in the field forecast offices, supplement the oceanographic and hydrologic activities of many of those offices, and assist those responsible for coping with climate-sensitive problems. The center, through its use of a large computer facility and together with numerical forecasting techniques, provides NWS, other governmental agencies, private industry, and foreign users with guidance forecasts out to ten days. When necessary, the center uses its dynamical hurricane computer model to provide guidance in tracking the eyes of hurricanes up to 72 hours or in forecasting the movement of large storms that are causing significant precipitation events. These data are processed, cataloged, and distributed widely to field offices, other governmental agencies, private subscribers, and overseas users via automatic and conventional communications systems.

SEVERE STORMS

NOAA also operates the National Severe Storms Forecast Center in Kansas City, Missouri. It is responsible for preparing and releasing messages of expected severe local storms, including tornadoes. These messages, called tornado or severe thunderstorm watches, include information for public use and aviation services. Meteorologists maintain a continuous watch of weather developments.

Watches are issued when needed, rather than on a scheduled basis. Warnings of tornadoes and thunderstorms are issued by local offices. All counties are assigned to specific field offices, depending on station staffing, coverage, and availability of methods of communicating with the public and public safety officials.

The National Aviation Weather Advisory Unit is also a part of the National Severe Storms Forecast Center. Its function is to provide aviation area, route, and terminal weather information (FIG. A-2) for safe and efficient flight operations within the United States. It also provides service for flights from the United States to Canada, and for most flights to Mexico and short-range Caribbean flights.

The responsibility for forecasting the path and intensity of hurricanes, other tropical disturbances, and associated sea conditions is divided among three hurricane forecast centers. These are the National Hurricane Center (NHC) in Miami, Florida, the Eastern Pacific Hurricane Center (EPHC) in San Francisco, California, and the Central Pacific Hurri-

FIG. A-2. A cloud ceiling recorder used at airports.

cane Center (CPHC) in Honolulu, Hawaii. A portion of the National Hurricane Center's responsibility for public warnings rests with the Hurricane Warning Office at San Juan, Puerto Rico.

When necessary or when requested by one of these centers, the National Meteorological Center provides forecast guidance on the track and location of the eye of the hurricane, as predicted by its dynamical hurricane model. Of the three centers, only Miami has a special hurricane forecasting staff. It bases its predictions, advisories, and warnings on subjective and objective methods, while the R&D staff focuses its efforts on objective methods alone. The hurricane-forecasting functions at the other two hurricane centers are integrated with the regular forecasting functions of the Weather Service Forecast Offices (WSFO) at their respective locations.

The Public Weather Service provides the general public with current weather information, warnings, and forecasts, primarily through the news media. These products also serve as the starting point for most interpretive and applied forecast services, including weather services provided by industrial and consulting meteorologists. For long-range weather-planning needs, local climatological information is available at each public service office.

Approximately 300 offices cooperate directly or indirectly in serving the public. The principal public forecast products are state, extended, zone, and local forecasts. The objective of the Weather Service Forecast Office is to furnish the public with general weather conditions expected for about 48 hours over its area of responsibility, and also give extended forecasts over the area up to 5 days. State forecasts are prepared every 12 hours and are given wide distribution to the various forecast offices. An extended forecast is prepared once daily for the same area, and covers expected weather for those areas up to 5 days.

STORM WARNING

Tornadoes, floods, hurricanes, and other natural disasters continue to take an inordinate number of lives and cause thousands of injuries every year, despite advances in technology and skill in forecast-

ing and warning. Cost to federal, state, and local governments are over $3.5 billion per year. The nation's natural disaster warning system is a cooperative effort on the part of the NWS and the Federal Emergency Management Agency (FEMA), state and local emergency service agencies, and the news media. The efficiency and success of this cooperative warning system requires close coordination and advance planning among these organizations. During the widespread tornado outbreaks of 1974 and 1984, NWS warnings, the relay of warnings by the news media, and the protective actions taken by community officials and agencies were credited with saving thousands of lives.

Between 1970 and 1980, there has been a 15 percent increase in population along the Atlantic and Gulf coastal areas. These coastal populations have witnessed many near misses and fringe effects of hurricanes. Yet more than 40 million people along the hurricane-vulnerable coasts have never experienced the devastation of a major hurricane. There is a need to provide education, improve dissemination of warnings, and help communities develop or update hurricane preparedness plans.

Floods and flash floods are more widespread than any other natural hazard and become the nation's number one stormy weather killer. Deaths from flash floods are now approaching 200 each year, compared to an average of less than 70 per year during the preceding 30-year period. Damages from flash floods are now nearly 10 times what they were in the 1940s. Still, urbanization of the nation's floodplains continues. Almost 85 percent of all federal expenditures for disaster relief are flood related. Flood and flash-flood warning systems require preparedness plans and services for specific flood-prone areas if warnings are to be effective and lives saved.

MILITARY WEATHER

In addition to using the public agencies, the branches of the armed forces also operate their own weather services (FIG. A-3). The weather is of vital importance to military operations and can make the difference between victory or defeat in battle. Often the military was required to fight the weather

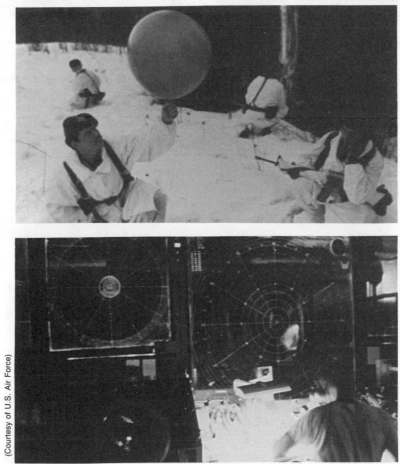

FIG. A-3. Weather operations of the U.S. military.

as well as the enemy. Even when this was done, however, it was seldom through ignorance of the adverse weather, and its effects were minimized in every possible way.

Many modern forecasting tools and methods came out of military research during World War II. Today, the military has a most sophisticated weather-watch program that includes an impressive array of weather, communication, and navigation satellites. The military also maintains weather ships and planes, and manned or automated weather stations in isolated outposts. Long-range weather forecasts are also extremely important for military strategy and war-planning purposes. Many studies are carried out by military weather services, which are closely geared to a specific military operation such as the bombing of an enemy target.

The applied studies in the field of military meteorology are carried out by the two primary military weather services—those of the Air Force and the Navy—and by smaller groups of weather specialists attached to research and development laboratories, to organizations concerned with operations analysis, to major commands of the Army, Navy, and Air Force, and to the General Staff.

The USAF Air Weather Service has weather forecasters stationed at all air bases, both at home and abroad, to provide the weather predictions necessary to the operation of military aircraft and of major Army and Air Force installations. The forecasting services of the Navy are centered at its Fleet Weather Centers at Norfolk, Virginia; Boston, Massachusetts; San Diego, California; Honolulu, Hawaii; Guam; and other localities around the world. The Navy also maintains forecast staffs aboard the flagships of all major fleet units.

In the event of war, the activities of these groups would be greatly intensified, while at the same time there would be an expansion of military forecasting activities throughout the world. The nucleus for such an expansion would be the forecasting systems and personnel that are now meeting peacetime requirements of the armed forces.

PRIVATE FORECASTERS

The National Weather Service is limited in its ability to provide industry and other private concerns with specialized weather forecasts tailored to individual needs. Therefore, many industries that depend upon the weather for their livelihood and with millions of dollars at stake hire their own meteorologist or use the services of a meteorological consultant. Most major cities across the country have radio and television stations that employ the services of a nongovernmental weather forecaster.

The private meteorologists all subscribe to the same meteorological data provided by the National Weather Service. The major differences are the interpretation of the data for specific areas, such as ski resorts or orange groves. Many large airlines maintain their own organizations to collect, distribute, and interpret information about the weather. The services of a skilled company or consulting meteorologist could maximize benefits when the weather is favorable and minimize losses when it is unfavorable.

Glossary

absorption—The process by which radiant energy incident on any substance is retained and converted into heat or other forms of energy.

adiabatic—Of or referring to changes in temperature that occur within air masses as a result of pressure changes, which cause them to expand or contract without gain or loss of heat.

advection—The horizontal movement of air, moisture, or heat.

aerosol—A mass made of solid or liquid particles dispersed in air.

air mass—An extensive body of air whose horizontal distribution of temperature and moisture is nearly uniform.

airstream—A substantial body of air with the same characteristics flowing with the general circulation.

albedo—The amount of sunlight reflected from an object.

anemometer—An instrument for determining the speed of the wind.

angular momentum—The product of angular velocity and mass, of an object or orbiting body.

anticyclone—The circulation of air around a central area of high pressure, which is usually associated with settled weather; pressure rises steadily when an anticyclone is developing and falls when it is declining.

aphelion—The point at which the orbit of a planet is at its farthest point from the sun.

asthenosphere—A layer of the upper mantle, roughly between 50 and 200 miles below the surface. It is more plastic than the rock above and below and might be in convective motion.

atmospheric pressure—The weight per unit area of the total mass of air above a given point; also called *barometric pressure.*

bar—The unit of atmospheric pressure at sea level that is equal to the pressure of 29.530 inches (750.062 millimeters) of mercury.

barometer—An instrument for measuring atmospheric pressure.

basalt—A volcanic rock that is dark in color and usually quite fluid in the molten state.

Beaufort Scale—A wind scale devised by Admiral Beaufort in 1806 to denote the strength of wind from 0 to 12, hurricane force; since revised to 0 to 17.

blackbody—An ideal black surface completely absorbing energy of any wavelength impinging upon it and reflecting no energy.

blackbody radiation—The electromagnetic radiation emitted by a heated blackbody; the theoretical maximum amount of radiant energy at all wavelengths that can be emitted by a body at a given temperature.

blocking high—Any high-pressure center that remains stationary, effectively blocking the usual eastward progression of weather systems in the middle latitudes for several days.

Buys Ballot's Law—A rule stating that if an observer stands with his back to the wind in the Northern Hemisphere, atmospheric pressure will be lower to his left than his right. The effect is opposite in the Southern Hemisphere.

Cenozoic era—An age known as recent life, spanning from 65 million years ago to the present.

center of mass—The center of gravity; the center of rotation in an orbiting system of objects.

chinook—A wind descending a mountain side and warming in the process of dynamic compression. It is a characteristic of the slopes of the Rocky Mountains.

circulation—The flow pattern of moving air.

circum-Pacific belt—Active seismic regions on the rim of the Pacific plate, coinciding with the ring of fire.

coalescence—The merging of two or more colliding water droplets into a single, larger drop.

coastal storm—A cyclonic, low-pressure system moving along a coastal plain or just offshore. It causes north to northeast winds over the land; along the Atlantic seaboard it is called a northeaster.

cold front—The interface or transition zone between advancing cold air and retreating warm air.

condensation—The process whereby a substance changes from the vapor phase to the liquid or solid phase; the opposite of evaporation.

conduction—The transmission of heat by direct contact through a material substance, as distinguished from convection, advection, and radiation.

continent—A slab of light, granitic rock that floats on denser rocks of the upper mantle.

convection—A circular, vertical flow of a fluid medium caused by heating from below. As materials are heated, they become less dense and rise while cooler, heavier materials sink.

convergence—A distribution of wind movement that results in a net inflow of air into an area, such as a low-pressure area.

core—The central part of the Earth with a radius of 2300 miles; consisting of a crystalline inner core and molten outer core composed of iron and nickel.

Coriolis effect—The apparent force that deflects the wind or a moving object, causing it to curve in relation to the rotating Earth.

cosmic rays—High energy charged particles that enter the Earth's atmosphere from outer space.

crust—The outer layers of the Earth's rocks.

cut-off low—A low-pressure center that has been displaced out of the basic westerly current so that it lies on the current's equatorial side.

cyclone—The circulation of air around a central area of low pressure that is usually associated with unsettled weather. In tropical latitudes, it can refer to an intense storm that does not attain full hurricane status.

deepening—The decrease of pressure at the center of a storm.

degree-days—A unit of heat measurement equal to a 1-degree per day difference from a standard temperature. The premise is that artificial heating or cooling is not needed at a mean temperature of 65 degrees Fahrenheit; used for estimating relative energy requirements. For example, 30 degrees above or below requires 30 cooling or heating degree days respectively.

density—The amount of any quantity per unit volume.

depression—An area of low pressure and often unsettled weather.

dew—Liquid water droplets caused by condensation of water vapor from the air as a result of radiation cooling.

dew point—The temperature to which air, at a constant pressure and moisture content, must be cooled for saturation to occur.

diffusion—The exchange of fluid substance and its properties between different regions in the fluid, as a result of small, almost random motions of the fluid.

discontinuity—The rapid variation of the gradient of the rate of pressure or temperature change at a front.

disturbance—An area of low pressure attended by storm conditions.

divergence—A distribution of wind movement that results in a net outflow of air from an area such as a high-pressure system.

drought—A period of abnormally dry weather sufficiently prolonged for the lack of water to cause serious deleterious effects on agricultural and other biological activities.

dry adiabatic lapse rate—The rate at which dry air cools with height when it is forced to rise into regions of lower pressure: 5.4 degrees Fahrenheit per 1000 feet (1 degree Celsius per 100 meters). Dry, sinking air warms at the same rate.

earthquake—The sudden breaking of Earth's rocks.

ecliptic—Of or relating to the plane in which the Earth's orbit traces an elliptical path around the Sun.

electromagnetic radiation—The energy from the Sun that travels through the vacuum of space to reach the Earth as electromagnetic waves.

electron—A negative particle of small mass orbiting the nucleus and equal in number to the proton.

element—A material consisting of only one type of atom.

equinoctial storm—A violent wind storm occurring at the time of year when the Sun crosses the equator.

equinox—Either of the two points of intersection of the Sun's path and the plane of the Earth's equator.

evaporation—The transformation of a liquid into a gas.

evolution—The tendency of physical and biological factors to change with time.

exosphere—The outermost portion of the atmosphere, whose lower boundary is at a height of 300 miles.

extratropical cyclone—An atmospheric disturbance that either originated outside the tropics or, after leaving the tropics, loses the characteristics of a tropical storm.

eye—The central portion of a tropical hurricane or typhoon. It is a roughly circular area of relatively light winds and fair weather.

filling—The increase of pressure at the center of a storm system.

foehn—A warm, dry wind on the lee side of a mountain range.

fossil—Any remains, impression, or trace in rock of a plant or animal of a previous geologic age.

frequency—The rate at which crests of any wave pass a given point.

front—The transition zone between two air masses of differing properties.

frost—Ice crystals formed on grass and other objects by the sublimation of water vapor from the air at below-freezing temperature.

geostationary satellite—A satellite that orbits above a particular point on the Earth's surface at the equator. The satellites are stationed at a height of 22,300 miles, at which altitude they orbit at the same angular speed as the Earth.

geostrophic wind—The horizontal wind resulting when only atmospheric pressure differences and the deflecting Coriolis effect are taken into account.

glaze—A sheath of transparent ice resulting from an ice storm.

Gondwanaland—A southern supercontinent of Paleozoic time, consisting of Africa, South America, India, Australia, and Antarctica. It broke up into present continents during the Mesozoic era.

granite—A coarse-grained, silica-rich rock consisting primarily of quartz and feldspar. It is the principal constituent of the continents and is believed to be derived from a molten state beneath the Earth's surface.

greenhouse effect—The global heating effect resulting from the atmosphere being more transparent to incoming, short-wave solar radiation than to outgoing, long-wave radiation.

groundwater—The water derived from the atmosphere that percolates and circulates below the surface of the Earth.

Hadley cell—Atmospheric circulation that distributes air from the tropics to the poles. It is sustained by large-scale convection currents in which hot air is replaced by cooler air.

helium—The second lightest and second most abundant element in the universe, composed of two protons and two neutrons.

high—An area of high atmospheric pressure within a closed circulation system; an anticyclone.

hydrocarbon—A molecule consisting of carbon chains with attached hydrogen atoms.

hydrogen—The lightest and most abundant element in the universe, composed of one proton and one electron.

hygrometer—An instrument for measuring the humidity of the air.

igneous rock—Rock that has solidified from a molten state.

inertia—Inherent resistance to applied force.

infrared—Of or referring to invisible light with a wavelength between red light and radio waves.

insolation—Solar radiation impinging on the Earth. The word is a contraction of "incoming solar radiation."

Intertropical Convergence Zone—The axis along which the northeast trade winds of the Northern Hemisphere meet the southeast trade winds of the Southern Hemisphere.

inversion—An increase of temperature with altitude through a layer of air.

ionization—The process whereby electrons are torn off previously neutral atoms.

ionosphere—The atmospheric shell, characterized by high ion density and extending from about 40 miles to very high regions of the atmosphere.

iridium—A rare isotope of platinum; relatively abundant on meteorites.

isobar—A line joining places of equal pressure on a weather map.

jet stream—Relatively strong winds concentrated within a narrow belt that is usually found in the tropopause.

Kelvin—A temperature scale, similar to the centigrade scale, having its zero point at absolute zero, or -273 degrees centigrade.

kinetic energy—The energy that a moving body possesses as a consequence of its motion.

knot—One nautical mile per hour, the unit of speed in the nautical system. A nautical mile is equivalent to $\frac{1}{60}$ of 1 degree or 1 minute of arc on the Earth's surface, or 1.15 miles (1.852 kilometers).

landslide—Rapid downhill movement of earth materials; often triggered by earthquakes.

lapse rate—The decrease of an atmospheric variable (usually temperature) with height.

latent heat—Heat absorbed when a solid changes to a liquid or a liquid to a gas with no change in temperature; heat released in the reverse transformations.

Laurasia—The northern supercontinent of the Paleozoic era, consisting of North America, Europe, and Asia.

lava—Molten magma after it has flowed out onto the surface.

light-year—The distance that electromagnetic radiation, principally light waves, can travel in a vacuum in one year; approximately 6 trillion miles.

limestone—A sedimentary rock composed of calcium carbonate that is secreted from seawater by invertebrates and whose skeletons comprise the bulk of deposits.

lithosphere—A rigid outer layer of the mantle, typically about 60 miles thick. It is overridden by the continental and oceanic crusts and is divided into segments, called *plates*.

low—An area of low atmospheric pressure; a cyclone or a depression.

magma—A molten rock material generated within the Earth that is the constituent of igneous rocks, including volcanic eruptions.

magnetic field reversal—A reversal of the polarity of the Earth's magnetic poles.

magnetometer—A device used to measure the intensity and direction of the magnetic field.

magnetosphere—The region of the Earth's upper atmosphere in which the Earth's magnetic field controls the motion of ionized particles.

mantle—The part of the Earth below the crust and above the core, composed of dense iron-magnesium rich rocks.

mean temperature—The average of any series of temperatures observed over a period of time.

mesosphere—A region of the Earth's atmosphere between the stratosphere and thermosphere, extending 24 to 48 miles above the Earth's surface. Also, the rigid part of the Earth's mantle below the asthenosphere and above the core.

Mesozoic era—Literally the period of middle life; the period between 230 and 65 million years ago.

metamorphic rock—A rock crystallized from previous igneous, metamorphic, or sedimentary rocks created under conditions of intense temperatures and pressures without melting.

meteorite—A metallic or stony body from space that enters the Earth's atmosphere and impacts on the Earth's surface.

micron—A unit of measurement equivalent to $1/1000$ millimeter.

midocean ridge—A submarine ridge along a divergent plate boundary where a new ocean floor is created by the upwelling of mantle material.

millibar—A unit of pressure equivalent to $1/1000$ bar.

monsoon—A seasonal wind accompanying temperature changes over land and water.

moraine—A ridge of erosional debris deposited by the melting margin of a glacier.

nautical mile—A unit of distance in the nautical system equivalent to 1 minute of arc on the earth's surface or 1.15 miles (1.852 kilometers).

nebula—An extended astronomical object with a cloudlike appearance. Some nebulae are galaxies; others are clouds of dust and gas within our Galaxy.

neutrino—A small electrically neutral particle having weak nuclear and gravitational interactions.

neutron—A particle with no electrical charge and roughly the same weight as the positively charged proton, both of which are found in the nucleus of an atom.

numerical forecasting—Forecasting the behavior of the atmosphere using mathematical models, usually on a computer.

occlusion—The boundary formed when warm air behind a warm front is lifted above the surface by an overtaking cold front.

orogeny—An episode of mountain building.

overrunning—The ascent of warm air over relatively cool air. It usually occurs in advance of a warm front.

ozone—A molecule consisting of three atoms of oxygen, which exists in the upper atmosphere above the tropopause and filters out ultraviolet radiation from the Sun.

paleomagnetism—The study of the Earth's magnetic field, including the position and polarity of the poles in the past.

paleontology—The study of ancient life forms, based on the fossil record of plants and animals.

Paleozoic period—The period of ancient life, between 570 and 230 million years ago.

Pangaea—An ancient supercontinent that included all the landmass of the earth.

Panthalassa—The great world ocean that surrounded Pangaea.

perihelion—The point at which the orbit of a planet is at its nearest to the sun.

phenology—The study of the times of recurring natural phenomena in relation to climatic conditions.

photon—A packet of electromagnetic energy, generally viewed as a particle.

photosynthesis—The process by which plants create carbohydrates from carbon dioxide, water, and sunlight.

placer—A deposit of rocks left behind from a melting glacier. Any ore deposit that is enriched by stream action.

plate tectonics—A theory stating that the major features of the Earth's surface are a result of the interaction of lithospheric plates.

polar air—An air mass conditioned over the tundra or snow-covered terrain of high latitudes.

polar front—A semipermanent discontinuity separating cold polar easterly winds and relatively warm westerly winds of the middle latitudes.

polar orbiting satellite—A satellite that circles the Earth over the poles and at right angles to the equator. The Earth rotates beneath the satellite during its orbit, allowing the satellite full coverage of the Earth for meteorological purposes.

precession—The slow change in direction of the Earth's axis of rotation resulting from gravitational action of the Moon on the Earth.

precipitation—Products of condensation that fall from clouds as rain, snow, hail, or drizzle.

prefrontal squall line—An unstable line of turbulence preceding a cold front at some distance, often accompanied by showers or thunderstorms.

proton—A particle with a positive charge in the nucleus of an atom.

radiation—1. The process by which energy from the Sun is propagated through a vacuum of space as electromagnetic waves. 2. A method, along with conduction and convection, of transporting heat.

radioactivity—An atomic reaction releasing detectable radioactive particles.

radiometric dating—The determination of how long an object has existed by chemical analysis of stable versus unstable radioactive elements.

radiosonde—A balloon-borne instrument that simultaneously measures and transmits meteorological data.

red shift—The shift of light toward the lower end of the spectrum, indicating that distant galaxies are receding.

relative humidity—The ratio of the amount of moisture in the air to the amount that the air would hold at the same temperature and pressure if it were saturated; usually expressed as a percentage.

ridge—An elongated area of relatively high pressure extending from the center of a high-pressure region.

St. Elmo's fire—Visible discharges of static electricity in the air, specifically in the masts and rigging of a ship during storms.

sandstone—A sedimentary rock consisting of cemented sand grains.

saturated adiabatic lapse rate—The rate at which a parcel of saturated air decreases in temperature as it rises vertically and cloud droplets form.

saturated air—Air that contains the maximum amount of water vapor it can hold at a given pressure and temperature. It has a relative humidity of 100 percent.

sea-floor spreading—The theory that the ocean floor is created by the separation of lithospheric plates along the midocean ridges, with new oceanic crust formed from mantle material that rises from the mantle to fill the rift.

secondary depression—An area of low pressure that forms in a trough to the south or east of the primary storm center.

seismic sea wave—An ocean wave related to an undersea earthquake.

semipermanent high or low—One of the relatively stationary and stable pressure and wind systems; for example, the Icelandic Low, or the Bermuda High.

shield—Areas of the exposed Precambrian nucleus of a continent.

solar flare—A short-lived bright event on the Sun's surface that causes greater ionization of the Earth's upper atmosphere from an increase in ultraviolet light.

solar wind—An outflow of particles from the Sun that represents the expansion of the corona.

solstice—The occurrence twice yearly when the apparent distance of the Sun from the equator is at its greatest. During summer solstice (June 22), the Sun appears to be at its most northerly position. The Sun is then directly overhead at a latitude of 23.5 degrees north. During winter solstice (December 22), the Sun appears to be at its most southerly position. The Sun is then directly overhead at a latitude of 23.5 degrees south.

source region—An area of nearly uniform surface characteristics over which large bodies of air stagnate and acquire a more or less equal horizontal distribution of temperature and moisture.

squall line—A well-marked line of instability ahead of a cold front accompanied by strong gusty winds, turbulence, and often heavy showers.

steering—The process whereby the direction of movement of surface pressure systems is influenced by the circulation aloft.

storm surge—An abnormal rise of the water level along a shore as a result of wind flow in a storm.

stratosphere—An upper layer of the atmosphere above the troposphere, between 12 to 30 miles above the Earth's surface. The air in this layer is usually stable, and the temperature increases with height.

subduction zone—An area where the oceanic plate dives below a continental plate into the asthenosphere. Ocean trenches are the surface expression of a subduction zone.

sublimation—A process by which a gas is changed into a solid or a solid into a gas without going through the liquid state.

subsidence—The descending motion aloft of a body of air, usually within an anticyclone. It causes a spreading out and warming of the lower layers of the atmosphere.

sunspot—A region on the Sun's surface that is cooler than surrounding regions and affects radio transmissions on Earth.

supercooling—The cooling of a liquid below its freezing point without it becoming a solid.

supernova—An enormous stellar explosion in which all but the inner core of a star is blown off into interstellar space, producing as much energy in a few days as the Sun does in a billion years.

supersaturation—The condition of air having a relative humidity greater than 100 percent.

synod—The alignment of the Sun, planets, and their accompanying moons.

synoptic weather mapping—The analysis of weather observations at many points over a large geographical area.

tectonic activity—The formation of the Earth's crust by large-scale earth movements throughout geologic time.

tendency—The local rate of change of barometric pressure.

tephra—All clastic material, from dust particles to large chunks, expelled from volcanoes during eruptions.

Tethys Sea—The hypothetical midlatitude area of the oceans separating the northern and southern continents of Gondwanaland and Laurasia during the Palezoic era.

thermalsphere—The outermost layer of the atmosphere in which the temperature increases regularly with height.

tide—A bulge in the ocean produced by the Moon's gravitational forces on the Earth's oceans. The rotation of the Earth beneath this bulge causes the rising and lowering of the sea level.

tropical air—An air mass conditioned over the warm surfaces of tropical seas or land.

tropical cyclone—A low-pressure area originating in the tropics having a warm central core and often developing an eye.

troposphere—The lowest 6 to 12 miles of the Earth's atmosphere, characterized by decreasing temperature with height.

trough—An elongated area of low atmospheric pressure, usually extending from the center of a low-pressure system.

typhoon—Severe tropical storms in the Western Pacific similar in structure to a hurricane.

ultraviolet—Of or referring to the invisible light with a wavelength shorter than visible light and longer than X-rays.

uniformitarianism—The belief that the slow processes that shape the Earth's surface have acted essentially unchanged throughout geologic time.

upper air—The atmosphere above the lowest 3280 feet (1000 meters) within which surface friction has an influence. No distinct lower limit is set, but the term is normally applied at pressures of around 850 millibars.

Van Allen belts—Region of high-energy particles trapped by the Earth's magnetic field.

virga—Wisps or streaks of water or ice particles that fall from clouds and evaporate before reaching the ground.

viscosity—The resistance of a liquid to flow.

volcano—A fissure or vent in the crust through which molten rock rises to the surface to form a mountain.

warm front—The boundary of an advancing current of relatively warm air that is displacing a retreating colder air mass.

warm sector—Warm air between a retreating warm front and an approaching cold front.

waterspout—A funnel-shaped, tornadolike cloud complex that originates over water.

water vapor—Atmospheric moisture in the invisible gaseous phase.

wet-bulb temperature—The temperature indicated by a ventilated thermometer by evaporating water on the bulb.

whirlwind—A rapidly whirling, small-scale vortex of air often seen on hot, still days.

wind chill factor—A number derived from the calculation of heat loss from exposed human skin as a result of the combination of temperatures and wind speeds.

Bibliography

THE SOLAR CONNECTION

Boss, Alan P. "Collapse and Formation of Stars." *Scientific American* Vol. 252 (January 1985): 40-45.

Burns, Jack O. "Very Large Structures in the Universe." *Scientific American* Vol. 255, No. 1 (July 1986): 38-47.

Christensen-Dalsgaard, Jorgen, et al. "Seismology of the Sun." *Science* Vol. 229 (September 6, 1985): 923-931.

Herbst, William and George E. Assousa. "Supernovas and Star Formation." *Scientific American* Vol. 241 (August 1979): 138-144.

Hughes, David W. "Comets colliding with the Sun." *Nature* Vol. 308. (March 1, 1984): 16-17.

Kerr, Richard A. "Where Was the Moon Eons Ago?" *Science* Vol. 221 (September 16, 1983): 1166.

Lewis, John S. "The Chemistry of the Solar System." *Scientific American* Vol. 230 (March 1974).

Leibacher, John W., et al. "Helioseismology." *Scientific American* Vol. 253 (September 1985): 48-57.

Maddox, John. "Alternatives to the Big Bang." *Nature* Vol. 308 (April 5, 1984): 491.

____. "Origin of Solar System Redefined." *Nature* Vol. 308 (March 15, 1984): 223.

"Making the Moon from a Big Splash," *Science* Vol. 226 (November, 30 1984): 226.

Schramm, David N. and Robert N. Clayton. "Did a Supernova Trigger the Formation of the Solar System?" *Scientific American* Vol. 239 (October 1978): 124-139.

Waldrop, Mitchell M. "Why do Galaxies Exist?" *Science* Vol. 228 (May 24, 1985): 978-980.

____. "Origin of the Moon." *Science* Vol. 216 (May 7, 1982).

Wetherill, George W. "The Formation of the Earth from Planetesimals." *Scientific American* Vol. 224 (January 1981): 163-174.

Weymann, Ray J. "Stellar Winds." *Scientific American* Vol. 239 (August 1978): 44-53.

WHAT A GAS

Allen, Oliver, E. *Atmosphere*. Alexandria, Va: Time-Life Books, 1983.

Cloud, Preston. "The Biosphere." *Scientific American* Vol. 249 (September 1983): 176-189.

Ford, Trevor D. "Life in the Precambrian." *Nature* Vol. 285 (May 22, 1980): 193-194.

Ingersoll, Andrew P. "The Atmosphere." *Scientific American* Vol. 249 (September 1983): 162-174.

Lewin, Roger. "Paleoclimatic Magic Numbers Game." *Science* Vol. 226 (October 12, 1984): 154-156.

Pimentel Report. "Ozone in the stratosphere." *Environmental Science and Technology* Vol. 20 (April 1986): 328-329.

Sanders, T. I. *Weather; A User's Guide to the Atmosphere*. Icarus, 1985.

Sootin, Harry. *The Discovery of Air*. Norton, 1967.

STORMY WEATHER

Brodt, Jan. "The Tri-State Tornado." *Weatherwise* (April 1986): 91-94.

Catton, Bruce. "The Great Lakes Hurricane." *Weatherwise* (October 1985): 248-253.

Galway, Joseph G. "Ten Famous Tornado Outbreaks." *Weatherwise* (June 1981): 100-109.

Hughes, Patrick. "The Blizzard of '88." *Weatherwise* (December 1981): 250-256.

Lelyveld, Joseph. "Ruin and Renewal in Bengal." *The New York Times Magazine* (June 23, 1985): 26-29.

Lyer, Pico. "Trail of Tears and Anguish." *Time* (June 10, 1985): 42-45.

Mogil, Michael M. "The Great Freeze of '83." *Weatherwise* (December 1984): 304-308.

Sanders, T.I. *The Weather is Front Page News*. Icarus, 1983.

Stommel, Henry and Elizabeth Stommel. "The Year without a Summer." *Scientific American* Vol. 240 (June 1979): 176-186.

WEATHER FOLKLORE

Derr, John S. "Luminous phenomena and their relationship to rock fracture." *Nature* Vol. 321 (May 29, 1986): 470-471.

Hanson, Jeanne K. "Are You a Weather Prophet?" *Readers Digest* (June 1983): 111-113.

Lee, Albert. *Weather Wisdom*. New York: Doubleday, 1976.

Lynch, David K. "Atmospheric Halos." *Scientific American* Vol. 238 (April 1978): 144-152.

Maranto, Gina. "Nature's Forecasters." *Discover* (April 1985): 13.

Savage, Joe. "Test Your Weather I.Q." *Organic Gardening* (February 1983): 127-130.

Thompson, Philip D. "Cricket; Natures Thermometer." *Weatherwise* (August 1983): 190-191.

THE FICKLE CLIMATE

Cullen, Christopher. "Was there a Maunder Minimum?" *Nature* Vol. 283 (January 31, 1980): 427-428.

Dansgaard, W., et al. "A New Greenland Deep Ice Core." *Science* Vol. 218 (December 24, 1982): 1273-1277.

Gough, Douglas. "What causes the solar cycle?" *Nature* Vol. 319 (January 23, 1986): 263-264.

_____. "Climate and variability in the solar constant." *Nature* Vol. 288 (December 25, 1980): 639.

Kerr, Richard A. "Milankovitch Climate Cycles: Old and Unsteady." *Science* Vol. 213 (September 4, 1981): 1095-1096.

_____. "Sun, Weather, and Climate: A Connection?" *Science* Vol. 217 (September 23, 1982): 917-919.

Morris, Simon C. "Polar forests of the past." *Nature* Vol. 313 (February 28, 1985): 739.

North, Gerald R. "The climate as natural oscillator." *Nature* Vol. 316 (July 18, 1985): 218.

Prospero, Joseph M. "Records of past continental climates in deep-sea sediments." *Nature* Vol. 315: 279-280.

Schneider, Stephen H. and Randi Lander. *The Coevolution of Climate and Life*. San Francisco: Sierra Club Books, 1984.

Williams, G.E. and C.P. Sonett. "Solar signature in sedimentary cycles from the late Precambrian Elatina Formation, Australia." *Nature* Vol. 318 (December 12, 1985): 523-527.

Williams, Gareth. "Sun-weather effects." *Nature* Vol. 285 (May 8, 1980): 71.

Wilson, Olin C., et al. "The Activity Cycles of

Stars." *Scientific American* Vol. 244 (February 1981): 104-119.

THE GLOBAL GREENHOUSE

Broecker, Wallace S. "Carbon dioxide circulation through ocean and atmosphere." *Nature* Vol. 308 (April 12, 1984): 602.

Collins, Elizabeth. "Upwind versus downwind." *Nature* Vol. 317 (October 3, 1985): 377.

Idso, S.B. "Industrial age leading to the greening of the Earth?" *Nature* Vol. 320 (March 6, 1986): 22.

Likens, Gene E., et al. "Acid Rain." *Scientific American* Vol. 241 (October 1979): 43-51.

Revelle, Roger. "Carbon Dioxide and World Climate." *Scientific American* Vol. 247 (August 1983): 35-43.

Sun, Marjorie. "Possible Acid Rain Woes in the West." *Science* Vol. 228 (April 5, 1985): 34-35.

Tarbuck, Edward J. and Fedrick K. Lutgens. *Earth Earth Science*. Bellevue, Wash: Merril Press, 1982.

Tuck, A.F. "Depletion of Antarctic ozone." *Nature* Vol. 321 (June 19, 1986): 729-730.

Weisburd, S. "Pole's ozone hole: Who NOZE?" *Science News* Vol. 130 (October 25, 1986): 261.

Woodwell, George M., et al. "Contribution to Atmospheric Carbon Dioxide." *Science* Vol. 222 (December 9, 1983): 1081-1085.

Woodwell, George M., "The Carbon Dioxide Question." *Scientific American* Vol. 238 (January 1978): 34-43.

Zwally, Jay, H. "Variability of Arctic Sea Ice and Changes in Carbon Dioxide." *Science* Vol. 220 (June 3, 1983): 1005-1012.

THE WORLD OF VOLCAN

Decker, Robert and Barbara Decker. "The Eruptions of Mount St. Helens." *Scientific American* Vol. 244 (March 1981): 68-80.

Gribbin, John. *Future Weather and the Greenhouse Effect*. New York: Delacorte Press, 1982.

Kerr, Richard A. "Domesday Book of the World's Volcanoes." *Science* Vol. 213 (August 21, 1981): 856-857.

Robock, Alan. "The dust cloud of the century." *Nature* Vol. 301 (February 3, 1982).

Simon, Cheryl. "Red Sky at Night." *Science News* Vol. 122 (August 21, 1982): 120-122.

Stommel, Henry and Elizabeth Stommel. *Volcano Weather*. Camden, ME.: Seven Seas Press, 1983.

Strothers, Richard B. "The Great Tambora Eruption in 1815 and Its Aftermath." *Science* Vol. 224 (June 15, 1984): 1191-1197.

POLAR FLIP-FLOPS

Carrigan, Charles R. and David Gubbins. "The Source of the Earth's Magnetic Field." *Scientific American* Vol. 240 (February 1979): 118-130.

Gribbin, John. *Forecasts, Famines, and Freezes*. New York: Walker, 1976.

Hones, Edward, W., Jr. "The Earth's Magnetotail." *Scientific American* Vol. 254 (March 1986): 40-47.

Jacobs, J.A. *The Earth's Core*. San Diego: Academic Press, 1975.

_____. "What triggers reversals of the Earth's magnetic field?" *Nature* Vol. 309 (May 10, 1984): 115.

Parker, E.N. "Magnetic Fields in the Cosmic." *Scientific American* Vol. 249 (August 1983): 44-54.

Prevot, Michel, et al. "How the geomagnetic field vector reverses polarity." *Nature* Vol. 316 (July 18, 1985): 230-234.

STREAMS IN THE SEA

Barber, Richard T. and Francisco P. Chavez. "Biological Consequences of El Niño." *Science* Vol. 222 (December 16, 1983): 1203-1210.

Broecker, Wallace S. "The Ocean." *Scientific American* Vol. 249 (September 1983): 146-160.

Cane, Mark A. "Oceanographic Events During El Niño." *Science* Vol. 222 (December 16, 1983): 1189-1194.

Holland, H.D., et al. "Evolution of the atmosphere and oceans." *Nature* Vol. 320 (March 6, 1986): 27-33.

Lewis, Brian T.R. "The Process of Formation of Ocean Crust." *Science* Vol. 220 (April 8, 1983): 151-156.

MacIntyre, Ferren. "The Top Millimeter of the Ocean." *Scientific American* Vol. 230 (May 1974): 62-77.

Philander, S.G.H. "El Niño Southern Oscillation phenomena." *Nature* Vol. 302 (March 24, 1983): 295-301.

Ramage, Colin S. "El Niño." *Scientific American* Vol. 254 (June 1983): 77-83.

Rasmusson, Eugene M. and J. Michael Hall. "El Niño; The Great Equatorial Pacific Ocean Warming Event of 1982-1983." *Weatherwise* (August 1983): 167-175.

Rasmusson, Eugene M. and John M. Wallace. "Meteorological Aspects of the El Niño/Southern Oscillation." *Science* Vol. 222 (December 16, 1983): 1195-1202.

Weiner, Jonathan. *Planet Earth*. New York: Bantam Books, 1986.

WEATHER OR NOT

Basu, Janet E. "Jerome Namias; Pioneering the Science of Forecasting." *Weatherwise* (August, 1984): 191-201.

Brownlee, Shannon. "Forecasting: How Exact Is It?" *Discover* (April 1985): 10-16.

Bruno, Mary and Jeff Copeland. "Keeping Up With the Weather." *Newsweek* (September 2, 1985): 70.

Gleick, James. "They're Getting Better About Predicting the Weather." *The New York Times Magazine* (January 27, 1985): 30-40.

Hardy, Ralph, et al. *The Weather Book*. Boston: Little, Brown & Co. 1982.

Huges, Patrick. "Weather Satellites Come of Age." *Weatherwise* (April 1984): 69-75.

Kerr, Richard A. "A Chance to Predict Next Month's Weather?" *Science* Vol. 220 (May 6, 1983): 590-591.

____. "Weather Satellites Coming of Age." *Science* Vol. 229 (July 19, 1985): 255-257.

Smith, W.L., et al. "The Meteorological Satellite: Overview of 25 Years of Operation." *Science* Vol. 231 (January 31, 1986): 455-462.

Wellborn, Stanley N. "High-Tech Tools To Spot Sudden Killer Storms." *U.S. News & World Report* (April 29, 1985): 81.

Williams, Gordon. "The Weather Watchers." *The Atlantic Monthly* (March 1986): 69-73.

MAN-MADE WEATHER

Battan, Louis J. *Weather in Your Life*. New York: W.H. Freeman, 1983.

Calder, Nigel. *The Weather Machine*. New York: Viking Penguin, 1974.

Halacy, David S. *The Weather Changers*. New York: Harper & Row, 1968.

Kerr, Richard A. "Cloud Seeding: One Success in 35 Years." *Science* Vol. 217 (August 6, 1982): 519-521.

____. "The Fine Points of Cloud Seeding." *Science* Vol. 223 (January 13, 1984): 153.

Maddox, John. "Towards understanding snowflakes." *Nature* Vol. 321 (June 12,1986): 645.

"Serendipity." *Weatherwise* (December 1985): 307.

Straten, Florence W. *Weather or Not*. New York: Dodd, Mead & Co., 1966.

Yulsman, Tom and Andrew C. Revkin. "Will We Ever Control the Weather?" *Science Digest* (October 1985): 40-44.

SEVERE STORMS

Clary, Mike. "Thunderstorms." *Weatherwise* (June 1985): 130-151.

"Facing Geologic and Hydrologic Hazards." *U.S. Geological Survey Professional Paper 1240-B*. Washington, D.C.: Government Printing Office, 1981.

Few, Arthur A. "Thunder." *Scientific American* Vol. 233 (July 1975): 80-90.

Idso, Sherwood B. "Dust Storms." *Scientific American* Vol. 235 (October 1976): 108-114.

Maddox, John. "Thunder and electric storms." *Nature* Vol. 311 (October 1987): 507.

McCarthy, John and Robert Serafin. "The Microburst." *Weatherwise* (June 1984): 120-125.

Snow, John T. "The Tornado." *Scientific American* Vol. 250 (April 1984): 86-96.

Witten, John. "Elena; She taunted us, she teased us & then she hit us." *Weatherwise* (October 1985): 259-261.

FUTURE WEATHER

Begley, Sharon and Bill White. "Alaska's Runaway Glacier." *Newsweek* (August 25, 1986): 52-53.

Bowen, D.Q. "Antarctic ice surges and theories of glaciation." *Nature* Vol. 283 (February 14, 1980): 619-620.

Campbell, Philip. "New data upset ice age theories." *Nature* Vol. 307 (February 23, 1984): 688-689.

Covey, Curt. "The Earth's Orbit and the Ice Ages." *Scientific American* Vol. 250 (February 1984): 58-66.

Crane, Robert G. "Remote Sensing and Polar Climate." *Earth and Mineral Sciences* Vol. 55 (Spring 1986): 38-41.

Fodor, R.V. "Explaining the Ice Ages." *Weatherwise* (June 1982): 109-114.

Kerr, Richard A. "Carbon Dioxide and the Control of Ice Ages." *Science* Vol. 223 (March 9, 1984): 1053-1054.

____. "How to Make a Warm Cretaceous Climate." *Science* Vol. 223 (February 17, 1984): 677-678.

Laorius, C., et al. "A 150,000-year climatic record from Antarctic Ice." *Nature* Vol. 316 (August 15, 1985): 591-595.

Lewin, Roger. "Extinctions and the History of Life." *Science* Vol. 221 (September 2, 1983): 935-937

Pittock, A. Barrie. "Cycles in the Precambrian." *Nature* Vol. 318 (December 1985): 509-510.

Radok, Uwe. "The Antarctic Ice." *Scientific American* Vol. 253 (August 1985): 98-106.

Rensberger, Boyce. "Mass Extinctions: What happened to the dinosaurs?" *Science Digest* (October 1985): 38-39.

Wigley, T.M.L., et al. "Scenario for a warm, high CO_2 world." *Nature* Vol. 283 (January 3, 1980): 17-21.

Williams, George E. "The Solar Cycle in Precambrian Time." *Scientific American* Vol. 255 (August 1986): 88-96.

CLIMATE AND HUNGER

Brown, Lewis R. "World Population Growth, Soil Erosion, and Food Security." *Science* Vol. 214 (November 27, 1981): 995-1001.

Demany, Paul. "The Populations of the Underdeveloped Countries." *Scientific American* Vol. 231 (September 1974): 149-159.

Holden, Constance. "World Bank, U.S. at Odds on Population." *Science* Vol. 225 (July 27, 1981): 396.

Kerr, Richard A. "Fifteen Years of African Drought." *Science* Vol. 227 (March 22, 1985): 1453-1454.

Larson, W.E., et al. "The Threat of Soil Erosion to Long-Term Crop Production." *Science* Vol. 219 (February 4, 1983): 458-464.

LeComte, Douglas. "The Year of Worldwide Extremes and Droughts." *Weatherwise* (February 1984): 9-17.

Lewin, Roger. "No Dinosaurs This Time." *Science* Vol. 221 (September 16, 1983): 1168-1169.

____. "What Killed the Giant Mammals?" *Science* Vol. 221 (September 9, 1983): 1036-1037.

"Population planning gone awry." *Nature* Vol. 310 (August 9, 1984): 439.

Raloff, Janet, "Famine: Is there a lesson from Africa?" *Science News* Vol. 127 (February 23, 1985): 118.

Revelle, Roger. "Food and Population." *Scientific American* Vol. 231 (September 1974): 161-170.

Sai, Fred T. "The Population Factor in Africa's Development Dilemma." *Science* Vol. 226 (November 16, 1984): 801-805.

Strasser, Steven, et al. "The Big Drought of '83." *Newsweek* (August 22, 1983): 14-16.

Trimble, Jeff. "Rain and aid save millions of Africans—for now." *U.S. News & World Report* (January 20, 1986): 32.

Walsh, John. "Sahel Will Suffer Even If Rains Come." *Science* Vol. 224 (May 4, 1984): 467-471.

Watson, Russell, et al. "An African Nightmare." *Newsweek* (November 26, 1986): 50-58.

Webster, Peter J. "Monsoons." *Scientific American* Vol. 245 (August 1981): 109-118.

NUCLEAR WINTER

Ehrlich, Paul R., et al. *The Cold and the Dark.* Norton, 1984.

____. "Long-Term Biological Consequences of Nuclear War." *Science* Vol. 222 (December 23, 1983): 1293-1299.

Lewis, Kevin N. "The Prompt and Delayed Effects of Nuclear War." *Scientific American* Vol. 241 (July 1979): 35-47.

McNaughton, S.J., et al. "Ecological consequences of nuclear war." *Nature* Vol. 321 (May 1986): 483-487.

"Nuclear Famine." *Scientific American* Vol. 253 (November 1985): 103-104.

Sagan, Carl. "On minimizing the consequences of nuclear war." *Nature* Vol. 317 (October 10, 1985): 485-488.

Thompson, Starley L. "Global interactive transport simulations of nuclear war smoke." *Nature* Vol. 317 (September 5, 1985): 35-39.

Turco, Richard P., et al. "Nuclear Winter: Global Consequences of Multiple Nuclear Explosions." *Science* Vol. 222 (December 23, 1983): 1283-1290.

____. "The Climatic Effects of Nuclear War." *Scientific American* Vol. 251 (August 1984): 33-43.

Index

Other Bestsellers From TAB

☐ **SUPERCONDUCTIVITY—THE THRESHOLD OF A NEW TECHNOLOGY—Jonathan L. Mayo**

Superconductivity is generating an excitement not seen in the scientific world for several decades! Experts are predicting advances in state-of-the-art technology that will make most existing electrical and electronic technologies obsolete! This book is the most complete and thorough introduction to this multifaceted phenomenon covering the full spectrum of superconductivity and superconductive technology. 160 pp., 58 illus.

Paper $12.95   **Hard $18.95**
Book No. 3022

☐ **LASERS—THE LIGHT FANTASTIC—2nd Edition—Clayton L. Hallmark and Delton T. Horn**

Gain insight into all the various ways lasers are used today . . . in communications, in radar, as gyroscopes, in industry, and in commerce. Plus, more emphasis is placed on laser applications for electronics hobbyists and general science enthusiasts. If you want to experiment with lasers, you will find the guidance you need here—including safety techniques, a complete glossary of technical terms, actual schematics, and information on obtaining the necessary materials. 280 pp., 129 illus.

Paper $12.95   **Hard $19.95**
Book No. 2905

☐ **PARTICLES IN NATURE: THE CHRONOLOGICAL DISCOVERY OF THE NEW PHYSICS—John H. Mauldin**

If you're interested in physics, science, astronomy, or natural history, you will find this presentation of the particle view of nature fascinating and informative. This guide makes particle physics seem less abstract—it shows significant spin-offs that have resulted from research done, and gives a glimpse of future research. 304 pp., 169 illus., Full-Color Pages.

Paper $16.95   **Hard $23.95**
Book No. 2616

☐ **SCIENCE FAIR: Developing a Successful and Fun Project—Maxine Haren Iritz, Photographs by A. Frank Iritz**

Here's all the step-by-step guidance parents and teachers need to help students complete prize-quality science fair projects! This book provides easy-to-follow advice on every step of science fair project preparation from choosing a topic and defining the problem to setting up and conducting the experiment, drawing conclusions, and setting up the fair display. 96 pp., 83 illus., 8½″ × 11″.

Paper $12.95   **Hard $19.95**
Book No. 2936

☐ **PUZZLES, PARADOXES AND BRAIN TEASERS—Stan Gibilisco**

This is a clear, concise, well-written exploration of the mysteries of the universe. It is an intriguing look at those exceptions that are as frustrating as they are amusing! The author's approach is entertaining, enlightening, and easy to understand. Although the topics are of a mathematical nature, the discussions are nontechnical. 122 pp., 83 illus.

Paper $8.95   **Hard $14.95**
Book No. 2895

☐ **COMETS, METEORS AND ASTEROIDS—How They Affect Earth—Stan Gibilisco**

Information on meteors, asteroids, and other related space phenomena is all here for the taking. It includes a spectacular eight-page section of color photos taken in space. Packed with little-known details and fascinating theories covering history's most memorable comets—including Halley's Comet—the origins of the solar system, and speculation on what may happen in the future. 224 pp., 148 illus.

Paper $14.95   **Book No. 1905**

Other Bestsellers From TAB